Praise For Ethan Brown's
MURDER IN THE BAYOU

*A *NEW YORK TIMES* BESTSELLER*
*A *SOUTHERN LIVING* 2016 BOOK OF THE YEAR*

"Ethan Brown's daring and dangerous exposé uncovers a murky inferno of violence and corruption in South Louisiana, where it's hard to tell the good guys from the bad, and the brutal murders of eight prostitutes go unpunished, though not necessarily unsolved."
—John Berendt, author of *Midnight in the Garden of Good and Evil*

"A deeply reported, and disturbing, true crime story that is as puzzling as it is intriguing. Ethan Brown's *Murder in the Bayou* raises as many questions as it answers, but never ceases to enrage. This is a book about power: those who wield it, and those who, tragically, fall victim to it."
—Janet Reitman, contributing editor at *Rolling Stone* and author of the *New York Times* Notable Book *Inside Scientology*

"By way of Jefferson Davis Parish, Louisiana, Ethan Brown casts light on an America that many people would prefer to believe is not there. *Murder in the Bayou* reveals a complicated web of violence, poverty, drugs, and corruption—it's a brave feat of reporting."
—Zachary Lazar, author of *Evening's Empire: The Story of My Father's Murder*

"Investigating what appeared to be a string of unsolved sex-murders that began in 2005, journalist Ethan Brown eventually uncovered a snake pit of small-town corruption in the bayou parish of Jefferson Davis, Louisiana. With its large cast of lost,

doomed, and sinister characters, its dense atmosphere of menace and dread, and, at its center, a dogged reporter pursuing a mystery with the fearlessness of a pulp-fiction private eye, Brown's *Murder in the Bayou* is a stunning work of real-life Southern noir."
—Harold Schechter, author of *The Serial Killer Files*

"Ethan Brown wades into the fetid political swamps of South Louisiana and emerges with a sordid yarn of sex, drugs, and death. With a depraved and threatening cast of characters, Brown delivers a dogged, courageous inquiry into the murders of eight women. Even those accustomed to institutional corruption in the Pelican State will be shocked by this tale."
—Doug J. Swanson, author of *Blood Aces:
The Wild Ride of Benny Binion, the Texas
Gangster Who Created Vegas Poker*

"Damn near hard to put down."
—Sarah Weinman, editor of *Women Crime Writers*
and author of *Among the Wholesome Children*

"Brown is a man on a mission. . . . [He] is especially enlightening when it comes to this region. . . . [He] gives the victims more respectful attention than they probably got in real life."
—*The New York Times*

"Mesmerizing . . . A snarled web of power dynamics and deeprooted corruption . . . symptomatic of a kind of system-wide brokenness that applies all over the country. . . . Brown is able to show each individual victim as a real person, who is mourned and who couldn't be silenced as easily as their murderers seemed to think."
—*Rolling Stone*

"Far truer than T*rue Detective* . . . Part murder case, part corruption exposé, and part Louisiana noir."
—Boris Kachka, NYMag.com

"The depths of the corruption detailed in the book by Brown . . . will make your head spin for days after you finish reading it."

—*Uproxx*

"[A] page-turning account . . . Filled with vivid characters . . . Startling and haunting."

—*Gambit Weekly*

"Doggedly researched and sensitively observed."

—*Gothamist*

"A gripping narrative that will revive curiosity about eight unsolved murders . . . Brown's spare but effective prose and measured analysis of the evidence makes this a must-read for true crime fans."

—*Publishers Weekly* (starred review)

"A complicated web of intrigue and murder and one that will haunt you long after you put the book down."

—*The Monroe News Star*

"Explosive."

—*The Huffington Post*

"Sweeping, rigorously reported . . . The story has all the elements of a sordid Southern Gothic."

—*The New Orleans Advocate*

"Brown's writing is clear and approachable, and his research is meticulous. . . . Readers will be shaken by the unpleasant implications of a narrative bearing similarities to the first season of *True Detective*. Compulsively readable true crime provoking questions about policing, poverty, and the ritualized brutality of the rural South."

—*Kirkus Reviews*

SEEKING
INFORMATION

MURDER VICTIMS
JENNINGS, LOUISIANA AREA

Loretta Lewis

Ernestine Patterson

Kristen Lopez

Whitnei Dubois

Laconia Brown

Crystal Zeno

Brittney Gary

Necole Guillory

THE DETAILS SURROUNDING THE CRIMES

A Multi-Agency Investigative Team led by the Jefferson Davis Parish Sheriff's Office located in Jennings, Louisiana, is seeking information regarding the murders of eight women; Loretta Lynn Chaisson Lewis, Ernestine Daniels Patterson, Kristen E. Gary Lopez, Whitnei Charlene Dubois, Laconia Shontell Brown, Crystal Shay Benoit Zeno, Brittney Gary and Necole Jean Guillory. The victims, who range in age from 17 to 30 years old, were found deceased in and around the Jennings, Louisiana area from May 2005 through August 2009.

For additional information relating to these crimes/cases, please see Crimes in Jefferson Davis Parish at http://www.jeffdaviscrimes.net.

REWARD

MURDER IN THE BAYOU

WHO KILLED THE WOMEN KNOWN AS THE JEFF DAVIS 8?

ETHAN BROWN

SCRIBNER

New York   London   Toronto   Sydney   New Delhi

SCRIBNER
An Imprint of Simon & Schuster, Inc.
1230 Avenue of the Americas
New York, NY 10020

Library of Congress Control Number: 2016031710

ISBN 978-1-4767-9325-2
ISBN 978-1-9821-2781-7 (pbk)
ISBN 978-1-4767-9327-6 (ebook)

Dedicated to the Jeff Davis 8 and especially to a group of fearless women in Louisiana and elsewhere who have fought selflessly for years to keep this case alive when few cared about it. This project would not exist without you.

Those who commit the murders write the reports.

—Ida B. Wells[1]

Contents

Key Figures

The Jeff Davis 8	
Loretta Chaisson (aka Loretta Chaisson-Lewis)	Jeff Davis 8 victim #1, slain in May of 2005.
Ernestine Patterson	Jeff Davis 8 victim #2, slain in June of 2005.
Kristen Lopez (aka Kristen Gary Lopez)	Jeff Davis 8 victim #3, slain in early March of 2007; cousin of Jeff Davis 8 victim #6, Brittney Gary.
Whitnei Dubois	Jeff Davis 8 victim #4, slain in May of 2007.
Laconia "Muggy" Brown	Jeff Davis 8 victim #5, slain in May of 2008.
Crystal Zeno (aka Crystal Shay Benoit Zeno)	Jeff Davis 8 victim #6, slain in late August/early September of 2008.
Brittney Gary	Jeff Davis 8 victim #7, slain in November of 2008; cousin of Jeff Davis 8 victim #3, Kristen Gary Lopez.
Necole Guillory	Jeff Davis 8 victim #8, slain in August of 2009.

Suspects	
Tracee Chaisson (pronounced SHA-sohn)	Longtime associate of Frankie Richard; cousin of Jeff Davis 8 victim Loretta Chaisson; charged as accessory after the fact to second-degree murder in slaying of Jeff Davis 8 victim Kristen Gary Lopez; charges later dropped.
Billy Conner, Sr.	Brother of Frankie Richard, father of Hannah Conner; suspected of assisting Richard in running his drug operation; deceased.
Hannah Conner	Niece of Frankie Richard; charged with second-degree murder in slaying of Kristen Gary Lopez; charges later dropped.
Kenneth Patrick Drake	Forty-four-year-old man from Welsh, Louisiana, who attacked Jeff Davis 8 victim Crystal Benoit Zeno with a metal pipe in the late summer of 2008, just before she was murdered; deceased.
Eugene "Dog" Ivory	Longtime associate of Frankie Richard; charged in 2007 rape of Elizabeth Clemens; charges later dropped.
Byron Chad Jones	Charged in 2005 killing of Ernestine Patterson, Jeff Davis 8 victim #2; charges later dropped.
Lawrence Nixon	Cousin of Jeff Davis 8 victim Laconia "Muggy" Brown; charged in 2005 killing of Jeff Davis 8 victim Ernestine Patterson; charges later dropped; charged in 2005 with rape of investigator Kirk Menard's daughter, Rosalyn Breaux; charges later dropped.

Suspects	
Frankie Richard (pronounced REE-shard)	Former pimp and drug dealer in Jennings; briefly charged in 2007 with the murder of Kristen Gary Lopez, Jeff Davis 8 victim #3; charges were later dropped; charged, along with Eugene "Dog" Ivory, in 2007 rape of Elizabeth Clemens; charges later dropped.

Law Enforcement	
Danny Barry	Former deputy with the Jefferson Davis Parish Sheriff's Office; frequent client of the Jeff Davis 8; died in 2010.
Dallas Cormier (pronounced COR-mee-yay)	Jefferson Davis Parish sheriff, 1980–92; indicted by the feds for using public funds for private purchases; plead guilty to one count of obstruction of justice.
Ramby Cormier	Detective with the Jefferson Davis Parish Sheriff's Office; serves on the Jeff Davis 8 Taskforce; former detective with the Calcasieu Parish Sheriff's Office.
Donald "Lucky" DeLouche	Former investigator with the VCTF (Violent Crimes Task Force) in Calcasieu Parish during the 1990s; chief of Jennings Police Department from late 1990s to the early 2000s.
Ricky Edwards	Jefferson Davis Parish sheriff, 1992–2012.
Warren Gary	Former chief investigator/chief of detectives of the Jefferson Davis Parish Sheriff's Office; in 2007 purchased a truck from a female inmate that had allegedly been used to transport the body of Jeff Davis 8 victim Kristen Gary Lopez.

Law Enforcement	
Terrie Guillory	Former warden of the Jefferson Davis Parish jail; also formerly with the Jennings Police Department; currently with Lake Arthur, Louisiana, Police Department.
Mark Ivory	Jailer under former Jefferson Davis Parish warden Terrie Guillory; defendant in a 2007 federal civil rights lawsuit for alleged sexual assault of female inmate Lisa Allen; committed suicide in the fall of 2007.
Phil Karam	Officer with the Jennings Police Department; in February 2000, killed fellow officer Kenneth Guidry and his wife, Christine; during an ensuing standoff, also killed Officer Burt LeBlanc; deceased.
Wayne McElveen	Former sheriff of Calcasieu Parish; son Richard McElveen was implicated—but never charged—in two murder cases in Calcasieu Parish during the 1990s.
Raymond Mott	Former detective with both the Jennings Police Department and the Lake Arthur Police Department; claims that he was instructed by Terrie Guillory not to arrest drug dealers in town; terminated by Lake Arthur PD after photo emerged of him at KKK rally.
Ivy Woods	Jefferson Davis Parish sheriff since 2012.

Other Victims	
Rosalyn Breaux	Daughter of private investigator Kirk Menard, who is investigating Jeff Davis 8 case; in 2005, allegedly lured to home in South Jennings by Jeff Davis 8 victim Laconia "Muggy" Brown and raped by a group of men, including Lawrence Nixon, Brown's cousin, who was briefly charged in the murder of Jeff Davis 8 victim Ernestine Patterson.
Harvey Lee "Bird Dog" Burleigh	Prescription-pill dealer; his home at 610 Gallup Street in Jennings was raided by law enforcement on April 20, 2005; Leonard Crochet killed during raid; associate of Jeff Davis 8 victim Whitnei Dubois's brother, Mike; stabbed to death in Jennings in the summer of 2007. His murder remains unsolved.
Sheila Comeaux	Informant beaten to death in Jennings in 1998; her murder remains unsolved.
Leonard Crochet	Killed by law enforcement on April 20, 2005, drug raid at 610 Gallup Street in Jennings; murder witnessed by Jeff Davis 8 victim Kristen Gary Lopez.
David "Bowlegs" Deshotel	Former boyfriend of Jeff Davis 8 victims Brittney Gary and Necole Guillory; his murder in July of 2011 remains unsolved.
Eric Ellender	One-half of Calcasieu Parish couple murdered in 1991.

Other Victims	
Pam Ellender	One-half of Calcasieu Parish couple murdered in 1991.
Lacie Fontenot	Twenty-seven-year-old woman from Lake Arthur, Louisiana, found dead by drowning from hypothermia in a ditch in that town on January 31, 2014; dated Alvin "Bootsy" Lewis, a former boyfriend of Jeff Davis 8 victim Whitnei Dubois's and father of a child with Dubois; associate of longtime Frankie Richard cohort Eugene "Dog" Ivory's.
Steven Gunter	Lake Arthur, Louisiana, man shot to death by Terrie Guillory of the Jefferson Davis Parish Sheriff's Office on June 9, 2007.
Christopher Prudhomme	Suspect in 1991 killing of Eric and Pam Ellender; found dead in Calcasieu Parish jail weeks later, allegedly by suicide.

Whistle-Blowers	
Jesse Ewing	Former detective with the Jennings Police Department who in December of 2007 took statements from two female inmates who claimed that high-ranking members of law enforcement—including Chief Criminal Investigator Warren Gary—conspired with Frankie Richard to destroy physical evidence in the murder of Jeff Davis 8 victim Kristen Gary Lopez.

Whistle-Blowers	
Nina Ravey	Jail nurse under Jefferson Davis Parish warden Terrie Guillory; in 2007, filed internal reports regarding sexual assaults at the jail by jailer Mark Ivory; then charged with falsifying medical documents; charges later dropped.

Jeff Davis 8 Milieu	
Roxanne "Mama" Alexander	Housed most—if not all—of the Jeff Davis 8 at her home on the north side of Jennings.
Mike Dubois	Brother of Jeff Davis 8 victim Whitnei Dubois; associate of slain Jennings street hustler Harvey "Bird Dog" Burleigh.
Jared Sauble	Informant for Jennings Police Department whose tips led to April 20, 2005, raid on 610 Gallup Street, the home of Harvey "Bird Dog" Burleigh; Leonard Crochet killed by law enforcement during the raid.

Note from the Author

I refer to the slain women collectively as the Jeff Davis 8, even though this descriptor was not utilized until 2009, after the eighth and final victim, Necole Guillory, was discovered by the side of Interstate 10. I often refer to key players by their first name or street name, not out of disrespect, but for the sake of clarity. In southwest Louisiana, surnames such as Chaisson (sometimes spelled Chiasson), Boudreaux, and Cormier are extraordinarily commonplace, reflecting the area's Cajun/Acadian roots. Many people in this story who share last names are of no family relation.

The narrative of this book was put together utilizing my own witness interviews and public records requests that resulted in thousands of pages of files from the Jefferson Davis Parish District Office, the Jennings Police Department, the Jefferson Davis Parish Sheriff's Office, and many other public entities in the area that were directly involved in investigating the case. Yet it is important to underscore that the Jeff Davis 8 murders remain unsolved: no one has been convicted; no one has been brought to trial; no charges are even pending. My chronicle of the case reflects only my best investigative effort at providing a theory as to how each of these women were slain and an account of other events that may help explain why they died, and why no one has been held responsible. I hope that this account will prompt responsible authorities to effectively employ their more substantial investigative resources to bring justice to the Jeff Davis 8.

CHAPTER 1

Loretta

On May 20, 2005, Jerry Jackson, a soft-spoken slim African-American retiree with a short salt-and-pepper Afro, prepared to cast a fishing line from a hulking bridge over the Grand Marais Canal on the outskirts of Jennings in southwest Louisiana. Jackson peered down at the muddy rush below, the corroded, cylindrical rain pipes along the canal belching water, the collapsed pedestrian bridge far out in the distance. As he prepped his fishing line, Jackson imagined the catch that day, white perch, a small bass with a strong spine that's so abundant in Louisiana it's the state's official freshwater fish.[1] In low-lying southwest Louisiana, where rain is constantly siphoned to prevent flooding, drainage canals are as common as the perch. These canals provide sustenance for poor Louisianans for whom fishing is both a generations-old tradition and a day-to-day necessity. For hobbyists such as Jackson, who made the approximately ten-mile trip to Jennings from his cramped trailer on a dead-end street in nearby Welsh, drainage canals democratize fishing. Expensive shrimp boats and fishing equipment aren't necessary — all one needs to do is drop a line into the water.

As Jackson peered deeper into the Grand Marais Canal, he spied the outline of a human body. "It had come up on the news that someone had stole some mannequins," Jackson told me, "so I thought that one of the mannequins ended up in the water somehow."[2] Jackson focused his eyes on the figure. "I saw flies, and mannequins don't attract flies."

Panicked, Jackson dialed 911 from his cell phone. His call was transferred to a dispatcher at the Jefferson Davis Parish Sheriff's Office. The parish is home to about thirty thousand residents (a "parish" is known as a county outside Louisiana).[3] The dispatcher at the Sheriff's Office took Jackson's call at 11:46 a.m. and noted:

"Caller adv fishing from bridge and seen body floating in the water."[4]

About five minutes later, over a dozen deputies and detectives arrived at the foot of the bridge. An emotionally overcome Jackson piled into his truck and sped back home—"I was afraid somebody might bump *me* off," he remembers. On the short drive he thought about whether he'd have the courage to ever go fishing again. "It's a bad feeling," Jackson told me. "Them things," he adds softly, "run across your mind all the time. I love to fish. But that broke me up."

That afternoon, a dead woman was hoisted over the bridge and laid on the banks of the Grand Marais. She was clad in blue jeans, blue panties, and a short-sleeve white blouse; her body was decayed but showed no evidence of injury aside from a small patch of blood under her scalp.[5] Fingerprints identified her as twenty-eight-year-old Loretta Lynn Lewis Chaisson, a Jennings sex worker.

Farther down Highway 1126, Barb Ann Deshotel, a longtime friend of the victim's, watched nervously as investigators set up a perimeter around the crime scene. Early that morning Terrie Guillory, a deputy from the Jefferson Davis Parish Sheriff's Office who had a thick, stocky build, a shaved head, and a scruffy goatee, had arrived at her home on West Division Street in South Jennings to question her about Loretta's whereabouts.

"Where was Loretta?" Deshotel remembers Guillory asking. "When was the last time I seen her? I said, 'After my son's birthday. What's the matter?'"[6]

Guillory's tone grew serious: "We think she's missing." Then he turned his back on Deshotel and left.

A confused and panicked Deshotel phoned Loretta's brother Nick, asking him to come over. But before he even arrived, the news had spread through the neighborhood: a body, found in the canal. She feared it was Loretta. When Nick finally made it to Deshotel's home, the pair took off down Highway 1126 in the direction of the Grand Marais.[7]

"We saw a CSI van on the road," Deshotel remembers, "and followed it to where the cops blocked the road off. Me and Nick watched the body come out of the water and onto the bridge. We were watching from afar but I knew it was her. She was wearing one of my shirts when they found her. It was pink, but the color had gotten so light that they said it was white in the police report."

For Deshotel, the sight of a friend being fished out of the murky Grand Marais was terrifying and traumatic. Afterward, she found herself thinking not about Loretta's passing but Terrie Guillory's early-morning visit. She and Loretta's brother Nick had been unaware of anyone—not her family nor her friends—reporting her missing (I was also unable to find any record of Loretta being reported missing to the Sheriff's Office or the Jennings Police Department; I obtained such records on other victims). "None of us called her in as a missing person," Deshotel insists. "So why were they looking for her? Unless they know something that other people didn't know?"

Deshotel would have known if Loretta was missing. The pair, after all, shared everything. Clothing, food, makeup, even Deshotel's West Division Street home. Loretta stood five foot three and weighed just 104 pounds. She had sandy-brownish-blond hair and a sly smile. At the time of her death she was deep in thrall to a crack addiction. After years of slow and painful dissolution, Loretta's marriage to a burly African-American shipyard worker, Murphy Lewis, had finally come undone. She'd sought refuge with friends and extended family, including, at the time, Deshotel.

"I knew she did drugs recreationally," says Lewis, who married Loretta in March of 2000 in the backyard of a relative's home in Jennings, "but two weekends out of a month developed into an everyday habit."[8]

Though Lewis and Loretta had two boys together—Keylan in 1999 and Kendrick in 2002—she would disappear into South Jennings's heady drug scene for days, sometimes weeks at a time, reemerging only to beg her husband for a few dollars to purchase meals at Popeyes or Sonic. By 2004, Lewis had persuaded Loretta to enter a local outpatient drug-rehabilitation facility. When the stint failed to help her, the pair separated but did not legally divorce.

Loretta's decline quickened after her separation from Lewis. On March 6, 2005, she snatched a checkbook out of a truck and wrote three checks, for $54, $265, and $226.[9] The petty crime crystallized Loretta's desperation: one of the checks was made out to local grocery store Hanson's Super Foods, and a receipt shows that the bulk of her purchases were cigarettes. Hanson's turned over surveillance footage to law enforcement and Loretta was quickly apprehended.

In a videotaped interview with the Sheriff's Office, Loretta admitted to taking the checks, but insisted it was all part of a routine cash-for-sex arrangement. According to the interview notes, Loretta insisted that the owner of the checkbook "give [*sic*] her money for sex all the time." Nonetheless, Loretta was charged with theft and forgery and, thanks to an outstanding cocaine-possession charge, faced the prospect of three years in prison.

In an April 11, 2005, letter to the District Attorney's Office, Loretta's attorney, David Marcantel, pleaded for leniency, citing her myriad mental and physical health problems: "You have her pleading to simple possession of cocaine, suspended all but three years is very harsh," Marcantel wrote. "Loretta, who is in jail on a bench warrant for missing court, has tuberculosis and takes 12 kinds of medicine for her TB, anxiety, bi-polar disorder, cough, breathing difficulties, depression. I am asking that she be allowed to plead to simple possession of cocaine, get a suspended sentence, parish jail time of four months, with credit for inpatient substance abuse treatment. She has no prior felonies. She has done three weeks in jail on these charges. I would like to get her out of jail and into substance abuse treatment as soon as possible, if you will agree."[10] Marcantel's push for mercy worked: she was given a six-month prison sentence, just about all of which—excluding sixty days—was suspended.

That spring, Loretta was released from lockup. Nothing in the court records indicates that she received the substance abuse treatment Marcantel requested. Even after jail Loretta's drug habit remained as ferocious as ever.

Loretta's husband isn't sure when he last saw his wife

alive; he thinks it may have been the late afternoon of Sunday, May 15, 2005, when Loretta emerged from a multiday bender, hungry, exhausted, and broke. Lewis gave her a few bucks to buy herself some chicken from Popeyes; she took the cash, thanked him for being a good daddy to their sons, then walked over to Tina's Bar, a popular South Jennings haunt with a rough-and-tumble reputation, bearing a sign encouraging patrons to PASS A GOOD TIME.

After Loretta was pulled from the waters of the Grand Marais Canal, Lewis, like Loretta's confidante Barb Ann Deshotel, took issue with the investigation. "After Loretta died, I was never questioned," Lewis says furiously. "The spouse is supposed to be questioned. What was in evidence that ruled *me* out as a suspect?"

Barb Ann Deshotel kept circling back to Terrie Guillory's visit. It felt like a linchpin, a crucial piece of the puzzle. Guillory had somehow known Loretta was missing before anyone else.

And, according to a law enforcement witness, Guillory was acquainted with Loretta long before her murder. Loretta's cellmate from the Jefferson Davis Parish jail, an outdated, sixty-two-bed facility built in 1964 and plagued with inadequate lighting and sewer backups, spoke to investigators and alleged that the pair maintained a sexual relationship.[11] One night, according to the cellmate, while the two were lying in their decrepit steel bunks, someone entered the cell unannounced. The cells were often hot. No air-conditioning even in South Louisiana's humid, subtropical climate. Scared, the cellmate feigned sleep. A short time later, she heard the sound of "heavy breathing coming from the bunk, which was directly beneath her." When the cellmate peered over the side of her bunk, she saw Deputy Guillory; Loretta's legs were spread and in the air. He and Loretta were having sex.

According to the cellmate, the encounter was followed by a period of quiet, then the sound of the cell door opening and closing again. With Deputy Guillory gone, the cellmate looked "over at Chaisson and Chaisson put her finger to her lips, meaning for her to be quiet." But Loretta Chaisson wasn't secretive about her illicit relationship. She admitted to having "sex with the deputy all the time," even when she was not incarcerated.

At the time Loretta was also engaging in sex work and partying with the parish's roughest street players. On the morning of May 17, 2005—the day she was murdered—Loretta was seen clambering into a vehicle at the Phillips 66 gas station with a much-feared South Jennings pimp and drug dealer named Frankie Richard. Later that day, she snorted cocaine at the Boudreaux Inn, a now-shuttered motel and bar on Highway LA 26 in Jennings, just off exit 64 on I-10, with street heavy Jermaine "Stymie" Washington and two fellow sex workers and, later, Jeff Davis 8 victims Muggy Brown and Necole Guillory. Certain investigators, I have learned, believe that Stymie suffocated Loretta at the inn as Muggy and Necole watched helplessly, a theory that fits with the coroner's report. Murder by suffocation often leaves no discernible wounds or marks, and indeed, the coroner later noted "no evidence of significant injuries." The manner of Loretta's death was left "undetermined."[12] The toxicology screen was more definitive: Loretta had the antidepressants Zoloft and Celexa as well as cocaine in her system. Her blood alcohol level was measured at 0.16, defined as a "sloppy drunk."[13]

Between 2005 and 2009, the bodies of seven more female sex workers would be discovered in and around the outskirts of Jennings and nearby Acadia Parish, in dirt roads, swamps, and canals, as well as along a highway; like Loretta's, the other victims' bodies were often too decomposed to determine the cause of death.

It's a staggering body count for a town of approximately ten thousand residents, a place that lies in the heart of Cajun country, a town once named "the boudin capital of the Universe."[14] For the uninitiated, boudin—pronounced *boo-dan*—is a Cajun sausage packed with herbs, spices, and rice. And the gumbo served up by Jennings's iconic Boudin King restaurant features a broth as murky as the area's swamps. Indeed, the landscape in and around Jennings is quintessentially Cajun. To the east sits the Atchafalaya Basin, the largest wetland and swamp in the entire United States.[15] To the west lies Calcasieu Parish, where oil and gas refineries, vinyl chloride production facilities, coal-fired power plants, and several major petrochemical manufacturers dominate.[16] These towering facilities release high levels of cancer-causing chemicals into the environment, contaminating fish and leaking toxins into groundwater. According to an environmental activist group based in Louisiana, one Citgo Petroleum refinery in Lake Charles—the parish seat of Calcasieu Parish—averages about fifty-five accidents per year, one of the highest accident rates in the state.[17] At times the parish seems shrouded in a thick chemical fog. "Got a bad taste out there," fictional Louisiana State Police detective Rust Cohle famously remarks as he rides through Calcasieu Parish in season one of the HBO series *True Detective*. "Aluminum, ash, like you can smell the psychosphere."

Yet along with Loretta, victims Ernestine Marie Daniels Patterson, thirty, Kristen Gary Lopez, twenty-one, Whitnei Dubois, twenty-six, Laconia "Muggy" Brown, twenty-three, Crystal Shay Benoit Zeno, twenty-four, Brittney Ann Gary, seventeen, and Necole Guillory, twenty-six—who are collectively known as the Jeff Davis 8—all resided in Jefferson Davis Parish.[18] Each of the victims was deeply mired in poverty, mental illness, and drug addiction—afflictions so prevalent that drugs "account for eighty to eighty-five percent of our cases,"[19] according to the long-serving parish DA, Michael Cassidy. Given the pervasiveness of addiction, one would think that treatment would be readily available. Not so, according to Cassidy: "We certainly don't have any inpatient treatment here," he admitted.

Drugs are plentiful in Jennings because of its critical location along the route of the Gulf Coast drug trade. Jennings sits along the nearly four-hundred-mile stretch of Interstate 10 that connects Houston to New Orleans, a route favored by marijuana and cocaine traffickers as well as prescription-pill "doctor shoppers." Turn on the local news in Jeff Davis Parish and you'll likely see deputies announce the latest I-10 drug bust. The amounts are usually staggering. In December 2011 during a routine traffic stop, police confiscated 116 pounds of marijuana from a Jeep Liberty.[20] In May of 2014, a drug bust in the Lake Charles area resulted in the indictment of fifty-one people, one of whom was accused of being the largest cocaine distributor in the entire southwest Louisiana region.[21]

The many threads that linked the Jeff Davis women in life (sex work) and in death (elevated levels of cocaine and anti-depressants, possible death by asphyxia) led local law enforcement to investigate the Jeff Davis 8 as a serial killer case. "The average time it takes to catch a serial killer is 7.8 years," District Attorney Michael Cassidy said in November of 2008. "That's alarming. We're not used to something like that happening in our little rural community."[22]

In December of the same year, a Multi-Agency Investigative Team (MAIT), composed of federal, state, and local law enforcement, was formed to investigate the unsolved sex worker slayings, which then totaled seven.[23] About one year later, the Taskforce more than doubled the reward—from $35,000 to $85,000—for information leading to the guilty party's arrest. They also launched a website, www.jeffdavis crimes.net, in which identifying information about the murdered women was posted (names, height and weight, and date of birth) along with the most basic facts about their deaths, such as the dates that they were last seen alive.[24] The Taskforce's website, which solicited tips directly from the public, is no longer functioning. It's unclear why this is so. The FBI also posted a flyer on its own website seeking information about the cases.[25] The flyer offered little else but the number to the Taskforce hotline.

"You have all asked whether or not this is a serial killer," Sheriff Edwards said in the first Taskforce press conference, which was held in December of 2008. "The facts that we currently have do not allow me at this time to say with certainty that these cases are all linked." But then Sheriff Edwards spent the remainder of the press conference ticking off the behavioral characteristics of serial killers.

About one year later, in another Taskforce press conference, Sheriff Edwards seemed more certain that a serial killer was at work in Jennings. "It is the collective opinion of all agencies involved in this investigation," he said, "that these murders may have been committed by a common offender."[26]

Law enforcement stuck by this theory, at least publicly; Sheriff Edwards even suggested that a "serial dumper" was behind the unsolved murders, a nonsensical phrase that he admitted to a reporter is "terminology I guess we're making up."[27] Behind closed doors, however, various members of the Taskforce were dubious. In the spring of 2015, a Taskforce investigator admitted to me, "We investigate under a dual-type situation." This is law enforcement speak for a case that they believe could just as likely have multiple suspects or a single serial killer.

The Taskforce had many reasons to cling to a serial killer theory. For one, it kept the public vigilant. Neighbors started keeping an eye out for suspicious behavior, suspicious people. A killer could be lurking among the canals, creeping through backyards, seeking shelter in abandoned houses. If you weren't careful, you could be next. The threat was tangible, concrete. And more important, the threat was external. A single killer, though horror inducing, was a more containable, less nefarious prospect than a network of killers, working in concert, hiding in plain sight.

This pronouncement about a "common offender" riled local media into a round-the-clock serial killer watch. The notion of a Ted Bundy or John Wayne Gacy–style murderer stalking the swamps of Cajun country brought a swarm of national media as well. "A big mystery is stalking a small town deep in Louisiana," said CNN anchor Don Lemon on *CNN Newsroom* in September 2009. "At least eight women in the town of Jennings, that's in Jefferson Davis Parish in Louisiana, have been found dead in the past few years."[28] In January of 2010, the *New York Times* ran a feature on the front page of its National section, "8 Deaths in a Small Town, and Much Unease."[29] It has been more than a decade since the first body of a Jennings sex worker—Loretta—was fished out of the Jennings canal, yet all eight of the murders remain unsolved.

But the Jeff Davis 8 cases are far from the only unsolved homicides in Jefferson Davis Parish. With nine other unsolved murders in the area since Loretta's body was discovered in 2005, Jefferson Davis Parish has one of the lowest homicide-clearance rates in the country—less than 7 percent, compared to a national clearance rate of 64 percent.[30] The result of so many unsolved murders in communities such as Jennings causes, as *Los Angeles Times* crime reporter and author Jill Leovy wrote in a 2015 *Wall*

Street Journal op-ed, "a doubling down on distrust . . . many conclude that the state seeks control, not justice."[31]

Complex murder cases such as the Jeff Davis 8 can remain open for years, sometimes even decades. The infamous killings of twenty-nine children in Atlanta during the late 1970s and early 1980s yielded the arrest of one suspect, Wayne Williams, who was charged in and then convicted of just two of the murders.[32] When the remains of four women—some sex workers—were discovered near the Long Island towns of Gilgo Beach and Oak Beach in December 2010, the media again circled around a serial killer theory, but the attention generated few leads, even though there may be as many as seventeen victims.[33] And like the Jeff Davis 8 case, the Gilgo Beach case has been characterized by law enforcement corruption and incompetence. In December of 2015, former Suffolk County police chief James Burke was indicted in federal court on civil rights charges for allegedly beating a robber after he stole items, including sex toys, from Burke's car. In February 2016, an outside medical examiner reexamined one of the victims' autopsies and concluded that, contrary to an earlier finding, "there is no evidence whatsoever that [the victim] died from drowning."[34]

"They can go unsolved forever," laments John Jay College of Criminal Justice forensic psychologist Louis Schlesinger of serial killer cases. "It's usually just luck that breaks a case."[35]

But it should have been obvious all along that the Jeff Davis 8 killings were not the handiwork of a serial killer. For one, the victims of serial killers (according to the FBI Behavioral Analysis Unit's own research) are almost always strangers, both to their assailant and to each other. Yet the Jeff Davis 8 all knew one another intimately. Some were related by blood, others lived together. The prime suspects, too, were directly connected to the victims.

All of the victims engaged in their sex work locally, several at the Boudreaux Inn, the motel where some investigators believe Loretta was murdered. Local law enforcement were dispatched to the Boudreaux Inn regularly to break up fights or bust patrons with drugs; on at least one occasion, the Jefferson Davis Parish Sheriff's Office was called to the Boudreaux Inn regarding a dead body on the premises.[36] Loretta was the subject of numerous complaints to the Sheriff's Office based on her activities at the motel.

All but one of the victims—Ernestine—were associated with the same fixture of the Jennings underworld: sixty-one-year-old pimp and drug dealer Frankie Richard.

"Most serial killing is solo," cautions Schlesinger. "Serial murder is very unusual." But the multiple suspects in the Jeff Davis 8 case do suggest serial murder. In 2006, two men—Byron Chad Jones and Lawrence Nixon (a cousin of the fifth victim, Muggy)—were charged with second-degree murder in the 2005 slaying of Ernestine Patterson. (The case eventually collapsed.) In 2007, Frankie Richard himself was briefly charged in the killing of one of the victims, Kristen Gary Lopez. But those charges were dropped after witnesses provided conflicting statements and a key piece of physical evidence was mishandled. He remains free and is often perched on the porch of his family home in South Jennings. According to case files, Jennings street hustlers with connections to Frankie were suspected in the deaths of some of the other women. In aggregate, we see a pattern more in keeping with serial murder than a lone serial killer.

More compelling than any serial killer theory is that most if not all of the Jeff Davis 8 were murdered for knowing too much: most compelling that they witnessed *other* murders. Indeed, women who provided information about the first few cases wound up victims themselves. Muggy Brown—the fifth victim—was interrogated about the killing of Ernestine, the second victim.[37] Muggy also claimed to have spotted the body of Loretta, the first victim, floating in the Grand Marais Canal before Jerry Jackson found her there. According to a Task-force report that I have obtained, a witness told investigators, "Laconia Brown were [sic] walking across a bridge and they found Loretta Chaisson's body." Detectives also interrogated Kristen Gary Lopez, the third victim, about Loretta. "She knew what was going on," Melissa Daigle, Kristen's mother, told me. She trailed off, tearing up at the memory. "They were scared, them girls. I think she knew about it [who was responsible for the murders] and was too scared to say."[38]

That women who were questioned in high-profile homicides were turning up dead all over Jeff Davis Parish should immediately have raised red flags. But it didn't. At least not with law enforcement, who were accustomed to maintaining inappropriately intimate connections with those on the wrong side of the law.

But one thing is for certain. All eight of the victims snitched for local law enforcement about the Jennings drug trade.

When I confronted Sheriff Edwards with the allegation, he stammered a nondenial: "I wouldn't respond. If they were informants, I would still continue to protect their anonymity. I don't know that's the truth. I won't comment on it."[39]

CHAPTER 2

Boom and Bust

In life and in death, the Jeff Davis 8 were cast as outsiders by the ruling elite. Sheriff Ricky Edwards infuriated friends and family of the victims by publicly proclaiming that the Jeff Davis 8 all shared a "high-risk lifestyle." Most interpreted this to mean that they were unworthy of sympathy or significant law enforcement resources.

While the Jeff Davis 8 were no doubt marginalized, the parish in which they lived—and indeed much of southwest Louisiana—was built by outsiders. In 1912, Jefferson Davis Parish, along with four other parishes, was created from nearby Imperial Calcasieu Parish—which translates to "crying eagle" from a language spoken by the Atakapa, an indigenous people who lived along the Gulf of Mexico[1]—an area known as a "Wild West," populated by undesirables (Imperial Calcasieu Parish is now known as simply Calcasieu Parish).

Jeff Davis Parish sits in the Acadiana region of Louisiana, which stretches from Lake Charles hundreds of miles east to Grand Isle, itself 108 miles southwest of New Orleans. This land was largely populated by the Acadians, a group of settlers from Acadia, a seventeenth- and eighteenth-century colony of New France, which comprised parts of eastern Quebec, the Maritime provinces, and what is now Maine.

When the British conquered Acadia in the early 1700s, the Acadians were told to swear fealty to the British crown. The Acadians refused, and many resettled in Spanish-controlled Louisiana. Yet the Spanish took a similarly dim view of the Acadians, allowing them to live in the areas no one else wanted to inhabit—the Louisiana swamps.

The Acadians—later Americanized to "'Cadien" or "Cajun"—believed that their place in Louisiana would improve under French control in the early 1800s. But the sale of Louisiana to the United States in 1803 simply perpetuated their caste ranking, which was just above slaves. Indeed, in late-1800s Reconstruction-era Louisiana, Cajuns were forced to compete with freed slaves for low-level jobs.

The beginning of the twentieth century saw a further diminishing of the Cajuns' status in Louisiana: the Americans forbade the speaking of Cajun French in schools. "They literally beat their culture out of them," explains Scott Lewis, a former reporter with the *Jennings Daily News*. "They couldn't speak French in schools and they were beaten when they did."

Cajuns were politically disenfranchised as well. Despite the majority of Louisiana's population living in the southernmost part of the state, most of its politicians were from elsewhere, namely North Louisiana and New Orleans. "That went on until Edwin Edwards was elected governor in the 1970s," says Lewis. "He was the first Cajun who had any significant political power."

Edwards was a hugely charismatic populist in the style of

Huey Long, and he became the first Cajun-born governor of the state. But while Edwards was enormously popular in Louisiana and his ascendance yielded some political clout for the Cajuns, a rise in their personal fortunes didn't accompany it. In the late 1990s, a federal jury found Edwards guilty on seventeen counts of racketeering, mail and wire fraud, conspiracy, and money laundering.[2] His fall was swift, and the Cajuns continued to occupy the bottom rungs on the economic ladder. While the Cajuns' economic status remained static, Edwards managed to parlay his political scandal into a short-lived reality series on A&E, where his acerbic, darkly truthful insights on Louisiana politics struck a nerve. "The only way I can lose this election," he once famously declared, "is if I'm caught in bed with either a dead girl or a live boy."

For the nineteenth and much of the twentieth centuries, Jennings residents found employment in decidedly blue-collar, working-class industries: farming, oil, and, later, at textile plants. A handful of elites, however, controlled most of the local commerce. One of the most prominent families in Jennings were the Ziglers, whose paterfamilias, George B. Zigler, migrated, penniless, to town from North Dakota in the early 1900s and quickly minted a huge fortune among Jennings's vast and newly discovered oil fields.[3] Passionate about Jennings and the riches the town had brought him, Zigler became a Johnny Appleseed for the business community. His son, Fred Zigler, owned and operated a prominent automobile dealership from the late 1930s to the mid-1950s, called Zigler Motors, which he later sold to another Jennings entrepreneur, A. J. M. "Bubba" Oustalet. The Oustalets remain one of the most powerful families in the area. Two sprawling car dealerships bearing the family's name sit in the heart of Jennings: a Chevrolet dealership on North Main Street and a Toyota dealership on North Broadway. Today, the hubs of activity in Jennings comprise just a few blocks around North Main. It includes the Oustalet dealership, a courthouse, a branch of the Jefferson Davis Parish library, and the sprawling Jennings Carnegie Library, with dramatic white columns by its entrance, built in 1908, which is the oldest library in Louisiana.

In the optimistic era of post–World War II economic expansion, Fred Zigler dreamed of building a grand hotel that would transform Jennings into a national destination. In 1948, Zigler took his hotel pitch public, urging fellow residents to buy shares in the hotel, to be named, naturally, for his father, George B. Zigler. He would build on a plot of family land on the corner of Broadway and Nezpique Streets in North Jennings. "If you do not build a hotel now," warned one of Zigler's partners in the *Jennings Daily News*, "you will pay the price of it every ten years in lost profits." Citizens of Jennings heeded the call. By the end of 1948, 125 hotel salesmen had sold 3,167 shares of stock, raising $316,700 (the equivalent of about $3 million today). For their efforts they were rewarded with gold watches and free groceries. Shareholders who purchased $1,000 in stock were paid back with a public nod to their civic pride: their names were published in the *Jennings Daily News*.

But the Zigler campaign was still hundreds of thousands of dollars short of the funding it needed to open the fifty-seven-room hotel. "We hit hotel firms, insurance companies, individuals, investment bankers, every place we thought we had a chance," Fred Zigler lamented to the *Wall Street Journal*. "But no luck—we had no operating record and they wouldn't take a chance on us." Finally, in 1952, the hotel's backers secured a sum—$600,000—in excess of their budget. The Zigler hastily opened.

The years of slow and frustrated financing efforts should have signaled to the Ziglers that the hotel's prospects would be dim. Shortly after opening, the Zigler was rocked by a series of disasters. In June of 1957, Hurricane Audrey brought torrential rains and 145-mile-per-hour winds, severely crippling infrastructure for the oil industry. Audrey was predicted to be a Category 2 storm at landfall, but defying forecasts, it intensified to Category 4, killing nearly 550 people in west Louisiana, including over 100 children. After Audrey, the region faced an even more destructive force: the interstate highway system. Now motorists could bypass dozens of small towns along US Highway 90 in favor of Interstate 10 (or I-10). "US 90 itself had abandoned the Zigler," wrote Lewis in a sprawling, eleven-part history of the Ziglers published in the *Jennings Daily News*. "At the end of the 1950s, the state adjusted the highway's route. Instead of running through the heart of downtown on Main Street, US 90 was shifted east to North Cutting Avenue. Even if motorists did go down US 90 instead of I-10, they could no longer clearly see the Zigler's welcoming sign."

If I-10 marked the beginning of the end of the Zigler era, the passing of Fred Zigler in 1960 was its culmination. With its founder gone and its finances imperiled, a hospitality company called Community Inns of America, based in Nacogdoches, Texas, assumed operations of the hotel in 1962, only to pull out a year later. Zigler's protégé, Bubba Oustalet, vowed to keep the hotel open and turned to the tactic that had kickstarted the project in the first place: seeking financial pledges from the public. In 1963, Oustalet led a new bond drive, which raised $160,000. "This hotel has already paid for itself at least once," Oustalet boasted to the *Jennings Daily News*, "and perhaps several times, in its benefit to the community during the last ten years."

The hotel's history, however, had already proven that financial backing did not ensure profits. The Zigler staggered through the 1960s and early 1970s until, yet again, death and the specter of financial ruin corroded it. On April 22, 1973, Zigler's wife, Ruth, passed away, and the Jefferson Davis Bank foreclosed on the property about a month later. During the summer of 1974, a court seized the property and set an auction for September. A familiar name—Bubba Oustalet—led the bidding for the Zigler and picked up the property with a partner for a fire-sale price of $65,000, one-tenth of the original cost of the hotel. But in a decision that baffled working-class Jennings, Oustalet decided to open an expensive white-linen dining establishment in the Zigler with an unfortunately apropos name, Chez Canard. To no one's surprise, the restaurant was an immediate failure, which put the Zigler on shaky financial footing yet again.

But Oustalet was prescient about a rise in property values in the area, and by 1980 he sold the hotel to a group of investors from Lafayette for $400,000, turning a huge six-figure profit for himself and his partner. The new Lafayette owners made better business decisions than Oustalet: they transformed Chez Canard into the casual Sally's Café, which provided affordable home-cooked meals to Jennings's blue-collar populace. "We were right next to the courthouse, so we had regulars from there, from city hall, from the downtown businesses, bus drivers after school, all kinds of people," its proprietor, Sally Landry, told the *Jennings Daily News.* "You get to know your town."

Another catastrophe, one that would far eclipse the damage wrought by Hurricane Audrey in 1957, was about to befall the owners of the Zigler. By the mid-1980s an oil bust drove prices of crude to $10 per barrel, devastating Louisiana's economy. In the late 1980s, the state's unemployment rate peaked at over 13.1 percent, nearly double the rate at the beginning of the decade (6.8 percent).[4] The hotel's operators struggled to maintain the massive property through the late 1980s and early 1990s, and in 1997 it finally closed for good. Jennings has never recovered from the oil bust or the decline in manufacturing of the mid-twentieth century: according to the Economic Innovation Group's "Distressed Communities Index" published in 2016, 49 percent of adults in Jennings are not working.[5]

The Zigler was built on a sense of grievance from the Jennings elite that the town—the birthplace of Louisiana oil—hadn't shared in the state's petrochemical profits. Major oil companies had opted to open offices in nearby cities such as Lake Charles and Lafayette. It was painfully ironic that the oil bust of the 1980s destroyed the hotel. The establishment, after all, was the product of the dreams of the Jennings elites who envied the surrounding parishes that had became vastly richer. The Zigler hotel, however, represented much more than a failed business venture. The constant bond drives in a small, poor community for the Zigler—in which hotel salesmen deployed boiler-room tactics under the banner of civic pride—could only end in calamitous financial ruin for everyone involved. "People were visited by the town elites," says Lewis of the *Jennings Daily News*. "They were told, 'You need to give your portion.' It was social coercion. You were expected to give to the town. People did give. But some gave more willingly than others. The financing of the Zigler was the power structure in action."

Power in Jennings—and in Jefferson Davis Parish—was exercised in a similar fashion by law enforcement. "Sheriffs in Louisiana have no oversight," says Lewis. "They answer to no one, except, theoretically, the voters. Sheriffs are elected, and generally stay in office for as long as they please. And anyone who wants to be anyone courts the sheriff's favor. Once a sheriff is entrenched, the parish's political structure works to keep him afloat."

The role of the sheriff in Louisiana as both king and *kingmaker*—particularly in small parishes like Jefferson Davis—often yields, unsurprisingly, widespread corruption. Dallas Cormier, who was the sheriff of Jefferson Davis Parish from 1980 to 1992, allegedly used public funds for all manner of personal purchases, including trucks, tires, and guns.[6] Cormier also used inmates in the parish lockup for his personal tasks, a highly unethical and illegal practice. A federal investigation into Cormier's activities yielded a sprawling indictment. In 1993, Cormier pleaded guilty to one count of obstruction of justice; he was ordered to pay a $10,000 fine and perform five hundred hours of community service.

Despite his misdeeds, Cormier, who sported senatorial gray suits, perfectly coiffed white hair, and a craggy face that conveyed deep seriousness, was beloved by his employees. "Dallas was no angel," remembers former Sheriff's Office radio dispatcher Ginger Reiley. "But he was a good man and he was good to his employees. Yes, he used the prisoners to go to work for him. That's why he got in trouble with the law. But back then, he wasn't the only one doing that. Calcasieu was doing that. That still goes on today. Dallas was good to us."[7]

The Cormier administration also earned the respect of the citizenry because major crime rates were extremely low during his time in office. When I asked Reiley if she could remember the number of calls she received about homicides under Cormier, she struggled mightily: "Only one. In 1990 or 1991. A set of twins were murdered. Black boys." Jennings residents have told me that there was not a single funeral in town that Dallas Cormier did not escort himself.[8]

While I-10 was beginning to emerge as a popular drug-trafficking route, key players often avoided Jeff Davis Parish, concerned that the sheriff's drug-interdiction officers would pull them over. "Fear of Jefferson Davis Parish in the drug community was strong in those days," says *Jennings Daily News* reporter Scott Lewis. "Drug dealers actually handed out maps which had directions to go *around* the parish."

One of the unit's drug-interdiction practices was the use of drug-sniffing dogs. "In the beginning of 1992, one of our dogs hit a green 4Runner on the Interstate," Reiley remembers. "We brought the suitcases in and started going through them; there were fine, formal dress clothes. But then I felt the shoulder pads and they were crunchy. I cut them and found forty thousand dollars. And drugs were sealed inside the car doors."

But a potent drug business was quietly taking shape in Jennings, aided by the ease with which one could travel to Houston, a two-hour-and-forty-five-minute drive straight down I-10. Once there, traffickers could connect with major cocaine and marijuana distributors. "Everybody made that trip back and forth to Houston," Jennings native Ty Anthony Cornelius, who grew up with the Jeff Davis 8, told me.[9] "Houston is part of our culture. Everybody in Jennings got hella family out there, everybody hang out there. Having all that family in Houston is helpful because it's a major drug hub. You can get whatever you want for a real low price. Motherfuckers in Jennings couldn't pass it up. Houston is so close that when we was all in high school, guys would take off from school, ride out there and pick up forty pounds of weed, and then come back to school again after missing just a few periods. Then they'd go home and break it down to sell."

Police misconduct also helped the drug business expand in Jennings and beyond. On March 2, 1990, nearly three hundred pounds of marijuana were stolen from the Sheriff's Office evidence room. One witness told investigators that the heist was an inside job masterminded by the then chief deputy and Frankie Richard, who would later become a prime suspect in the Jeff Davis 8 murders.[10] The witness who fingered the chief deputy of the Sheriff's Office as a suspect passed a polygraph test, and several of the individuals he named—including a Jennings man named Ricky Breaux—were charged, and later convicted, in the burglary.

While Jennings's strict drug-interdiction program appeased the public, it had a darker side as well. Mike Dubois, a former prescription-pill dealer in Jennings, whose sister Whitnei was the fourth victim in the Jeff Davis 8 case, told me that one of the top drug sources in town worked in narcotics at the Sheriff's Office. "I had a friend of mine who said, 'I got a buddy, my connection, he wants to meet with you, he wants you to work with us,'" Dubois told me. "I said, 'Man, I just got out, I'm not interested. Who is this guy?' 'He wants to talk to you before I tell you.' Okay. So I agreed to meet with him. . . . All of the sudden there's this car coming down the road. I said, 'You set me up.' I grabbed him by the neck. It was a guy from narcotics. Coming down the road. *That* was his connection."[11]

The narcotics officer then pitched Dubois on selling drugs seized off I-10. "He said, 'Look, Mike, I tried to break you in every way I could,'" Dubois remembers. "'You never gave us your sources, you never gave nothing. I know you can sell for me and you won't ever give me up. I'll tell you what I do, I'll let you know whenever narcotics are coming in, I'll let you know everything, I'll keep you as safe as I can. Just turn my stuff out on the street.'

"So I started selling drugs for the cops."

Dubois claims to have sold drugs under the protection of local law enforcement from the late 1980s through the early 1990s. He also owned and operated a now-shuttered Jennings nightclub called the Blue Jay Lounge, which was frequented by none other than Sheriff Cormier. "It was at my lounge that the sheriff was brought down," Dubois says.

The federal investigation into Dallas Cormier (which did not involve allegations of drug dealing) ended his tenure as sheriff, and in 1992 a new sheriff, Ricky Edwards, was elected. Unlike Cormier, Edwards didn't have a law enforcement background. He had worked in real estate as a personal properties supervisor for the parish assessor, and his curt, dismissive, and impersonal managerial style immediately alienated his employees, who were accustomed to the folksy, familial feel of Cormier's office. Beyond his gruff demeanor, Edwards betrayed his own elitism, letting class divisions dictate his agenda. The fissure between Jennings's impoverished south side and the relative opulence of the north was deeply entrenched, and Edwards did little to hide his disdain for the south side. According to former Sheriff's Office employees, Edwards once said, "You were raised on the wrong side of the tracks," to Sue Reiley, a south-side resident and employee of the Sheriff's Office. Shortly after, Sue and her sister Ginger (the radio dispatcher) were terminated in an office reorganization. The sisters, joined by other fired employees, sued the sheriff in federal court, claiming age discrimination, gender discrimination, and intentional infliction of emotional distress.[12] In 1995 a judge ruled in Edwards's favor and dismissed all of the plaintiffs' claims with prejudice.

The notion that South Jennings is the "wrong side of the

tracks" is a sentiment widely shared by the Jennings elite. South Jennings is literally located on the other side of the train tracks that run along South Railroad Avenue, in the heart of town. For decades, the north side has been home to the professional class in Jennings—lawyers, judges, district attorneys, and businessmen. The south side, conversely, is where the working class—oil-field workers, mechanics, housepainters—reside. The class division has yielded a racially mixed south side, though the African-American presence there is so deeply felt that in 2008 South Cutting Avenue was renamed for Jennings's only black mayor, Wilbert D. Rochelle.[13] Still, the divide, Ginger Reiley says, is "not skin color. It's *money*. It has always been that way." There are, however, profound divisions by race within the minuscule south side: African-American families dominate long thoroughfares to the east, while whites populate streets on the southwest. "South side has two different versions," explains Ty Anthony Cornelius. "It's G. C. Chaney Street for poor black people and West Division for poor white people. But we all cliqued together. I moved to Delaware and I experience more racism here than I *ever* experienced in Jennings."

Yet Sheriff Edwards didn't clash with his employees on issues of class alone. Soon after getting elected, sheriff's deputies claimed that Sheriff Edwards dismantled the drug-interdiction program and issued a shocking ultimatum about its drug-sniffing dog, a black German shepherd named Armin, to his handler at the Sheriff's Office, Jimmy Horner: *You can buy him or we kill him.* The animal was saved by Horner, who purchased Armin for $10,000.

Beyond allegedly dismantling the drug-interdiction program, Edwards jettisoned Cormier's careful approach to I-10 traffic stops and searches. Probable cause, a constitutional prerequisite for any search, was disregarded entirely, ensnaring the sheriff in a series of high-profile civil rights lawsuits.

In the early 1990s, Karen Bryant, from Austin, Texas, was returning home from a church convention in Florida on I-10 when she spotted a white sports car trailing her.[14] The sports car had a flashing blue light on its dashboard, but Bryant was unsure if the vehicle belonged to a cop. She nervously pulled to the side. As cars zoomed by her on the highway, Bryant was confronted by parish deputy Dennis Fontenot, a weight lifter who struck an imposing figure. When Bryant rolled down her window, Fontenot began to shout. Because he was so red faced and furious, Bryant feared that he was not a real deputy. She sped away to a nearby gas station, where she hoped to call the police. When Deputy Fontenot caught up to her, he threw her against her car and took her to the parish lockup, where she was strip-searched. "The type of strip search they issued or ordered was a cavity search," Bryant later told *Dateline NBC*.[15] "I felt subhuman." In 1993, Bryant sued Deputy Fontenot and Sheriff Edwards in federal court for violating her civil rights. The lawsuit was later settled and Deputy Fontenot was terminated.

But Fontenot was far from an outlier at the Jefferson Davis Parish Sheriff's Office. The pattern and practice of illegal stops under Sheriff Edwards continued well into the 1990s. Just after midnight on November 28, 1995, Albert and Mary Gonzales, a Hispanic couple, were traveling down I-10 when they were pulled over by Deputy Darrell Pierce without probable cause.[16] Like Bryant, the Gonzaleses sued Sheriff Edwards and the Sheriff's Office, but this time with a race-based claim, specifically that "it was . . . custom, habit and routine practice of Deputy Pierce to detain and question minority citizens, including Hispanics . . . and to disproportionately pull [over] out of state travelers." The Gonzaleses later settled their case for an undisclosed amount.

Such law enforcement misconduct in a rural part of the country rarely merits national media coverage. But on January 3, 1997, *Dateline NBC* ran a forty-five-minute exposé on illegal traffic stops in Jeff Davis and Calcasieu.[17] *Dateline*'s producers had been tipped off that the region's deputies were targeting motorists with out-of-state license plates and unlawfully seizing their cash. Under a Louisiana drug-forfeiture law, citizens who had their assets seized—and were uncharged— bore the burden of both proving their innocence and having to pay the highest bond in the nation (10 percent of the value of the property or $2,500, whichever was greater) to sue for their return.[18] Perversely, the 1989 law insured that forfeited assets were distributed in a manner that invited corruption. Sixty percent of the proceeds went to the law enforcement agency that seized the property, 20 percent to the district attorney, and 20 percent to a state judges' judicial-expense fund.

To prepare for its exposé, *Dateline* rigged a test car with Florida license plates, installed several hidden cameras, and set the vehicle's cruise control to sixty-three miles per hour, clearly below the posted speed limit of sixty-five. The *Dateline* crew then drove through Jeff Davis and Calcasieu parishes on I-10. Moments into their trip they were pulled over. The deputy told them, "You were speeding up and slowing down. You were going from line to line." The next day, the *Dateline* crew was pulled over yet again by a deputy, who provided an equally false rationale for the traffic stop: "The first reason why I'm stopping you, sir, is because you're slowing down real fast in traffic right there." Incredibly, this deputy also looked in the wallet of the driver—a *Dateline* cameraman— and asked him how much cash he had on him.

When confronted on camera, Sheriff Edwards defiantly denied that his deputies made illegal traffic stops: "Are you insinuating that we are targeting out-of-state people? I can only tell you that we are not." But when *Dateline* offered their hidden-camera footage and victim interviews to members of local law enforcement, many came forward—their identities hidden—to slam Edwards's department. "They got their own rules," one officer told *Dateline*, "their own laws. . . . This is the South."

The *Dateline* exposé garnered huge ratings—it was watched by an estimated 12.7 million households—and embarrassed not only the parish but the entire state of Louisiana.[19] *Dateline* boasted that its report "hit Louisiana like a thundercloud," and that was no exaggeration. Louisiana's lieutenant governor, Kathleen Blanco—who later famously battled George W. Bush over federal resources during the Katrina crisis—estimated that the negative publicity generated by *Dateline* would cost the state $150 million in tourism revenue.[20]

Despite the media firestorm surrounding Sheriff Edwards, the most egregious police misconduct was alleged to be occurring in neighboring Calcasieu Parish. A series of murders in Calcasieu during the 1990s—in which suspicion fell on the relative of a high-ranking member of law enforcement, and investigations were marred by corruption and incompetence—would haunt the region for the next decade.

CHAPTER 3

Lucky and LeDoux

At approximately 2:00 p.m. on February 12, 1991, a seventy-six-year-old Calcasieu Parish woman, Nella Haygood, rushed next door to check on her granddaughter Pam Little-ton Ellender.[1] It was Mardi Gras and no one had heard from Pam or her husband, Eric, since Lundi Gras, the Monday before Mardi Gras. Lundi Gras is usually reserved for friends and family to prepare meals and make last-minute alterations to costumes for Fat Tuesday. Pam's absence was conspicuous.

Nella peered into the carport and saw only Eric's car. Concerned, she walked to the front of the house and looked in the window. A gun lay on the floor surrounded by shotgun shells.

Eric was the proud owner of a Remington 7 mm rifle and a 12 gauge shotgun, so the sight of the weapon didn't alarm her, but the chaotic scene in the room did. "Pam never went to bed with the house messed up," Nella later told investigators. Panicked, she went to the side door, which was often left open. To Nella's relief, the door was ajar and she went inside and up to the bedroom.

Eric and Pam were in bed, under the covers, but not

31

moving. When Nella pulled back the sheets, she found Eric lying faceup in nothing but white underwear, his left eye wide-open and his right eye closed. Pam lay next to him, naked from the waist down. Just then, Nella heard her year-and-a-half-old great-granddaughter, Erica, crying from her crib in an adjoining room. Nella rushed to Erica, scooped her out of the crib, and ran to a neighbor's house. "I told Huey," Nella later said to investigators, referring to her son, "to call the law and bring them out there."

The law arrived quickly; just moments after the 911 call was made, Deputy Michael Williams of the Calcasieu Parish Sheriff's Office greeted Nella in the driveway of her granddaughter's home, where she was clutching Erica. Williams inspected the bedroom. "I approached the bed and pulled the covers back," he wrote in his investigative report, "to see massive gunshot wounds to the victims' heads."[2] The murders in this sleepy section of Calcasieu Parish resembled an execution.

Pam and Eric were atypical murder victims. Eric, twenty-seven, worked as an adjuster for his father-in-law's insurance company, while Pam, twenty-five, raised Erica at home and worked at the insurance company as needed. "Whoever did this," thought Huey Littleton, Pam's father, "killed two of the finest people in Calcasieu Parish."[3]

The mystery of the Ellender homicides lasted barely a few hours. In the early evening of Mardi Gras, the Baton Rouge Police Department, acting on a tip, apprehended four white men, all in their late teens or early twenties—Christopher Prudhomme, Robert Adkins, Robert Gentry, and Robert Messick—in a Toyota 4Runner owned by the Ellenders. The police searched the suspects' apartments and found Eric's 12 gauge shotgun, which had been freshly sawed off. Adkins confessed that he and Prudhomme had disposed of an infant seat and a baby stroller from the Ellender home in a Sulphur drainage canal. Those items were later recovered exactly where Adkins had said they were discarded.

Law enforcement also took a series of incriminating statements from friends and associates of the suspects. One friend told investigators that he was watching *Helter Skelter* with Christopher Prudhomme just before the murders and that later, in the early-morning hours of February 13, both Robert Adkins and Prudhomme visited his home, visibly shaken. "Chris looked very scared," the friend admitted to detectives. "He told us that he had done something bad. I asked him about what he did, and he told me not to worry about it, he didn't want me in on it." The friend then walked Prudhomme and Adkins to the door and watched them get in a truck he had never before seen.

Sensing that he was facing insurmountable evidence against him, Prudhomme confessed to the slayings and insisted that he acted alone. "I went and shot 'em," he said in a videotaped statement to investigators. "I shot the guy. . . . He had a hole in his head. . . . The lady, when she jumped, I shot her, too . . . in the face." In the wake of Prudhomme's statement, Prudhomme was indicted on two counts of first-degree murder—punishable by life in prison without the possibility of parole, or death. Adkins was charged with being an accessory after the fact.

It was a remarkably ugly murder case for Sulphur, Louisiana, a quiet, small town of about twenty thousand. But given the quick resolution, it seemed the criminal justice system had worked a real miracle.

Two weeks later, Prudhomme was found hanging from a shower stall at the Calcasieu Parish jail. The noose was fashioned from torn bedsheets. Prudhomme left a long suicide note in which he proclaimed the innocence of codefendants Robert Adkins and Robert Messick. In the note, Prudhomme asserted—again—that he was solely responsible for the Ellender slaughter: "Neither of them knew positively of my actions and had no reason to believe in my acts of violence, which I would also like to say that I enjoyed very much in the taking of those two individuals lives." Prudhomme signed off by quoting lyrics from a song by Houston thrash rockers D.R.I.: "FUCK THE SYSTEM IT CAN'T HAVE ME I DON'T NEED SOCIETY."[4]

With the demise of the alleged perpetrator, the parish considered the Ellender case closed. But Huey Littleton, Pam Ellender's father, wasn't convinced that justice had been served. He hired private investigators, who interviewed witnesses. According to those interviewed, more than a dozen people were in the Ellenders' bedroom when they were killed.

Littleton also found Prudhomme's repeated assertions of responsibility—sole responsibility—to be suspicious. "I will not be able to testify in court," Prudhomme wrote in his suicide note, a statement of defiance, given that the question of guilt was not settled, but also a bizarre one, too, since he had already confessed. Was Prudhomme saying that he would not be used to convict others who were perhaps more culpable? Whom was he protecting and why?

Huey Littleton was a skeptic by nature. He investigated insurance claims for a living. He spent his days determining whether the people around him were being untruthful. In the case of his daughter's murder, the facts didn't match up. Something was off. He sensed a cover-up. Later the following month, after he hired the raft of private investigators, new witnesses emerged whom law enforcement had never contacted. In the fall of 1991, Littleton prodded the new district attorney, Rick Bryant, to reopen the case. Bryant and Sheriff Wayne McElveen were both resistant, but Littleton's unyielding pressure and prominent stature in the community led them to forge a highly unusual deal. The Ellender case would be reopened and Littleton himself could present information directly to the grand jury.

Littleton and his team of hired private investigators collected dozens of witness statements. Perhaps the most stunning statement they obtained came from a former deputy sheriff who worked at the intake section of the Calcasieu Parish jail. He told one of Littleton's investigators that the shower where Prudhomme was found could only be accessed by deputies, who possessed special "rover's keys." Prudhomme was let into the shower by the jail's intake officer, Dave Carson, who he claimed later gave another inmate a fabricated witness statement that he was forced to sign. The statement characterized Prudhomme's death as a suicide.[5]

Carson was connected to another, earlier death similar to Prudhomme's. On May 7, 1988, twenty-one-year-old patrolman Stephen Sandlin, who worked under Carson in Mountainair, New Mexico, was found dead in the department's offices, felled by a gunshot. Carson discovered Sandlin's body and service weapon just hours after the two had been arguing over traffic tickets.[6] Sandlin's autopsy results were inconclusive, but only insignificant traces of gunpowder were found on his hand, essentially ruling out the possibility that Sandlin shot himself. Sandlin's family has long maintained that Sandlin was murdered. "Steve's death was a homicide," Sandlin's father, Tom, told *Unsolved Mysteries*. "I think they killed him to keep him quiet."

Littleton's witness who implicated Carson in the death of Prudhomme offered a similar theory: he was killed to prevent other, more powerful people, including the Calcasieu Parish sheriff's son, from being implicated in the Ellender case.

Carson is currently a licensed private investigator in Louisiana. He runs an investigative shop called "A Carson Agency." According to state guidelines, investigative agencies must register their contact information with the state board so it can be searchable online. However, the phone number on the state website for A Carson Agency was out of service, and therefore I was unable to reach Carson for comment.

Littleton's investigators uncovered other bizarre links between the Ellender slayings and law enforcement. Several witnesses claimed to have seen Sheriff McElveen's son, Richard McElveen, at the crime scene. Both Sheriff McElveen and his son strenuously denied the allegations, and the sheriff even took out a newspaper ad to proclaim his son's innocence, claiming that "this office is aware of no credible evidence placing Sheriff McElveen's son at the Ellender home before, during or after these homicides."[7] To one reporter, Sheriff McElveen blasted Littleton as a "sick man" obsessed with the investigation into his daughter's murder. He claimed that Littleton paid witnesses in exchange for their statements, allegations Littleton categorically denies.

The increasingly public and pitched battle between Littleton and McElveen led the Ellender case to be transferred to the Louisiana attorney general. In February 1995, Robert Adkins was charged with two counts of second-degree murder and Christopher Prudhomme's associates Philip LeDoux and Kurt "Dragon" Reese were indicted as accessories after the fact. Reese pleaded guilty and received a two-year sentence. LeDoux went to trial and was convicted, but only received four years. The relatively lenient sentences were a major disappointment to Littleton, who had pushed so hard to see LeDoux and Reese brought to justice. But for Sheriff McElveen, the paltry sentences were further validation of Prudhomme's guilt. "What did they get?" he asked a reporter from the *Times-Picayune* in 1998 (referring to Littleton and his investigators). "A couple of dopers who tried to cover up for Prudhomme." But Assistant Attorney General Fred Duhy praised Littleton's work, telling the *Times-Picayune*, "Huey Littleton is the reason this case is alive. He refused to accept what Chris Prudhomme said. He refused to say no."

Littleton's persistence in the investigation, however, never yielded a clear theory of the Ellender case: law enforcement suspected it was a botched robbery, while defendants such as LeDoux, who said that Prudhomme watched *Helter Skelter* before the slayings, darkly hinted at some sort of ritual killing. Yet one Littleton witness supported Littleton's suspicions that Prudhomme was a fall guy. Chip Richard, a confidant of several of the Ellender suspects, said that Prudhomme wasn't even present at the Ellender house the night of the murders. He had taken the fall for LeDoux and Adkins (though Richard wasn't clear why). Chip also told Littleton's investigators about a cop who was supplying the Prudhomme crowd with drugs seized from I-10: Calcasieu Parish detective Donald "Lucky" DeLouche. The drugs, Chip said, were seized from vehicles traveling on I-10, then put back on the streets for sale by local law enforcement, a common practice in both Calcasieu and Jeff Davis. Local hustlers call this phenomenon "dope on the table, dope on the streets"—meaning drugs are seized from I-10, proudly displayed for the press, then resold by the cops.

Throughout the 1990s, Detective Lucky DeLouche was the director of Calcasieu's Violent Crimes Task Force (VCTF), an elite homicide investigation unit comprising officers from the Sheriff's Office, the Louisiana State Police, and area police departments. VCTF investigators were tasked with solving the parish's most high-profile homicides.

Their most significant case came on July 6, 1997.

Early that morning Stacie Reeves, Nicole Guidry, and Marty Leboeuf were killed in an apparent armed robbery at KK's Corner, a convenience store and gas station near the corner of Highway 14 and Tom Hebert Road in Calcasieu Parish.[8] The victims were shot multiple times and their bodies were tossed in the store's cooler. Because the perpetrators left no physical evidence and had even removed the store's surveillance tape, the crime went unsolved for more than a year. The parish called in the FBI, and Sheriff McElveen offered a reward of up to $100,000 for information leading to the arrest and prosecution of the killers.

By all appearances the KK's Corner case appeared to be cold. No suspects were named, no official leads were announced. But behind closed doors the Sheriff's Office was sitting on essential intelligence. And this secret information linked the KK's Corner murders to the Ellender homicides.

After the KK's Corner slayings, the department received "thirty to forty tips or more" implicating Sheriff McElveen's son, according to a former Calcasieu Parish sheriff's deputy.[9] A decade before, young Richard McElveen had allegedly been spotted at the Ellenders' on the night of their murder. Now he was being implicated in another murder case.

"Some of the people who talked about the murders said [Richard McElveen] was drunk and high and he was bragging about it," said a former sheriff's deputy, who asked that she remain anonymous, "and they said he was there. I still say to this day that boy killed those people at KK's Corner. No doubt in my mind." The former sheriff's deputy points to McElveen's rap sheet of assault charges: "Wayne always got him out of trouble."

More damningly, with his thick shock of brown hair, heavy-lidded eyes, and wide nose, Richard McElveen closely resembled a composite sketch of the KK's killer.[10] The features of the sketch came from a witness who had purchased $10 worth of gasoline at KK's just moments before the murders. The witness observed two people enter the front of the store and saw some activity that frightened her (she never specified what), so she left before filling her gas tank.

Sheriff McElveen held an internal meeting to quell the allegations. "We got called into a meeting at the Sheriff's Department right after KK's Corner on Tom Hebert Road," the former deputy told me, "and it was to tell us his son was not involved in it and we were not to speak to anyone about the case. Everybody that knew that boy, he was the one who murdered the people at KK's Corner." In early May of 2016, I called Richard McElveen on his home phone for comment; a woman who answered the phone hung up on me when I introduced myself.

In addition to the flood of tips regarding the sheriff's son, an eyewitness told investigators that just after the killings occurred, he observed an unmarked police unit pull into the Fairview Mobile Estates, a trailer park just yards from KK's Corner. The car parked beside a trailer, and moments later a white man—whom the witness was unable to identify—approached the unmarked car and passed two paper bags to the driver. The white man then climbed into his own vehicle, described as a Mitsubishi Eclipse–type sports car with a hatchback, and sped away heading north, toward Highway 171, on the outskirts of Lake Charles.

The witness then spoke to an employee of KK's Corner who identified the occupant of the unmarked police car as Johnny Lassiter, a detective from the Jennings Police Department who would later become police chief. At the time, Lassiter resided in the Fairview Mobile Estates. Intriguingly, so did Richard McElveen.

Was the man with the paper bags Richard McElveen? Did the paper bags contain evidence that could incriminate him? Was Lassiter involved in a cover-up? It's a frustratingly incomplete tip and raises more questions than it settles. But this kind of suspicious activity is a hallmark of law enforcement in the region. And it would not be the last time that Johnny Lassiter appeared to wear the black hat.

Lucky DeLouche, who was both the director of the VCTF and the lead investigator on the KK's Corner case, focused the investigation solely on one suspect, Thomas Frank Cisco, an acquaintance of one of the victims who had also been identified by a witness in a physical lineup conducted by DeLouche.* Cisco claimed that he was in Metairie, Louisiana, the weekend of the KK's Corner murders, but investigators couldn't confirm his alibi.

The police arrested Cisco and placed him in an isolation cell. Cisco received a court-appointed lawyer, Evelyn M. Oubre, who, according to court records, was also representing DeLouche in "family court matters" at the time, a clear and undeniable conflict of interest. Oubre rightly raised the conflict with the courts but, incredibly, remained on the Cisco case anyway.

DeLouche and VCTF investigators continued their interrogations throughout 1998 and 1999. Cisco, too, implicated Sheriff McElveen's son. According to Cisco, Richard

---

*I previously worked as a staff investigator at the Louisiana Capital Assistance Center (LCAC), a nonprofit law office that represents defendants charged in capital cases in the Deep South. Thomas Cisco, the man who was charged and convicted in the KK's Corner triple homicide, was represented by attorneys at LCAC. I did not work on Mr. Cisco's case in any capacity.

McElveen paid him $10,000 out of a promised $20,000 to kill KK's victim Stacie Reeves "because she knew too much about how her former boyfriend, Kevin Abel, had been killed in a drug-related matter in which McElveen was involved." The Sheriff's Office claimed that Abel's death was a suicide, which Reeves told a friend was false. Her insight may have put her in danger and possibly led to her death.

The case against Cisco was plagued by serious ethical problems, from the conflicts inherent in Cisco's legal representation to the credible leads about the sheriff's son that should have led to a recusal of the Sheriff's Office from the case. Nonetheless, in the fall of 2000 Cisco was tried and convicted on first-degree murder charges and sentenced to death by lethal injection. In 2003, the Louisiana State Supreme Court reversed the conviction and ordered a new trial because Cisco did not knowingly and intelligently waive his right to conflict-free representation by appointed counsel. But Cisco's attorneys ultimately brokered a deal to avoid the death penalty, convincing Cisco to plead guilty to three counts of manslaughter and serving a sentence of ninety years in prison.[11]

Both the Ellender case and KK's Corner were marred by accusations involving the sheriff's son, but allegations of misconduct were also directed at DeLouche of the VCTF. Pursuing Cisco in 1997, DeLouche faced serious criminal charges of his own. His ex-wife accused him of sexually molesting their daughter. According to allegations made in an incident report, DeLouche and his girlfriend allegedly penetrated the four-year-old's vagina with their fingers and performed oral sex on her.[12] DeLouche was hit with aggravated rape and aggravated oral sexual battery charges on October 22, 1997. Later, a pair of videotaped statements from the four-year-old were given to the state Attorney General's Office.

This was not the first time that DeLouche was accused of sexual misconduct. According to multiple sources close to the KK's case, the lawman made dozens of sex tapes that portrayed him and a girlfriend in a number of sexual acts, including copulation with a dog. In at least one of the tapes DeLouche was wearing a VCTF T-shirt. One investigator close to the KK's case told me that he and his coworkers personally reviewed the videos and identified DeLouche.

It is unclear what, if any, actions were taken by the Louisiana Attorney General's Office, and there is no record of the molestation case ever being prosecuted by Calcasieu Parish.[13] Over the course of several weeks in the spring of 2016, I left multiple messages for DeLouche on his home phone seeking comment; he did not return any of my calls.

Still, in the late 1990s, the case against Cisco had yet to collapse. The abuse allegations against DeLouche remained a secret because of the age of the alleged victim, and the DeLouche videotapes were viewed only by a handful of people in law enforcement and never publicly discussed. Local citizens remained oblivious. All the community knew was that DeLouche was a swaggering lawman nicknamed Lucky who handled Calcasieu Parish's most high-profile homicides.

In the fall of 2000, DeLouche was lured from the VCTF to the Jennings Police Department. Much later, Johnny Lassiter, who was allegedly seen near KK's Corner the night of the murders, became chief of police in Jennings. One Taskforce witness would later maintain, Sheriff McElveen "was involved in trafficking and distributing drugs and many, if not all, of his law enforcement associates moved from Calcasieu Parish to Jeff Davis Parish, where they conveniently slipped into positions of power."[14]

Jefferson Davis Parish would prove to be an ideal locale

for a lawman such as DeLouche. In 1999, just months before DeLouche took over as the Jennings police chief, Sheriff Ricky Edwards was reelected in a landslide victory over his opponent, Arnold Benoit (Edwards received 6,416 votes to Benoit's 3,802).[15]

On election night, unbeknownst to his constituents, Benoit received threats from a group of men who claimed to be Edwards supporters. Benoit was attending an election party at the American Legion hut in Jennings when three African-American men strode in and confronted him.

"You know you're not gonna beat Ricky until you play the game," the men warned him, all within earshot of his supporters, two of whom were so frightened that they vomited after the encounter. Benoit told me that he was surprised by the juvenile-sounding taunt but absolutely shocked by what the trio of men said next: "We can kill anybody we want in this town and nobody is gonna question it." Benoit says that the group of men then swiftly exited the American Legion hut—and he was never able to determine who they were. "But they were right," Benoit told me. "You *can* kill in this town and no one will question it. Just look at the Jeff Davis Eight."

After Sheriff Edwards's re-election, then Jennings mayor Greg Marcantel appointed Lucky DeLouche police chief. Local media celebrated the mayor's decision, praising DeLouche's decades-long career in law enforcement.[16] DeLouche himself touted his connections, both personal and professional, to the Sheriff's Office: "I'm looking forward to our two departments working together."

DeLouche had gotten lucky in Calcasieu, but his tenure in Jennings was quickly consumed by further sexual scandal. One female officer claimed that DeLouche forced her to videotape her nipples getting pierced and then displayed the video to visitors in his office. A police captain working directly under DeLouche allegedly told a female cop, "You know I like to lick pussy, I can numb it all night," and then demonstrated the sexual act with his mouth. The same captain was alleged to have driven a young female officer to a dead-end road in his patrol unit where he threatened to rape her. "You know what I want," he said, "it's time to prove yourself." A female prisoner said that she performed oral sex on this captain to get the position of cook in the jail. And a male lieutenant in DeLouche's employ waved a knife at a female officer, threatening, "Girl, I'll cut you." These sexual assault allegations and threats of violence—along with countless others—formed the basis of a sprawling civil rights lawsuit filed in federal court against DeLouche, a gaggle of male cops, and the City of Jennings, by eight female cops in 2003.[17]

The routine victimization of female officers at the Jennings Police Department pushed the organization to near collapse, just as it was beginning to recover from a murder by one of its own. On February 5, 2000, Jennings police officer Phil Karam shot and killed retired officer Kenneth Guidry and his wife, Christine, who was suffering from cancer, at their Jennings home. Johnny Lassiter of the Jennings Police Department was also shot in the encounter, though he survived.[18] When help arrived, Karam answered the door and said, "Yeah, I did them both." He then shot at several officers, killing one. When Karam was transported to the police station, he allegedly told a Jennings officer, "Well, who else did I kill today besides Kenneth and Christine, of course?"

Unsurprisingly, Karam entered a plea of not guilty by reason of insanity. "Phil was pushed over the edge by what he was seeing at the Jennings Police Department," a former law enforcement source in Jennings told me. "He couldn't take it anymore. He broke." Karam was tried on three counts of first-degree murder and was ultimately sentenced to three life terms. The ugly saga didn't truly conclude until Karam died of an apparent heart attack in a North Louisiana prison in 2011.

The Jennings Police Department and the Jefferson Davis Parish Sheriff's Office shared a long and deep history of corruption, evidenced by the illegal I-10 traffic-stop and asset-forfeiture scandals of the 1990s. But the misconduct of the new millennium in Jennings was much darker than the get-mine-while-nobody's-looking days of the 1990s. Murder and rampant sexual violence now reigned in the ranks of local law enforcement.

"This is a place of sin," one patrolman said of the Jennings Police Department just before resigning. "There is nothing but sex going on here."

Facing mounting pressure from the Jennings business and city government elites over the growing disarray of his department, Chief DeLouche hurriedly submitted his resignation letter on August 19, 2003.[19] Reporters covering DeLouche's resignation noted the pending harassment complaints from female police officers as well as accusations made by his ex-wife of "many immoral explicit sexual acts." DeLouche's attorney Ric Oustalet denied all of the sexual misconduct allegations and insisted that his client's resignation from the Jennings Police Department was voluntary. DeLouche left the Jennings Police Department consumed in scandal. Later he was named assistant chief of police in Welsh.[20] The Sheriff's Office, meanwhile, was still reeling from the torrent of lawsuits leveled by I-10 motorists. This near-anarchic time in Jennings and Jefferson Davis Parish was the perfect moment for a savvy homegrown hustler to seize power.

CHAPTER 4

Frankie

"It was wide-open."

Frankie Richard, a onetime pimp, strip-club owner, drug dealer, meth addict, and muscle-for-hire, has just eased back into a rocker on the front porch of his family home in South Jennings. "The drugs, the prostitution, the bars, the crooked cops."[1] It was an unusually warm and muggy late afternoon in Jennings in the spring of 2012, and Frankie was reminiscing about the bracing days of the Jennings underworld in the early 2000s. He wore blue jeans and tennis socks. No shoes, no shirt, his paunchy upper body collecting sweat. We were shaded by the blue metal roof of his cramped shotgun-style home. He was mostly motionless as he talked, stopping occasionally to scratch his salt-and-pepper goatee. Frankie's vacant brown eyes rarely met mine, and as day turned to night, he retreated to the kitchen for water served in mason jars.

The good times for Frankie are long gone. In the summer of 2011, he was temporarily exiled to Breaux Bridge, Louisiana, nearly fifty miles east of Jennings, after years of being fingered as a prime suspect in the Jeff Davis 8 murders. But the exile was merely temporary. Frankie is a true native son.

The trajectory of his life has mirrored the rise and decline of Jennings, from the oil fields to the killing fields.

Frankie Joseph Richard was born on July 24, 1955, the son of a trucking-company owner and a housewife. He has four siblings, three brothers and a sister. As with many young men in Jennings, Frankie's first job out of high school was in the oil business. It was well-paying but dangerous work: an oil-field accident in the late 1980s left him with a broken back, but also a significant legal settlement that he used to start a dump-truck business.

Frankie soon flipped the dump-truck company and opened a strip club. He prefers a more unvarnished description: "I sold my trucks," he proudly exclaimed in his distinctly raspy voice, "and opened a whorehouse."

Frankie had a great run with strip clubs in Lafayette during the fizzy 1990s—the Padlock, the Foxy Lady, Club 26, Paradise Island—but his penchant for drinking and violence unwound his success. "Alcohol makes me *nigger* angry," Frankie declared. "I think I'm nine foot tall and bulletproof." His arrest record in the 1990s, on charges ranging from battery to aggravated assault, vividly illustrates the pugilistic path he pursued back then. When the brawling and the beefs in Lafayette became too dangerous, he moved back in with his mother in South Jennings. There, he quickly broke into the burgeoning prescription-pill hustle and garnered a reputation for his raw street muscle, which anyone who dared cross him would encounter. "Let me tell you something. I hope you put this in this interview." Frankie stabbed a finger into my notepad. "I used to hire me and my fuckin' pick handle out. If somebody wanted a leg broke and they give me five hundred dollars, you can bet tomorrow you'd be wearing a fucking cast."

Better still, Frankie's South Jennings home base endeared him to the poor and working-class whites and African-American pill poppers, drug dealers, and pimps alike, who all saw him as an outsider much like themselves. One of Frankie's many African-American associates once told me, "Frankie ain't nothing but a white nigger."

When Frankie wasn't hustling at home, he was doing business at the Boudreaux Inn. With its sloping blue-metal roof and white-painted façade, the Boudreaux Inn could be mistaken for a storage facility. But with Frankie running drugs and sex workers out of its rooms, the Boudreaux Inn was one of the key places in town to trade sex for drugs or drugs for sex. Central to the motel's underworld appeal was its proximity to the highway. It's just yards from I-10, literally in the shadow of drug trafficking on the interstate. Platinum-selling, Baton Rouge–born rapper Lil Boosie was even known to sport a diamond-studded pendant that read I-10 DOPE ZONE. The Boudreaux Inn sat just down the street from another drugs-and-sex hot spot in Jennings, the Budget Inn, on LA 26.

The Boudreaux lot contained two buildings, a restaurant and bar out front and, just behind it, a tiny motel with fourteen rooms. Both buildings were surrounded by a sprawling gravel parking lot, allowing patrons to pull their cars right up to the door of their room. That the Boudreaux Inn served as both bar and motel allowed transactions to run smoothly. Sex workers could pick up a john at the bar and then have sex with him in one of the rooms. "You bought dope at the bar," one former Jennings sex worker told me, "and then you rented a room in the back to have sex. If you didn't have money, you gave head or had sex in the motel so you could buy dope."

By the mid-2000s, Frankie pimped out a growing cadre

of women from the motel, including soon-to-be Jeff Davis 8 murder victims Loretta Chaisson, Kristen Gary Lopez, and Whitnei Dubois. "I would pick 'em up when I seen 'em," Frankie told me, "get 'em off the street, take 'em, spend my money, get high. If they wanted to go make money, we'd hustle. If they didn't want to, the party was over." Though he describes himself as their pimp, Frankie insists that he forged deep bonds with the slain sex workers because of their mutual addictions. "We shared something," Frankie says mournfully. "When we were at the lowest point of our life and no one wanted to have anything to do with us, we had something to do with each other. And that means something to me. . . . No matter how fuckin' low their life was."

But with Frankie and his women deep in the thrall of crack and prescription-pill addiction, business at the Boudreaux Inn rarely ran smoothly. In 2004, Loretta Chaisson (victim one) was banned from the motel after being involved in numerous incidents, including threatening a motel worker. Around the same time, cops were called to the motel when Frankie brawled with Kristen Gary Lopez's father, Andrew Newman, and broke his nose. (Kristen was victim three.)

To most Jennings residents, the Boudreaux Inn was simply a dingy motel off the interstate. But to workers at the motel and players in the South Jennings underworld, the run-down inn had an outsize reputation. Powerful people, it was whispered, patronized the motel. Those who ran the business were well connected in Louisiana politics.

Frankie Richard may have sat atop the drugs-and-sex trade in South Jennings, but he was not without competition, particularly in prescription pills. Just blocks from Frankie's McKinley Street base, a hustler named Harvey Lee "Bird Dog" Burleigh moved prescription pills by the thousands from his home in South Jennings. Bird Dog's business partner was Mike Dubois, a veteran of the South Jennings drug scene.

Dubois was an ideal prescription-pill conduit. He was recovering from two epithelioid trophoblastic tumors in his neck that were, he says, "the size of golf balls," and as a result he was prescribed a plethora of pain medication. "Lortabs, Xanax, muscle relaxers, Somas, morphine," Dubois told me, "I had so much stuff that it was unreal."[2] Because of his legitimate medical needs, Dubois was the perfect doctor shopper. He hit medical clinics all over East Texas. "After my cancer surgery, the doctor-shopping thing was big," Dubois explains. "Harvey Burleigh [Bird Dog] and myself and Wendell Breaux, we were the three original doctor shoppers in town. When Harvey, myself, and Wendell started going to Houston and comin' back and selling 'em, there was nobody else. We were the only game in town."

But by the spring of 2005, Bird Dog's prescription-pill business at 610 Gallup was imperiled. One of his suppliers in Orange, Texas, had its medical license suspended when it was discovered that nearly every patient at the clinic during a six-month period received 120 hydrocodone pills, 90 Soma pills, and 60 Xanax pills.[3] And Burleigh dangerously boasted to his street associates that his drug suppliers were troopers from the Louisiana State Police's Troop D, located just west of Jennings in Lake Charles. Troop D has a long history of drug-related misconduct, culminating in a 2010 internal affairs investigation into its captain, Chris Guillory, for violating the State Police drug policy. (Despite admitting that he obtained prescriptions from three different doctors and that he had "maybe a hundred" pills at his home, Guillory received only a letter of reprimand.)[4] Finally, in February of

2016, after years of mounting allegations of misconduct by Captain Guillory, he was reassigned to the Louisiana State Police's headquarters in Baton Rouge.[5]

Worst of all, unbeknownst to Bird Dog, one of the men living with him, Jared Sauble, was a confidential informant. Sauble told law enforcement, "There was ongoing narcotics activity . . . at 610 Gallup," and "Bird Dog, also a renter at the residence, had gone to Houston to acquire a large amount of prescription medication."[6]

Sauble also told investigators that a fugitive from the Louisiana Department of Corrections was hiding out at his house. Like many informants, Sauble was himself in deep trouble with the law: in the spring of 2005, he was suspected of robbing an elderly couple. By turning on his roommate and partner, he could soften his sentence.

Working off Sauble's information, the Jennings Police Department, along with state Probation and Parole agents, and investigators from the DA's office, plotted a raid. At approximately 6:00 p.m. on April 20, 2005, the multiagency team converged on 610 Gallup. The tiny, raised white clapboard home was typical of the distressed housing that dominates the south side (in Louisiana, homes are often raised off the ground, sometimes even by a foot or two, as a flood-protection measure).

Local law enforcement invited reporters from the *Jennings Daily News* and the *American Press*, a newspaper from Calcasieu Parish, to come along for the raid. Around 8:15 p.m., the team began its final preparation for the raid; the reporters were instructed to remain in the cop cars, out of harm's way and, perhaps more important, with no true vantage point to view the raid.

About two hours later, at 10:20 p.m., the multiagency

team stormed 610 Gallup. When they burst through the front door and yelled, "Police," they found a chaotic scene: more than a dozen drug users crowded inside the darkened home. The electricity had been turned off because, Sauble said, the occupants had spent all of their money on drugs. The only light came from the beams of police flashlights and a battery-powered lamp in the kitchen. Just moments after entering, John Briggs Becton, a Probation and Parole agent, encountered an addict, Leonard Crochet, forty-three, his hair in a ponytail, standing in the living room. Briggs Becton told Crochet to show his hands and claimed Crochet failed to comply. Instead, Crochet "made a sudden movement with his hands toward his belt line." Believing that Crochet was reaching for a weapon, Briggs Becton fired and struck Crochet with a single shot to the chest. He collapsed. Briggs Becton used his foot to roll him onto his side. "Oh shit, oh shit," Briggs Becton muttered, according to a statement provided later by one of his fellow agents. An ambulance finally arrived at 11:45 p.m., over an hour after the raid began. Crochet was pronounced dead at a local hospital. Meanwhile, the inhabitants at 610 Gallup were taken into custody and transported to the Jennings Police Department for questioning.

Most of those in the house said they didn't see the shooting—one said she simply heard someone yell, "Police," and then heard a gunshot. Another, however, said that Crochet "was standing with his hands in the air when he was shot." Louisiana State Police investigators were "unable to locate any items in the immediate vicinity of Crochet's location in the residence which could have been construed as a weapon."

In the summer of 2005, Jefferson Davis Parish prosecutors presented their case to a parish grand jury. They argued that Briggs Becton committed negligent homicide. The jury came back with a "no true bill" decision—meaning no probable cause or evidence to show that a crime had been committed.[7]

The outcome of the Crochet case is similar to that in many police-related killings around the country. Grand juries who heard evidence in the 2014 killings of Michael Brown, a Ferguson, Missouri, teenager shot by a cop, and Eric Garner, a New York man who died after being put in a choke hold by NYPD officer, both came back with a "no true bill," sparking worldwide protests.[8] Indictments are extraordinarily difficult to secure in police-killing cases. Police officers have wide legal discretion in responding to perceived threats and tend to have strong relationships with district attorneys over shared criminal cases.

In the rare instances when prosecutors do pursue charges against cops, the DA's office feels the backlash. In January of 2015, a district attorney in New Mexico filed murder charges against two Albuquerque cops who shot and killed a homeless man, only to have her prosecutor physically blocked by cops from attending a briefing.

Like all grand jury hearings, the Crochet case was held in secret, with no public record. But little in law enforcement's own accounts of the raid suggest that the killing was justified. Crochet was unarmed, with no weapons of any kind anywhere near him. The claim that he reached for his waistband is disputed by numerous witnesses; at least one law enforcement witness said that Crochet was hiding a crack pipe, not reaching for a weapon, when he was shot. I reached out to Sauble, the informant whose information prompted the raid. He refused my request for an interview, but sent me a Facebook message on August 21, 2014:

Although I know more than people would like to think in regards to this matter that is a chapter in my life that I wish to not discuss. Do like almost everyone else and LET IT GO. Please do not contact me about this matter. I will give you 1 clue: Jennings City Police Department (former employees).

Sauble has, however, talked about the killing of Crochet—and the events that precipitated it—in numerous e-mails and private Facebook messages that I've obtained. His motives for becoming an informant, I learned, were twofold. He was facing armed robbery charges and needed to make a deal. But he also claims Bird Dog was stealing from him.

In these e-mails and Facebook messages, Sauble explained that in the spring of 2005 he not only lived with Bird Dog at 610 Gallup, but also played a critical role in his booming prescription-pill business. "Being I was the only one with a valid driver's license," Sauble wrote, "I was taking Bird Dog and others all over Texas and Louisiana to doctor shop for doctors who would easily write perscription drug scripts [*sic*]." Sauble claimed that, despite his bringing in $5,000 per month in drug revenue, Bird Dog was stealing from him. "I was on parole at the time and done [*sic*] an armed robbery against an elderly man," Sauble wrote. "I was being investigated for this. To get my ass out of the jam I put myself in I made a deal with the police to set up the bust at Bird Dog's house."

Sauble's account differs from the State Police investigation in one significant respect. He told investigators that he watched the raid at 610 Gallup from a ditch on nearby Jefferson Street, but in the messages I've obtained, he said that not only was he inside the home, but he was seated *next* to Crochet. "I was sitting right next to Leonard Crochet when he was shot," Sauble wrote. "Leonard just happen [sic] to be an innocent bystander that night and the police told him to stop reaching for whatever he was reaching for under the couch."

An opportunistic and unreliable snitch looking for retribution against his partner in the drug business initiated a drug raid that yielded, according to the Louisiana State Police's own account, merely a bottle of ibuprofen, one bottle of tizanidine (a muscle relaxer), and "one bottle of assorted pills." The negligible haul was made all the more perverse by the profound human cost it carried. Yet Crochet's fateful encounter with law enforcement was apparently not his first. In the years before his death, Crochet told friends and relatives that cops from the Jennings Police Department were harassing him because he refused to sell drugs for them. "I know a lot about a lot," Crochet told relatives. "Jennings isn't a place for me to be."

By April 2005, Crochet reported that the harassment from local law enforcement had escalated. He told a family member that he encountered a group of law enforcement gathered at a Waffle House in Jennings that included John Briggs Becton, the same officer who would later kill him. "They said they're gonna kill me," Crochet said, to which his relative replied, "If you throw your hands in the air, they're not gonna kill you. They can't shoot you with your hands in the air." I left several messages for Briggs Becton on his home phone in May of 2016 seeking comment; he did not return any of my calls.

Crochet's friends and family insist that he was murdered by law enforcement. As of now, there is not enough evidence to support that claim. But an unarmed man was killed by law enforcement after weeks of clashing with them. That alone begs a new investigation by a more independent body. The Crochet case is particularly critical to the Jeff Davis 8 case because those who witnessed his murder constitute much of the milieu of its victims: Kristen Gary Lopez (victim three), Bird Dog, and Alvin "Bootsy" Lewis, who was related to two of the victims. "The victims were being killed because they were present when Leonard Crochet was killed by the police," one witness told Taskforce investigators. "The girls were being killed because they had seen something they were not supposed to see."

At least one of the Jeff Davis 8 victims, Kristen Gary Lopez, witnessed the slaying of Leonard Crochet—a man who had told friends and relatives that he'd refused to sell drugs for the police—at the hands of law enforcement. Crochet's murder occurred at the Jennings home of Harvey "Bird Dog" Burleigh, a prescription-pill dealer who claimed that much of his supply came from a source within Louisiana State Police's Troop D. The Leonard Crochet killing was steeped in law enforcement misconduct—it was an unnecessary use of lethal force, and both the victim and his roommate (Bird Dog) claimed to have had close ties to corrupt police—all of which the Jeff Davis 8 were suddenly perilously aware of.

CHAPTER 5

Ernestine

With the shooting death of Leonard Crochet at the hands of law enforcement in April and the unsolved slaying of Loretta Chaisson in May, the spring of 2005 was Jennings's bloodiest in contemporary memory. Just after midnight on June 18, 2005, the body count grew once again. Three friends—Byron Roy, Jason Smith, and Aaron Dupuis, all of Jennings—were frogging (catching bullfrogs by hand) in the Louisiana swamps to later eat, by a bridge over the Aguillard Canal just south of Jennings along Highway 102. In the impenetrable darkness of an early-summer night, the trio saw what appeared to be a corpse floating near the west bank of the canal. Smith hurriedly called 911, which brought a phalanx of Sheriff's Office detectives, including Sheriff Ricky Edwards himself. The officers took brief, incomplete statements from the trio, an investigative failure made all the more egregious given that Loretta's body had been fished out of a Jennings canal just weeks before. "I was frogging and we found a body," Byron Roy wrote in a statement written after midnight on June 18.[1] "I was out frogging and found what I thought was a body," said Smith, also in a statement provided around midnight, "then called 911."

Detectives fished the body of a partially clothed African-American woman out of the canal and then transported it to the coroner. The only identifiable piece of clothing on the decomposing corpse was a pair of jean shorts with the number 34 stitched on one leg.

The cause of death was clear even before the body reached the coroner. Detectives noted a large incision on the neck. Indeed, at 10:15 that morning the Calcasieu Parish coroner determined that the woman had died from three incisions on the front of her neck, and the death was declared a homicide.[2] It took just a few hours for local law enforcement to determine that the victim was Ernestine Marie Daniels Patterson, a thirty-year-old sex worker who frequented South Jennings and had been missing since at least June 16, 2005.

Excluding her race, Ernestine was much like Loretta. Both were slight physically—Ernestine weighed just eighty-two pounds and stood at five foot four—and their deaths followed a cascade of personal problems, including failed marriages, drug abuse, mental illness, and, for Ernestine, home foreclosure. Before she became immersed in drugs and sex work, Ernestine—whom friends called by her middle name, Marie—was a devoted churchgoer. She attended Greater First Apostolic Church on West Division Street with her four children and husband, Calvin. According to her sister, Jessica Daniels, Ernestine's downward spiral began when her marriage to Calvin dissolved. She left church, lost her home, moved in with a violent, drug-addicted boyfriend, and began hustling the streets of South Jennings.

Slim, petite, and sweet-faced with a wide, dimpled smile, Ernestine was extremely attractive to potential johns in Jennings. In an interview with investigators, two men who would later be charged in her murder described her as a "good-looking skinny girl who would do anything for crack."[3] Ernestine's naïveté also made her easy prey for the police. Her sister Jessica told me that late one night during the winter of 2004 the pair were walking along Cutting Avenue in South Jennings when they were stopped by an unmarked police car. "It was eleven or twelve o'clock at night," Jessica remembers. "He said, 'What y'all doin' late at night like that?' And I said, 'We ain't doin' nothing but goin' home.'"[4] The encounter was all too typical for African-American residents on the south side of Jennings. There wasn't probable cause for the stop. They were simply being pestered. The officer snarled at Jessica, "Yeah, I know your sister. Your sister ain't nothing but a crackhead. She's a sex worker. I'm gonna arrest y'all 'cause you ain't got no business walking late at night." Jessica protested—"I was like, 'No, you're not, you're not gonna arrest nobody'"—even though Ernestine tried to persuade her to stop arguing. "My sister was like, 'Jessica, shut up, c'mon,'" she remembers. The officer continued his tirade. "He was saying our family is crazy, nobody like us out here, we some crazy motherfuckers out here," says Jessica. "Then he said, 'Next time I see y'all, I'm gonna *kill y'all*.' Then he popped the trunk. I called the police and told them about it, and they were laughing like I was crazy."

The last night Ernestine was seen alive—June 16, 2005— she faced similar abuse, but this time from powerful street players. She was searching for potential clients near Renshaw, a tiny street off South Main, the long, ragged strip featuring Jay's Lounge, a run-down nightspot with the warning STRICKLEY ADULTS, NO ONE UNDER 21 painted on its pink clapboard siding. After sex with one client, Ernestine walked along the strip, searching for a South Jennings man named Larry West. During the spring of 2005, Ernestine crashed at West's home and did sex work in the abandoned house next door. That night she would make use of the house for the last time.

Ernestine had sex with Byron Chad Jones, a man from nearby Lake Arthur with a long criminal record, including charges of robbery and rape. While they were occupied, Jones's friend Lawrence Nixon waited for his turn. When they returned to the main house, Nixon was ready. He carried three black-colored condoms: two for Jones, one for himself. Nixon fantasized about a threesome with Jones and Ernestine, but it's not clear that Ernestine had sex with anyone other than Jones that night; indeed, what transpired among the trio after Nixon obtained the black condoms is disputed by everyone involved.

Nixon's wife Lucenda Kagy's account is that she was cooking fried chicken and french fries that night when her husband barged through the front door. He and Jones were carrying a massive, bulging, blood-soaked garbage bag. Nixon confessed that he had held Ernestine down while Jones sliced her throat. They dropped the bag on the back porch until a white vehicle appeared outside. The men loaded the bag—which Kagy described as large enough to hold a human body—and drove off. Kagy then hosed down the porch.

Kagy's story was partly corroborated. Her teenage daughter Ashley told investigators that Nixon came home covered in blood. And a neighbor (Ernestine's uncle) had given Nixon an industrial-size garbage bag just hours before.

Nixon and Jones both disputed the accounts. Nixon claimed that Jones came to his home covered in blood and said "he did something wrong and then left." Yet Jones had an alibi for at least part of the night. At 3:04 a.m. on June 17, 2005, he had checked himself into the American Legion Hospital in Jennings for psychological evaluation. He told doctors that he was living in an abandoned house and had smoked both formaldehyde and crack.

With so many competing narratives, the investigation stretched on for months without an arrest. But Nixon's troubles persisted into that fall. Just before 8:00 a.m. on November 28, 2005, Rosalyn Faith Breaux was riding through South Jennings with her friend Muggy Brown.[5] Earlier that night, Breaux had downed multiple beers and Somas (a muscle relaxant) in Lafayette. During the approximately forty-mile drive back to Jennings, Breaux passed out in the backseat. She awoke to find Muggy at the wheel, navigating the streets of South Jennings in search of a buyer for an Alpine CD player that she had just stolen. When Muggy couldn't find any takers, she pulled over at her cousin's home.

Her cousin was Lawrence Nixon.

"Why don't you come in this house real quick," Muggy told Breaux as they parked outside Nixon's home. Thinking that she and Muggy might ease their comedown with a joint of marijuana, Breaux went inside, passing Lucenda Kagy on the way to the bedroom. Inside the bedroom, Muggy closed the curtains and then promptly turned around and left. Just then, a hulking local drug dealer named Jarriel "Mooney" Palfrey walked in and removed his shirt.

"I done gave them some dope," Mooney allegedly said, referring to Nixon and Muggy. "Let's get this over with." Before Breaux could phone for help, Mooney pinned her down on the bed.

"I screamed out for Muggy," Breaux remembered later.

"Quit hollering," Mooney replied.

"If you're going to do this," a desperate Breaux said, "please put on a condom."

Mooney refused.

Breaux had no choice but to submit. "All I could do," she later told investigators, "was cry." When it was all over, Mooney ejaculated on the bedsheets and then Kagy returned to the bedroom, under Nixon's instructions, to clean up the mess.

A terrified Breaux ran outside and straight into a cluster of detectives, who were questioning Nixon about the stolen CD player that Muggy had just been hawking. Breaux raced over and told them about the assault.

Investigators discovered that Mooney had given Muggy Brown nine rocks of crack to deliver Breaux, and $10 to Kagy for use of the room. Mooney, Muggy, and Nixon were all indicted by the Jefferson Davis DA on charges of conspiracy to commit forcible rape. All three denied the charges, though Muggy corroborated many of Breaux's allegations. She admitted that Mooney had taken Breaux's cell phone, that Breaux didn't want to have sex with Mooney, and that she had seen semen on the bed after Breaux ran out of the bedroom. The cruelty of the alleged setup—Mooney told her, "You been traded for some crack cocaine and I'm going to get it"—was matched by Muggy's confrontational interrogation. She dared the Sheriff's Office to prove the rape case against her and even proudly bragged about getting high off Mooney's supply. "I smoked mine right there," Brown boasted. "I walked clean outside and smoked it."

Between Brown's bold defiance and Nixon's suspected involvement in Ernestine's murder, Breaux grew fearful; on March 27, 2006, she walked into the DA's office and dropped all charges.[6] The case was then "nolle prossed"—a legal term meaning a refusal to prosecute. But the collapse of the Breaux case did not signal an end to Nixon's legal troubles.

On June 23, 2006, Nixon and Byron Chad Jones were indicted on second-degree murder charges in Ernestine's murder.[7] With Nixon now officially charged, the circumstances of the Breaux case suddenly took on more relevance. After all, if women in Jennings could be sold off for drugs or small amounts of cash, then they could certainly be slaughtered and disposed of in canals around the parish. That the Breaux and Patterson cases had the same central players—Nixon, Kagy, and Brown—also pointed to the cliquishness behind the killings. Even then, with the body count at just two, it was likely that this was a case of serial murder, not the work of a single serial killer.

Muggy Brown was a particularly important figure in both cases. During the summer of 2005, Brown was interrogated about Ernestine's homicide. She said she'd heard that Ernestine had "robbed some Mexicans" in Jennings.[8] But Muggy knew much more than she let on.

According to multiple sources, Muggy witnessed Nixon and Jones kill Ernestine in the abandoned house on Garage Alley. Though she never reported this information to the police, her story is frighteningly plausible. Muggy was a frequent visitor to Garage Alley and a close associate of Nixon's and Jones's. In all likelihood she was there that night, either engaging in sex work, procuring drugs, or both. Muggy's confessions, however, also provided a crucial clue. According to her, Ernestine was murdered with a hunting knife.

Where did the knife come from? Whom did it belong to? Where was it hidden?

This potential piece of evidence could have cracked the case open, and police officers were well aware of the suspicious weapon. In an interview with investigators, Lucenda Kagy said that "a jagged hunting knife" lay in an abandoned home on Garage Alley that she and Nixon once shared. Incredibly, nothing in the homicide file indicates that investigators ever followed up on this lead.[9] A woman had died of laceration wounds to the neck on Garage Alley and someone had seen an out-of-place knife on Garage Alley. How could law enforcement have overlooked such an elemental piece of the case?

The Breaux rape brought the increasingly violent milieu of drugs and sex work in South Jennings to the attention of a Jennings-based private investigator named Kirk Menard. Menard was also Breaux's father. He had long known of his daughter's struggles with addiction and her dangerous circle of friends. And he knew firsthand about the corrupting powers of Jeff Davis law enforcement. His first wife, Kalanie Bourque, was a former Jennings police officer and one of the many plaintiffs in the sprawling civil rights lawsuit against Lucky DeLouche in 2003.

But Menard only truly grasped the dangers posed by South Jennings hustlers in the spring of 2006 when his daughter disappeared. Fearing she might become victim three, he initiated a frenzied search through the Jennings canals as well as the abandoned homes and drug houses that dot South Jennings. Menard received a tip that Breaux was hiding in a camper belonging to Frankie Richard's brother Billy Conner. The camper sat on the Richard family property on McKinley Street. Menard and his wife, Jessica, piled into their Chevy Suburban and gunned it toward McKinley Street. Jessica was armed with a tiny .38 special.

Menard and his wife knocked on the camper door. Billy Conner answered.

"Is Rosalyn there?"[10]

Getting no response, Jessica flashed her .38 special and Billy nervously stammered, "Rosalyn, somebody's here for ya." A flustered Breaux hurried past Billy Conner and joined her parents in the car.

When the newly reunited family arrived home, Menard pondered his own convoluted connections to the Jennings underworld. He was related by blood to the pimp Frankie Richard—Menard's brother Eldridge was married to Richard's aunt Caroline—and Menard's daughter had been raped by a suspect in one of the Jeff Davis 8 homicides, and one of its underworld's central players.

Menard, who is now in his late forties, is short, sweaty browed, and often clad in jeans and a company-issued red polo shirt bearing the name of his firm, Advanced Investigative Technologies. He works mostly on civil, not criminal, cases. Like most private investigators, he specializes in divorce and child-custody cases. Back then it was difficult for Menard to imagine investigating homicides, though in some ways he seemed destined to work the Jeff Davis 8 case. Born at the Jennings American Legion Hospital off I-10 to Rosita, a housewife, and Robert, an oil-rig worker, Menard, like the outcast women of the Jeff Davis 8, had a host of family problems that alienated him from his home life. His parents divorced when Menard was just five years old. Rosita got custody of Menard and his four siblings, then took up with a local Cajun musician named Eli Stutes, whom Menard says was abusive toward his mom.

By his early teens, Menard began to feel like a burden to his mother, who supported the entire family with a job in the meat department at the Piggly Wiggly supermarket. At fifteen, Menard ran away from home, thinking he would strike out on his own somewhere in southwest Louisiana. "I was gone for about a week and I was staying about two blocks away," Menard remembers. "A sheriff's deputy came and found me. He talked to me in my mom's kitchen—we were living in the projects in Jennings at the time—and said, 'Look, we got a program we're starting up called Sheriff's Explorers.'" Local police and sheriff's departments across the country maintain after-school "explorer" programs for teens who display an interest in law enforcement. Menard enrolled. He instantly loved carrying a law-enforcement-styled ID and kept busy with activities ranging from softball to shooting at a local firing range.

Sheriff's Explorers was not the only way the teen's life would intersect with the criminal justice system. When Menard was fifteen, his mom met a new man—Walter Dave Hickock—at a bar in Mermentau, a town of about seven hundred located near Jennings. Walter Dave had left his Kansas City home to escape the notorious reputation of his brother Dick. Dick and an acquaintance had brutally murdered four members of the Herbert Clutter family on November 15, 1959—the case that became the subject of Truman Capote's totemic work, *In Cold Blood*. Despite Walter Dave's notoriety, Menard's mother married him anyway, and when Menard was just a teen, the specter of the *In Cold Blood* murders hung heavily over his new family, an unspoken burden. "He wouldn't hardly ever talk about it," Menard remembers. Much later, however, Walter Dave told his story to Jefferson Davis Parish Library director Linda LeBert-Corbello, with whom he collaborated on an "as told to" book about his life called *In the Shadow of My Brother's Cold Blood*.

When Menard was just eighteen, his high school girlfriend, Shirley Marie Breaux, gave birth to Rosalyn. They had a second daughter, Chassity, two years later. Menard and Breaux never married, however, and when Menard was twenty-five he got engaged to seventeen-year-old Kalanie Bourque. The marriage to Bourque, who went on to become a Jennings police officer, lasted only two and a half years. In

1998, Bourque filed a protective order against Menard (Bourque claimed that Menard was stalking her, a charge Menard denies).

While Menard experienced a turbulent personal life, he found fast success in his career. In 1994, he took a job with oil giant Phillips 66 as an entry-level operator on an offshore rig. Six months later, he was promoted to an investigator position, a heady job in the accident-prone world of offshore rigs. The work was not unlike that of a crime scene investigator. "I seen guys get their fingers cut off, broken legs, broken backs, cracked skulls," Menard says.

In 2000, he found employment as a repo man for a major Jennings bank—called simply The Bank—and then in 2004 he took the forty-hour class required by the Louisiana State Board of Private Investigators and started his own PI agency, Menard Investigations Services LLC.

By early 2006, just one year after the first of the Jeff Davis victims was discovered, Menard found himself drawn to the case. The homicides quite literally hit home: his daughter Rosalyn's alleged attackers were charged in the murder of Ernestine. And Menard says his daughter's case collapsed because of witness intimidation and bribery, not lack of evidence. "One of the guys involved said he would pay [Rosalyn] ten thousand dollars to drop the charges," Menard says, "then he said he would kill her. Then he paid her five hundred dollars. My daughter was scared to pursue the case and she dropped it." Menard also pointed to the involvement of Muggy Brown in the incident as proof that sex workers in Jefferson Davis Parish could be both victims of—and accomplices to—crimes. "Muggy knew what was going to happen," Menard says. "This is a common practice—the luring of girls to certain guys."

Menard sensed that the unsolved homicides could be Jennings's undoing. Even though there were just two slain sex workers at that time, it seemed to Menard that the murders were the poisoned fruit of a tree that had been growing roots for decades. "Jennings is like an undisciplined child," Menard says. "If you never hold that child accountable, you're gonna have huge problems."

The chaos, incompetence, and corruption of law enforcement in Jefferson Davis Parish that so concerned Menard culminated in the sad and surprising outcome of the Ernestine Patterson slaying. By all accounts the investigation was doomed by shoddy police work and incomprehensibly bad decision-making. Not only had investigators failed to follow up on the substantial leads about the abandoned home on Garage Alley, the very place where Lucenda Kagy admitted that a "jagged edge hunting knife" would be found under a bed, but they also mishandled part of the crime scene itself. The lab didn't test the floorboards of Nixon and Kagy's home until October of 2006, nearly eighteen months after Patterson's homicide, even though witnesses had reported seeing pools of blood on their floor the night of the murder. Unsurprisingly, all of the floorboard tests "failed to demonstrate the presence of blood."

CHAPTER 6

Kristen

By 2006, frequent busts at the Boudreaux Inn drove parish sex workers to the home of Roxanne Alexander. At sixty-five, Roxanne was a maternal figure to the marginalized. She empathized deeply with the women who would be called the Jeff Davis 8, and they needed all the support they could get. They were poor, addicted to drugs, and often ostracized for dating African-American men. "One of the reasons they were so disliked in town is that they paid more attention to black men than white men," Roxanne told me, noting that many of the Jeff Davis 8, including Loretta Chaisson and Whitnei Dubois, had children with African-American men.[1]

In Roxanne, the Jeff Davis 8 found a loving and protective guardian whose north-side Jennings home at 403 North Craig Street sat far from the predatory pimps and hustlers across the tracks. "They all lived with me," Roxanne told me. "Loretta used to come around here and leave the children with me. Muggy stayed with me. I would give Kristen my ID. Just so that there would be something to identify her if she got into trouble. All of 'em stayed here. They would come to my house for refuge, when they were tired and didn't have no place to go." Roxanne admits that she, too, was a drug addict at the time and that her own struggles helped her forge bonds with the Jeff Davis 8. Still, she says, her domestic, tranquil life—a home on the quiet north side of Jennings—was far from the nomadic existence the Jeff Davis 8 otherwise clung to. "I was in the same lifestyle they were in," Roxanne says, "but I was more secure, so I helped them out. They called me Mama."

As Mama to the Jeff Davis 8, Roxanne was privy to their most closely held secrets. "Just before Loretta was killed, she lay with me in bed," Roxanne remembers. "She said, 'I'm scared. I'm tired of sucking dick for crack. I want to take my kids and go away.' She was tired and crying. The police came to my house a few days later, asking if I'd seen her. I told them she was just here yesterday. Then later I found out that they found her."

Loretta often confided in Roxanne; she once told her that several men in law enforcement were among her best clients. Roxanne remained highly skeptical of the claim until years later when she encountered a middle-aged man at a crack house on South Cutting Avenue. The man, Danny Barry, was a deputy with the Sheriff's Office. He and his wife, Alexander soon learned, were patronizing the Jeff Davis 8 so often that she asked the pair, "You sure you're not killing them girls out there?" (Barry would later become a suspect in the murders and was even interrogated by the Taskforce; he died of cancer in 2010.)

But while Roxanne possessed a fierce, motherly protectiveness, she could not spare her friends from the dangers of their world. Just before noon on March 18, 2007, James Aucoin, a Lake Arthur fisherman, reported a "body floating" in the Petitjean Canal on the outskirts of Jennings.[2]

Aucoin's 911 call came in at 11:54 a.m. that day—"James said he was going fishing when he found the body," wrote detective Angie Theunissen. "Everyone responded." Investigators from the Sheriff's Office, the DA's office, and the Calcasieu Parish forensics unit converged at 12:02 p.m. The victim was naked, save for a gold ring and white sock with red hearts. She was identified as Roxanne's beloved friend Kristen Gary Lopez. A missing person report had been filed for her on March 15. Investigators confirmed her identity by the tattoo on her lower right leg: interlocking hearts.

Yet the passage of time from Kristen's last-known sighting—sometime around March 5, 2007—to the date her body was discovered, March 18, made the task of determining a cause of death difficult. The Coroner's Office ruled her cause of death "undetermined" and noted that the body was significantly decomposed.[3] The notes describe "no obvious injuries: no scalp injuries, no facial or rib fractures," but instead "horseshoe-shaped puncture wounds consistent with the frontal jaws of alligators. I feel all of the injuries . . . were due to marine predators, after her death, chewing on her."

Kristen's fate was particularly cruel because she was so vulnerable. At twenty-one, she was physically gawky—wide forehead, thin nose, outsize ears, and a choppy, severe haircut that rested just above her shoulders. She was intellectually disabled and received Supplemental Security Income checks every month; when she was growing up in Jennings, she participated in Special Olympics events in Baton Rouge. Tougher still, a thirty-five-year-old man had sexually assaulted her when she was just thirteen. She had hardly any family support.[4] Her parents, Andrew Newman and Melissa Daigle, struggled with substance abuse problems and Newman was a regular at the Boudreaux Inn. Between the ages of eight and ten, Kristen was forced to live with her grandmother Nancy. In her preteen years she returned home but was placed in what her mother dubbed the "slow-learning class." Angry and frustrated as an outsider, Kristen dropped out of school in the eighth grade, only to get lost in the South Jennings underworld. Like the victims who preceded her, Kristen had become so alienated from friends and family that she was little more than a spectral presence. "She was out in the streets, she'd go from one place to another, she'd sleep on porches and in barns," Kristen's grandmother told me. "She'd say, 'Mama?' And I'd say, 'What, baby?' And she'd say, 'Do you have something to eat?' I'd fix her two or three ham sandwiches and two Cokes, put it in a bag, and off she'd go."[5]

In Frankie Richard, Kristen found both a father figure and a protector and took to calling him Uncle Frankie. In true Jennings fashion, their lives had intersected for many years: Frankie's sister Tabatha babysat Kristen when she was a toddler. Frankie told me that his family assisted in the raising of Kristen because her mother, Melissa, was addicted to drugs and unable to care for her. Melissa does not deny past drug problems nor that Frankie's kin babysat for her slain daughter. In fact she believe Frankie holds the answers. "I still say Frankie and Tracee [Chaisson] know what happened to my child," Melissa told me.

In Frankie's room at the Budget Inn—down the road from the Boudreaux Inn—Kristen found both sex work and shelter. Just before Mardi Gras in 2007, Kristen and fellow sex worker Tracee Chaisson (cousin of the first Jeff Davis 8 victim, Loretta) were viciously beaten by a Jennings drug dealer over a dispute about money. They were traumatized and deeply concerned for their safety. That spring they stuck closely to Frankie and strayed only from the Budget Inn to pick up fresh clothes. Sometimes, Kristen and Tracee avoided putting on new clothes altogether. Kristen could often be seen wandering near Frankie's house wearing Tweety Bird pajama pants and flip-flops.

When Frankie booked Room 114 at the Budget Inn for a two-week stretch—February 23, 2007, through March 8, 2007—Tracee and Kristen could breathe easily knowing they were temporarily safe from drug dealers.[6] At the time Frankie was one of the most respected and feared street hustlers in Jefferson Davis Parish. If you stuck with Frankie, you were safe.

But soon after the trio checked into Room 114, tensions emerged. Frankie suspected Tracee and Kristen were ransacking his room for everything from cash to motel shampoo bottles. "If they caught you slipping, you was got," Frankie told me, "and you don't leave a hundred-dollar bill laying around or no dope or nothing of any value hanging around because they had a habit to support."[7] Fed up, Frankie banned both Tracee and Kristen from Room 114. The women were devastated. They had nowhere else to go.

Late in the evening of March 5, 2007, Tracee and Kristen approached Frankie outside his home on McKinley Street and begged to be taken back to the safety of his room at the Budget Inn. "Kristen come give me a hug and said, 'Uncle Frankie, you don't want me back to your room?' And I said, 'No, because you don't have no respect, you want to steal everything.'" According to Frankie, the women then left and "went over to Frank Street," just blocks away, to have sex with clients. This was the last time Frankie saw Kristen.

Taskforce investigators conjecture that Kristen stopped at Frank Street just hours before she was murdered. Several of Kristen's personal items were seized from the Frank Street home, including a gray bra with pink trim, a pair of orange shorts, and a white undershirt.

At first, Tracee Chaisson corroborated Frankie's version of events. She told investigators that she last saw Kristen on the night of March 5th at 214 Frank Street, the home of a mutual acquaintance, which also served as a base for drugs and sex in South Jennings. Tracee had begged Kristen to go home because the pair had been partying for days, and the Frank Street location was unsafe. Tracee eventually left, but Kristen stayed. When a week passed with no word from Kristen, Tracee grew worried. On March 15, she called Kristen's mother, Melissa Daigle.

"Tracee was the one that led me to my daughter's murder," Daigle told me. "She called me—I was living in Evangeline Parish at the time—and she said that something really bad happened to Kristen. I said, 'What are you talking about? Get your fuckin' ass ready because I'm coming to get ya.' I got into my car with a picture of Kristen and picked up Tracee and went to the police station."[8] There, they filed a missing person report, and just three days later Kristen's body was discovered in the Petitjean Canal.

CHAPTER 7

Whitnei

At about 2:00 a.m. on May 11, 2007, Whitnei Dubois—the younger sister of Mike Dubois, who hustled prescription pain medication with Harvey "Bird Dog" Burleigh—was furiously searching for drugs in South Jennings. She stopped at her older brother's house and, just afterward, Frankie Richard's. Whitnei, twenty-six, stood at a petite five foot three and possessed a wide, engaging smile. She had thick brown bangs that hung just above her eyes. Like her fellow Jeff Davis 8 victims, Whitnei struggled with drug addiction and came from a troubled background. When she was six months old, she was abandoned by her birth mother and taken in by Elery and Dorothy Dubois, who had a large family of their own.[1] The Dubois clan cared for Whitnei until she was two, when the courts ordered that she be placed back into her biological mother's care. Years later, after enduring physical and sexual abuse at the hands of several of their mother's boyfriends and husbands, Whitnei and her sister were officially adopted by the Dubois family. Mike Dubois was more than twenty years Whitnei's senior. His daughter Brittany was Whitnei's aunt, but the pair were raised as sisters. "We tried to shelter Whitnei as much as we could," Mike Dubois said.

The love and protectiveness of her new Jennings family, however, could not erase Whitnei's long history of trauma. One of the men who dated her mother attacked Whitnei's brother Cody with a butcher knife. "Me and Whitnei would huddle in the closet and cry," Whitnei's sister Taylor told the *Jennings Daily News*.[2] "We could hear our brother screaming, but we couldn't do anything to stop it." Whitnei remained angry and rebellious into her late teens and developed a fierce crack-cocaine habit with her boyfriend, Jennings drug dealer Alvin "Bootsy" Lewis. (Bootsy had myriad connections to the Jeff Davis 8 milieu: he was a witness to the 2005 murder of Leonard Crochet and his brother was married to the first Jeff Davis 8 victim, Loretta Chaisson.) "It was a battle between her and Bootsy," Mike Dubois remembers. "She loved Bootsy and Bootsy loved her. But they fought. Whitnei had a temper. She was a fighter, man. She was sweet as gold, but don't make her mad. Even though she and Bootsy would fight, they were pretty much irreplaceable to each other. But the big trouble was, Bootsy couldn't stay out of jail. Bootsy would get busted for dealing crack, Bootsy would get busted for stealing, Bootsy would get busted for this, that, and the other, you know. And it left Whitnei hanging out there."

The loneliness that Whitnei felt when her relationship with Bootsy faltered eased when she became pregnant in 1996. She gave birth to a daughter, Beyoncé Dubois in November of that year. But Whitnei's problems with drugs and with the law persisted. In 2001, she was charged with cocaine possession (the case was dismissed),[3] and on April 8, 2006, she and Bootsy got into a brawl in Room 204 at the Boudreaux Inn. When investigators arrived at the scene, they found a large pool of blood in the bathroom. Whitnei had been stabbed in the back of the head with a screwdriver.[4] The deep wound measured two inches long and a quarter of an inch deep.

By 2006, Whitnei had hit rock bottom. "Our daddy passed," explained her brother Mike. "That was traumatic again for Whitnei because she was Daddy's girl. She had all of the other problems from her past and then Daddy died. When Daddy died, she lost her sanctuary, 'cause Daddy's house was there and she could go. When Daddy died, that was gone. Daddy was her protector. Whitnei could do no wrong in Daddy's eyes. So when Daddy died, Whitnei probably got worser at everything. She was already bad, but she got worser at everything." Mike Dubois added, "The rest of our family judged her, looked down on her."

Mike was one of the few remaining family members Whitnei felt she could trust. In the early-morning hours of May 11, 2007, on a quest for drugs and shelter, she stopped at his home. "Whitnei walked to my dad's house," Mike Dubois's daughter Brittany Jones told me. "She got something to eat and said she wanted to stay there. She was stealing and nobody could trust her and my dad didn't want her to stay. They started arguing. Whitnei told my grandma, 'You always favor him.' Then she took off out the front door. When my grandma went through her purse, she noticed that Whitnei had stolen all of her medicine. [Whitnei] took her pain medicine, her nerve medicine, anything she could get high off of. Then she turned the corner and went to Frankie's. She didn't stay long. Her and Frankie were arguing about something in the front yard. She took off. Some people say that Frankie took off after her."[5]

Frankie confirmed to me that Whitnei stopped by his house sometime late in the evening of May 10 or early on

May 11, but refuses to say what she was doing there. And he insists he had nothing to do with her murder a few hours later. "I'm on the side of the road when Whitnei died," Richard says. "I'm on the side of the road getting searched by the police. I was getting searched by Jennings City Police. And they still tried to put that on me. I think that Mike Dubois had something to do with that. I really and truly do."[6]

No one connected to the Dubois case disputes what happened next. At approximately 7:30 a.m. on May 12, Jamie Trahan, a Jennings man with close ties to Frankie, discovered a body at the intersection of Bobby and Earl Duhon Roads, on the outskirts of Jennings. The desolate area is surrounded by vast soybean and rice fields and shallow, murky crawfish ponds. Trahan told investigators that he spotted Whitnei's lifeless body from Highway 102, about a half mile away.

Was it really possible that Trahan had spotted the body at such a distance? Even though the sun had risen and the sky was clear, it would have taken laser-sharp vision to discern a human figure from his vantage point. It makes one wonder whether Trahan had been actively searching for Whitnei, whether he had really been driving on Highway 102, and whether he knew ahead of time where the body had been dumped. I don't have any evidence that suggests investigators followed this line of thinking. Reporter Scott Lewis, who covered the Dubois homicide for the *Jennings Daily News*, also questioned how her body could have been seen from Highway 102. "Whitnei was further south on Earl Duhon," Lewis told me, "completely out of sight of La. 102. Unless police moved her body out of the intersection, it would have been absolutely impossible to see her body from the highway."[7]

Word of the body spread rapidly. "I heard it was a woman," said a nearby resident to the local news. "I don't know the age, or anything like that, just that the body was found in the middle of the road. Some of the guys were talking this morning about how this was the fourth female body found within a year and a half in this general area. It's scary. I have two kids and I'm scared. I hope they do something about it."[8]

While the other Jeff Davis 8 victims were sparsely dressed when they were found, Whitnei was completely naked save for two elastic bands—one brown, the other white—hanging from her right wrist. An earring also lay near her body. Like the previous three victims, Whitnei had a high level of alcohol and drugs—cocaine and Xanax—in her system. The coroner deemed the cause of death "undetermined" and noted "non-specific" bruises on her lower extremities. He also found "no evidence of significant injuries or natural disease."

Whitnei's final hours are shrouded in mystery, and as with all of the Jeff Davis 8 victims, no one has been brought to justice in her murder. But I've obtained an interview conducted by the Taskforce of a witness whom I believe provides the most credible account of what happened to Whitnei Dubois on that May night. Out of concern for this witness's safety, I will identify him only as Witness A.

Witness A told investigators that on the night of May 11, 2007, he, Jamie Trahan, and an unidentified woman partied at the Budget Inn, just down the road from the Boudreaux Inn. Late that evening, Trahan left the Budget Inn and did not tell friends where he was going. Hours later, Trahan returned and at approximately 5:15 a.m., Witness A and Trahan drove from the Budget Inn to the outskirts of Jennings: "We turn a corner and Whitnei was in the middle of the road," said Witness A. Trahan attempted to convince A that what they'd just seen was not a corpse but a dead deer. "That wasn't no deer," A told Trahan, *that was a body.*" Despite A's pleas to pull over,

Trahan returned to the Budget Inn, where he and his girlfriend took a shower. According to A, Trahan then drove back alone to where Whitnei had been dumped and called the police.

Trahan then rendezvoused with Frankie Richard and his street associate Brandon "Disco" Wise. "We was past Lafayette," Wise told me, "and partner and I"—Wise gestures at Frankie—"were out there getting fucked up."[9]

Just then, the pair were approached by Trahan. "Man, I found a body," Trahan told Disco.

"What the fuck is you telling *me* for?" Disco shot back. "What you mean you found a body, dude?"

Disco remembers Trahan muttering, "I wish there was something I could do."

Disco replied. "Why?"

Bringing, finally, a fuller explanation: "I found Whitnei's body on the gravel road."

Frankie took immediate action: "Disco and I put him [Trahan] in the car because I know Mike Dubois. I was raised with him. And I brought [Trahan] there, introduced him, and went outside and sat with Disco. I thought maybe he could give him some answers and some closure."

But instead of answers, the visit—in which Trahan shocked the grieving Dubois family by offering to put up $2,500 for Whitnei's funeral—posed only questions. What was Trahan doing at the desolate intersection of Earl Duhon and Bobby Roads that night to begin with? And what role, if any, did Frankie Richard play?

Witness A's Taskforce interview doesn't answer all of these questions, but it provides what I believe is the most complete account of Frankie's involvement in the Dubois slaying. In early 2009, two years after Whitnei's murder, Witness A and Frankie were enrolled together in a drug rehabilitation program in Logansport, Louisiana. During that time Frankie spoke openly about the Dubois murder. It was there, Witness A told the Taskforce, that Richard confessed. "He and James Trahan had killed Whitnei and . . . two other girls and he didn't mention their names." Witness A was unable to elicit many specifics from Richard about the killings, but Richard admitting to utilizing a "fifty-five-gallon drum behind his mama's house." There were, A told Taskforce investigators, "chemicals in the drum." The drum could have been used to store the Jeff Davis 8 victims and preserve them in formaldehyde before the bodies were dumped. Indeed, Frankie himself has admitted to Taskforce investigators that he and his associates had purchased formaldehyde from Jennings-area funeral homes, most likely to sell and smoke as "wets," a marijuana cigarette dipped in formaldehyde. But the mystery of the alleged fifty-five-gallon drum and what chemicals were inside it remains just that. Multiple witnesses have alleged that Frankie used a barrel to store his victims, but police chose not to follow the lead. Nor did they pay heed to Witness A's specific and highly credible account of the behavior and activities of Jamie Trahan. This deeply unsettling investigative oversight would have fatal consequences down the road.

Soon after Witness A gave his statement, police discovered yet another victim with close ties to Frankie Richard. In the early-morning hours of May 14, 2007—just two days after Whitnei's decomposing body was found—thirty-five-year-old crack addict and sex worker Elizabeth Dawn Clemens clambered into a rusted truck with Frankie and his associate Eugene "Dog" Ivory.[10] The previous night Clemens had slept in Roxanne Alexander's garage. Roxanne, the Jeff Davis 8's maternal protector, didn't know Clemens; she had simply allowed her to stay at her home because she was an associate of

Dog's. Just moments after pulling onto West Division Street, Frankie and Dog turned onto a gravel road. There, according to Clemens, Dog held her down in the backseat while Frankie raped her. Then the pair switched. "If you tell anyone, bitch," warned Frankie, "you will end up like the others." Clemens took Frankie's threat as a clear, unmistakable reference to the four murdered sex workers—Loretta, Ernestine, Kristen, and most recently, Whitnei.

After the alleged assault, Clemens fled to a home on Sheridan Street in South Jennings, where she called the cops. When the police arrived, Clemens was sobbing uncontrollably in the living room. She refused to answer any questions. "They'll kill me," she wailed. "They'll kill me like they did the others." After Clemens calmed down, she provided a statement and was transported to the American Legion Hospital. A swab found a "sperm fraction" inside Clemens's vagina that contained Dog's DNA. In the wake of the test results, Dog and Frankie were both charged with rape; Frankie has long denied that he assaulted Clemens. He told me that he was the victim of a "fuckin' bogus-ass rape charge" in the case.

Behind bars during the spring of 2007, Frankie lamented his bad luck. A judge set his bond at $750,000. At the time, he had expanded his seedy underworld empire to include both the Boudreaux Inn and the Budget Inn. Now, with two more murder victims—Kristen and Whitnei—who had strong personal connections to him, Frankie's business stalled out. Worse, as a habitual offender in Louisiana, Frankie faced the possibility of a "natural life" sentence without parole.

Frankie's legal woes would only deepen. On May 16, 2007, a warrant for his arrest was issued in Jefferson Davis Parish on second-degree murder charges in the slaying of Kristen Gary Lopez, the third victim.[11] It was the first significant break in a

Jeff Davis 8 murder case since the arrest of Byron Chad Jones and Lawrence Nixon in the 2005 killing of Ernestine. Sheriff Edwards eagerly announced the huge catch to local media.

"I'm sitting there watching the five o'clock news on Channel 7," Frankie remembers, "Here comes Ricky Edwards on the TV and he says, 'We have the killers in custody.' And I say to myself, 'All right, they got that motherfucker, *ya know*?' Then, here comes *my* picture on the TV. Mine and my godchild. They charged my godchild with second-degree murder and told her, 'Just say your uncle done it and you helped him clean it up and we'll give you a manslaughter charge and let you walk.' She said, 'No, I ain't doing it because he didn't do it.'" Richard's niece, Hannah Conner, was a crack addict at the time. She frequently partied with Frankie, Kristen, and Tracee Chaisson. A warrant was issued for Conner's arrest on May 16, 2007, on second-degree murder charges.

Frankie and Conner were justifiably shocked; Frankie had not been interrogated in the investigation, and Conner had asserted that she had nothing to do with Kristen at the time she went missing. Tracee Chaisson had also offered little of use. She was simply one of the last people to see Kristen alive. She hadn't implicated anyone.

But during a second interrogation (that was, until now, part of the DA's file on the Lopez case that has never been made public), Tracee broke down weeping. She told investigators that on the night of March 9, she, Frankie, Kristen, Hannah Conner, and a Jennings sex worker named Connie Siler had been driving around in Siler's Chevy Silverado. They stopped in South Jennings to purchase drugs, did rails of cocaine in a trailer Frankie owned on Martin Roy Road, then traveled to the outskirts of town along dirt roads. Richard was furious with Kristen for stealing from him, and at one point he stopped the truck, dragged her outside, and beat her severely. As she lay wounded, he pulled her into a nearby canal. Tracee claimed that Hannah Conner held Kristen under the water, and as Kristen went lifeless, Frankie threatened to kill Tracee and all of her children if she said a word. Frankie then dropped Tracee back at Frank Street, where she and Kristen had been engaging in sex work.

After offering the surprise confession, Tracee led a group of investigators on the route she said that she had taken with Frankie, Kristen, Siler, and Conner in the Silverado on the night of the murder. Tracee claimed the truck traveled through a rural area south of Jennings, to the intersection of Highways 380 and 99. From there, they took a right on Cherokee Road and parked by a levee near the Petitjean Canal. Here, Tracee told investigators, Frankie and Conner killed Kristen. When they drove off, Siler "kept whispering to be quiet and to say nothing because I was going to be next."

Based almost entirely on her new statements, Tracee Chaisson was charged with accessory after the fact to second-degree murder, and Frankie and his niece Hannah Conner were hit with second-degree murder charges.

Both Conner and Tracee have refused multiple requests for interviews, but Frankie has talked to me about Kristen's murder on several occasions. He not only denies any involvement, but claims to know who is responsible. "They left here," Richard says of Tracee and Kristen, "here" being his home on McKinley Street. "They went over to Frank Street. Tracee and Connie [Siler] set Kristen up. The dudes they had ripped off were there. They made Tracee hold Kristen under the water."[12]

Frankie's story about Kristen's fate lacks specifics: he couldn't answer when I pressed him for details about where Tracee killed Kristen or why the drug dealers would kill her over a drug debt. Indeed, as we discussed his theory about Kristen's murder, he seemed to realize the gravity of his implications and began to backpedal. "That's what I was *told*," he stressed, adding that he can only corroborate details about Kristen's last days, which were mostly spent with him at the Budget Inn. "When Kristen asked me if she could go back to my room, I said no. I feel bad about that because she really had no place to go," Richard laments. "If I had let her come back to my room, she might still be alive today."

Tracee's inconsistent statements on Kristen's murder put the case on shaky factual ground from the get-go. Indeed, after Tracee stopped cooperating with investigators in late May of 2007, the second-degree murder case completely collapsed. "Obviously the judge was convinced they [Frankie and Hannah Conner] should be arrested because he issued a warrant," one Taskforce investigator told me. "But the DA decided not to prosecute." Frankie was sent back to the streets of South Jennings, and Jeff Davis law enforcement now had four unsolved sex-worker homicides. Worse, charges had been brought only to be dropped.

The summer of 2007 brought even better legal news for the once-beleaguered Frankie Richard. Like Rosalyn Breaux before her, Elizabeth Clemens walked into the DA's office and asked to drop rape charges against her assailants, Frankie and Dog.[13] The collapsing cases against Richard transformed him into a Teflon Don of the South Jennings underworld. For the moment, it seemed, no charge against him—be it rape or murder—could stick.

With four victims in two years, the milieu of the Jeff Davis 8 was quickly shrinking. The streets of South Jennings took another significant hit on July 25, 2007, when Harvey "Bird Dog" Burleigh, a witness to the Leonard Crochet killing, was stabbed to death inside a home on West Jefferson Street. A family member had discovered his body just after midnight after shopping at a local grocery store. "When she tried to get in the door, she noticed blood," Jennings police chief Johnny Lassiter told the media. "The victim was found on the floor, just on the other side of the door. He had been stabbed multiple times."[14]

Chief Lassiter assured reporters that the police were pursuing "several leads," but like the Jeff Davis 8 case, Bird Dog's murder remains unsolved. The lack of closure in the slaying was particularly disheartening because Bird Dog told friends that he'd gathered crucial intel in the Jeff Davis 8 slayings. "Just before he was killed," Mike Dubois remembers, "Bird Dog told me, 'I'm close to finding out who killed your sister. I almost got everything I need.' And then—boom—somebody murdered him."

A growing fear was rising across Jennings, transcending racial and economic divides. "It was just one murder after another, and suddenly there were different strands connecting all of them," remembers Scott Lewis, the former reporter with the *Jennings Daily News*. "These people all knew each other. And now we were hearing all of the people killed knew Bird Dog. Every single one of these victims had been through Bird Dog's living room. He knew all of them. This was far beyond one crazy person committing these murders."[15] Mounting public pressure for justice led Sheriff Edwards to lash out at the *Jennings Daily News*, which had preempted traditionally extensive coverage of the Jennings Bulldogs high school football team to focus more on the sex-worker slayings. During a visit with the sheriff by a member of the newspaper's sales department, Sheriff Edwards tossed a copy of the paper in the direction of a garbage can. "You know where I keep my newspaper," he said icily.

CHAPTER 8

Gunter and Guillory

Late in the evening of June 8, 2007, Lake Arthur couple Steven Gunter and his girlfriend, Lorritta Lacoste, were fighting outside their home at 507 Bliss Street.[1] Gunter was a thirty-nine-year-old self-employed carpenter with a big, bushy mustache and a thick, messy mop of brown hair. He was an alcoholic and a crack addict. He was friendly with the Jeff Davis 8 and often drank with them at Tina's Bar. During the late 1990s and early 2000s, he lived in a trailer park adjacent to the Boudreaux Inn. Furthermore, he was related to Jeff Davis 8 victim Crystal Shay Benoit Zeno, who was a cousin by marriage. Gunter had close relationships with local law enforcement, too: he drank at local bars with Terrie Guillory, the parish warden.

On that early June day, Gunter and Lacoste argued loudly over his excessive drinking. The dispute attracted the attention of a neighbor, who called the Lake Arthur Police (LAPD), but it's unclear if anyone from the LAPD was dispatched to the scene. As the argument escalated, Lacoste realized that Gunter would be too inebriated to drive the next morning, so as Gunter stumbled into bed, Lacoste remained outside and disabled her truck so that it could not start. "When Steve would drink, he liked to drive," Lacoste explained later, "and he didn't have no license. And I was protecting him."[2]

The fighting continued the next afternoon, again attracting the attention of a neighbor. When Gunter tried to wrestle the truck keys from Lacoste, he grabbed her by the left arm. "Don't worry about it," Lacoste told the concerned neighbor, and slipped from Gunter's grasp. But the neighbor called the LAPD again. Moments later, an officer arrived. Gunter fled inside. The officer asked Lacoste if Gunter was armed. "Yes," she replied, "he owns a gun," adding that Gunter kept the weapon unassembled and stored in a case. That Gunter was a gun owner didn't alarm Lacoste outright. Many Jefferson Davis Parish residents owned firearms, and Gunter kept a .22-caliber rifle in his home for protection.

Lacoste attempted to mitigate the situation. "There's no problem here," she insisted, but the officer ordered her to hand over the house key. When the officer opened the door, Gunter grunted, "Go away. I don't want y'all here. Leave my property."

Despite Lacoste's and Gunter's assurances, someone—it's unclear who—called the LAPD chief, Cheryl Vincent. When she arrived, Lacoste, talking about Gunter, insisted, "All he did was pull me out of my truck. I'm not hurt." But Chief Vincent approached the front door to talk with Gunter. "Get off my property," Gunter growled at her. "Leave me alone. I want some peace. Give me my peace."

Inexplicably, more law enforcement arrived, among them Sheriff's Office detective Chad Romero and parish jail warden Terrie Guillory. Again, it's unclear who summoned them.

Gunter had barricaded himself inside. Romero and Guillory later told state investigators that Gunter claimed he was armed with an SKS assault rifle and fourteen rounds of ammunition. Fearing that the standoff was about to turn violent, Guillory shot several tear gas canisters into the home's windows.

"Go home!" Gunter yelled. Undeterred, Guillory, who was armed with a shotgun, ran to the back of the house and used a battering ram to smash open a locked rear entrance. "Steven!" Guillory shouted as he entered. "This is Terrie! Where are you? Steven, it's Terrie. Come out! Come out!" When Guillory moved toward the living room, he observed Gunter sitting on the couch where (Guillory later claimed) Gunter fired two rounds at him. As Guillory ran for cover, he "could hear bullets pinging behind" him. When he reached the kitchen, Guillory fired several rounds—he estimated five to six—back at Gunter, who then collapsed to the floor.

Guillory's fellow officers stormed the house, but the sting of tear gas forced them to carry Gunter's lifeless body into the front yard. After a call to the Sheriff's Office chief, Guillory was instructed to "leave everything at the crime scene as it was." So Gunter's body lay outside for hours in the oppressive June heat. He was pronounced dead at 2:53 p.m. A coroner determined that he'd succumbed to shotgun wounds to the trunk, right arm, and left leg.

A Louisiana State Police investigation determined that "Deputy Guillory was justified in using lethal force to protect himself and others at that location" because "Gunter fired several rounds at officers with a .22 caliber rifle."

Law enforcement also claimed that Gunter had pushed Lacoste violently to the ground, giving them license to rush the scene, a claim that Lacoste vehemently disputes. But it's clear, even from law enforcement's own accounts, that both

Lacoste and Gunter insisted that they didn't need police assistance. Yet officers not only called the LAPD chief, they released the scene to Terrie Guillory, the man who ran the jail and had no experience handling hostage situations.

Guillory later admitted that he had "never read" procedures and policy manuals on confrontational imprisonments or confrontational hostage situations. He also had myriad personal connections to Gunter—they drank together at the American Legion Bar and Delia's Lounge in Lake Arthur (Guillory later insisted in a sworn deposition that he merely "drank beer in the *same place as* Steven"). Given his lack of hostage experience, Guillory seemed an unlikely ambassador for such negotiations.

Guillory also claimed that Gunter fired upon him both while sitting on the couch and, moments later, while standing near the kitchen. It was then, Guillory said, that he returned fire with five to six rounds, killing Gunter. But if Gunter had been holding and firing an assault rifle when he was killed, then why did the autopsy report show a cluster of entrance wounds to the palms of his hands, which would have been wrapped around the assault weapon at the time?

Even the coroner was suspicious. After Gunter was killed, Richard Dupont, the parish coroner at the time, telephoned Gunter's sister Beth. "This is a cover-up," he said. "Steven didn't have any gunpowder residue [which would indicate that he fired a weapon] on his hands."[3] Beth was stunned by the call from Dupont and pressed him for more details about her brother's death. Perhaps fearing retribution, Dupont refused to reveal any more and never voiced these concerns on record. He is now deceased.

Law enforcement had acted with fatal ineptitude, and Gunter's death, it seemed, had been entirely avoidable. It makes sense, from a public relations standpoint, that all involved would want to brush the tragedy under the rug as quickly as possible. But law enforcement may have had darker motives for lying about Gunter's death. Gunter's family told me that, just before he was killed, he revealed that he had information about the Jeff Davis 8 slayings, though he refused to be specific about what the information was. Had Gunter committed "suicide by cop," as the authorities' account suggests? Was he the victim of needless police escalation? Or was he the victim of a strategic, elaborately staged crime of opportunity?

There is certainly evidence suggesting a cover-up. Investigators claimed to have found a suicide note supposedly written by Gunter on his computer at 11:34 p.m. on June 8, 2007, the night before he was killed by law enforcement. I've obtained a complete copy of the note. It's inexplicably stiff and legalistic. Gunter's friends and family doubt its authenticity.

> *I Steven Gunter being of sound mind and do here by [sic] leave all my worldly possessions to Johnnie T. Gunter.*
>
> *I love you son, you are the only person who ever loved me unconditionally I'm sorry I'm a pussy and took the easy way out. Go live your life and learn from the mistakes I made it is said a wise man does not learn from his mistakes but from the mistakes of others well son I have made many mistakes and I'm sorry I was not there for you like I should have been.*
>
> *I LOVE YOU SON, PLEASE BE A BETTER MAN THAN I WAS!*
>
> *I LOVE YOU SON YOU ARE ONE AWSOME [sic] MOTHER FUCKER. . . . I REALLY WISH I*

*COULD HAVE BEEN THERE FOR YOUR WED-
DING I'm SORRY SON I love you, goodbye*
Daddy

Gunter's family members have told me that he had no prior history of suicide threats or attempts. They claim that the writing style of the suicide note does not in any way resemble Gunter's voice, and that he never referred to himself—especially to his young son, Johnnie, to whom the suicide note is apparently addressed—as Daddy.

And law enforcement accounts of the standoff—in which they claim Gunter shouted that he wanted to be left alone to die—are heavily disputed by both the Gunters and Lacoste. Lacoste insists that when confronted by cops, Gunter simply wanted to be left in peace.

Every account of the Gunter standoff—law enforcement's and Lacoste's—provides a picture of a rapidly evolving confrontation and not the actions of a man with a pre-existing death wish.

When the Gunter family held the funeral on June 14, 2007, they hoped to put Steven—and their concerns about his killing—to rest. But to the shock of everyone, Leonard Crochet's family members and his neighbors appeared at the funeral with a warning. "They said the same cops that shot Steven shot Leonard," Gunter's sister Beth told me.

That statement might not be strictly accurate. According to Louisiana State Police reports, John Briggs Becton fired the fatal shot at Crochet, while Terrie Guillory killed Gunter. Yet some of the same officers (Chad Romero of the Sheriff's Office and Derrick Miller of the Jennings PD) had responded to both scenes. And some of the same officers may have been complicit in both their deaths. Jared Sauble, the informant whose information led to the Crochet raid in 2005, told me that it was an (unspecified) member of the Jennings Police Department and not John Briggs Becton of the Louisiana State Police who killed Crochet.

Family and friends of Gunter's were not the only ones to raise concern. On August 15, 2007, a grand jury was impaneled in Jefferson Davis Parish to consider charges against Terrie Guillory: that his act of manslaughter was done "with the specific intent to kill or inflict great bodily harm," and "did kill Steven Gunter." The grand jury came back with the same decision handed down in the Leonard Crochet killing and in many recent cases involving police killings: "no true bill," meaning no probable cause or evidence to show that a crime had been committed. I've obtained a handwritten document from the grand jury and discovered that they determined the Gunter killing "a justifiable homicide."

Warden Guillory—the man who ended Gunter's life—was also presiding over a jail where sexual abuse and violence were alleged to have run rampant. One of the ugliest incidents involved Lisa Allen, who was incarcerated on bad-checks charges. From the end of 2006 to early 2007, Allen alleged that she was subjected to a series of brutal sexual assaults by jailer Mark Ivory, who worked under Guillory.[4] He exposed himself to her. He taunted her. He tricked her into going to the phones, where he pulled down her pants and attempted to touch her with his exposed penis. He even placed his fingers into Allen's vagina and warned her that she if she told anyone, "he would make her life miserable." Allen claims she attempted to report the incidents to Warden Guillory, but he never responded.

Allen's allegations were documented in internal reports from jail nurse Nina Ravey. "She told me that there was a black guard and he had raped her," Ravey told me. Ravey was legally required to document claims of abuse and entered the complaint into a logbook, according to the jail's regulations. Because she believed that Allen's allegations were credible, she warned Warden Guillory to act on them, which he failed to do.[5] Instead of notifying the sheriff, Warden Guillory turned on Ravey. He called in the Louisiana State Police, and, after an aggressive interrogation by trooper Jarrett Dobson, who would later become a key investigator on the Jeff Davis 8 taskforce, Ravey was charged with falsifying medical documents to support Allen's lawsuit.[6] Louisiana State Police investigators alleged that Ravey conspired with Allen to trump up rape charges against Ivory. They suspected the two were planning to share the financial rewards of a potential lawsuit.

By all indications, Ravey had done the right thing, both morally and legally, but by the time the charges were dropped, the damage was already done. Ravey's husband divorced her, she was unable to practice nursing during the years the investigation was ongoing, and her home went into foreclosure. "They discredited me," Ravey told me, "and ruined my life in the process."

During her tenure, Ravey had treated many of the Jeff Davis 8 victims when they were incarcerated. "One of 'em even worked in my office," Ravey remembers, "Crystal [Benoit Zeno]." When Ravey talked to the women of the Jeff Davis 8, she heard a common refrain: "I was present at a drug deal gone bad."

Ravey said she warned the Jeff Davis 8, "Y'all better not talk about this in front of these police." But they persisted anyway.

Lisa Allen filed a civil rights lawsuit against Terrie Guillory, Mark Ivory, and Ricky Edwards that referenced Ravey's internal reports. On the same day that Allen took a polygraph test—"on or about October 2–3, 2007," according to court records—jailer Ivory killed himself. The circumstances surrounding Ivory's suicide remain unclear, but there's no doubt he was steeped in law enforcement misconduct. And it's worth noting that, as a cousin of Eugene "Dog" Ivory, Frankie's codefendant in the 2007 rape of Elizabeth Clemens, he was connected, at least peripherally, to the Jeff Davis 8 milieu. (The Allen case was settled in 2010—terms of the settlement were not made public.)

Allegations of abuse and misconduct seemed to permeate even the highest rungs of the jail's institutional ladder. Several Taskforce witnesses claimed that Terrie Guillory ran the Jefferson Davis Parish jail like a Boudreaux Inn behind bars. According to their statements, Guillory prostituted female inmates out to johns on the outside and released inmates (both male and female) from the jail in exchange for sexual favors. Recall, too, that a separate Taskforce witness allegedly observed Guillory having sex with Loretta Chaisson (the first victim) in the bunk beneath hers. Loretta had been released and was murdered shortly thereafter. Yet another witness told Taskforce investigators that he saw "Terrie Guillory picking up girls on the south side of Jennings on several occasions." And a former law enforcement official told me that a female family member who was addicted to drugs regularly had sex with Guillory in exchange for narcotics. If, as certain Taskforce witnesses suggested, the Jeff Davis 8 were slain because they knew too much about high-ranking members of law enforcement, then Terrie Guillory would be a plausible suspect. The women of the Jeff Davis 8 were intimately acquainted with Terrie and his ex-wife, Paula, as informants, as sexual partners, and as witnesses to their misconduct. That said, while I do believe that the fear of "knowing too much" indicates a grave systemic problem, I do not believe that, with the exception of Danny Barry, members of law enforcement committed the murders.

Against this backdrop of law enforcement incompetence and corruption, a veteran Jennings cop made a decision that would forever change the course of his career and the Jeff Davis 8 investigation.

In December 2007, Sergeant Jesse Ewing of the Jennings PD, who had worked in law enforcement for nearly two decades and was known as a straightforward, reliable investigator, received word that two female inmates at the city jail wanted to talk about the unsolved sex-worker homicides (then totaling four). He was stunned by what he heard: "higher-ranking officers" had been involved in the murders.[7] The inmates' statements were tape-recorded.

Ewing had long been wary of his fellow cops and feared the audiotapes would vanish from the department's evidence room, just as drugs and cash often did, so he handed the interview tapes to private investigator Kirk Menard, who rushed copies to the Lake Charles office of the FBI.

Ewing's gambit apparently backfired. He was charged with malfeasance in office and sexual misconduct. (One of the female inmates claimed that Ewing touched her inappropriately during the interview. Ewing denies it, and that charge was later dismissed. I've listened to audio of Ewing's interviews with the two inmates—nowhere does either inmate complain of sexual advances from Ewing.)

Ewing and I sat in his home in the Paradise Park development in Jennings in July 2011. Short and wide-shouldered, he has a cleanly shaved head, a graying goatee, and the bulky frame of a rugby player. His home was decorated with little more than a TV set and a couch—a no-frills lifestyle that he blamed on employment troubles since his termination after twenty years on the job. "I felt screwed for doing the right thing," he told me.

The contents of Ewing's interview tapes have never before been made public. They offer specific information about the murders of two of the slain sex workers—Whitnei and Kristen—as well as local law enforcement's efforts to cover up Frankie Richard's role in at least one of the killings. I'm withholding the names of these witnesses to protect them from retaliation by cops or suspects, and because these interviews are not part of any public record.

The first female inmate told Ewing that when she was in the camper that belonged to Frankie's brother Billy, waiting to purchase drugs, she encountered Frankie's niece Hannah Conner, who was smoking crack cocaine. She asked Conner about the murders, and Conner confessed that she was present when Kristen Gary Lopez was killed. Kristen, Conner allegedly said, was killed in a "designated area off of Highway 26" and then "put . . . in a barrel." According to the first female inmate, Frankie transported the barrel containing Kristen's body in a truck, then sold the truck to "an officer named Mr. Warren—I don't know his exact name. He bought the truck to discard the evidence."

By "Warren," the inmate meant the chief criminal investigator at the Sheriff's Office, Warren Gary.

Below is a transcript of the interview with the first inmate:

So you're saying that this officer knew about the DNA [evidence, in the truck in which Kristen's corpse was allegedly transported]?

Yes, sir.

Did Hannah say that?
Yes, sir.

Did he know about the killing?
Yes, sir, because him and Frankie Richard were good friends. . . .

What did Hannah tell you about the officer?
That him and her uncle Frankie are good friends and that he bought the truck so that the evidence wouldn't come back to her uncle Frankie. He discarded it. He cleaned the truck at the car wash.

Who cleaned it at the car wash?
Officer Warren.

What car wash did he clean it at?
Ray's.

Ray's Laundry and Cleaners, at 108 South Lake Arthur Avenue in Jennings, has a car wash out back. Later, the storefront would sit directly across from the Taskforce offices.

The second female inmate spoke about the night that Whitnei died, in May 2007. She claimed that Tracee Chaisson had told her about Whitnei's murder. Tracee, Frankie, Hannah Conner, and Whitnei had all been getting high in the camper when Frankie asked for sexual favors from Whitnei. When she refused, Frankie "got aggressive, he started fighting with her, and when she started fighting back, he got on top of her and started punching her." According to the inmate, "Hannah held her head back and drowned her."

Like the first female inmate, the second female inmate said that Kristen, too, was murdered by a similar group, that Frankie had placed her body in a barrel and transported the barrel in a truck that was sold to a cop named Warren, who at Ray's cleaned the vehicle of any physical evidence.

Such secondhand accounts might inspire skepticism. But the first and second female inmates claimed their information came directly from Hannah Conner and Tracee Chaisson, who are describing their own involvement in the murders.

Public records also corroborate both witnesses accounts of a truck sale by the former chief criminal investigator, Warren Gary. On March 29, 2007, Gary purchased a 2006 Chevy Silverado truck for $8,748.90 from Connie Siler, the Jennings sex worker who was allegedly present when Kristen was murdered.[8] Siler used the small profit she made from selling the truck to pay fines and fees to the DA's office for bad checks she had issued. Less than a month later, Warren Gary resold Siler's Silverado for $15,500, a nearly 100 percent profit. We don't know to whom he sold it, or how he managed to turn such a large profit.

Gary's purchase of the truck was possibly illegal and definitely unethical—he was later fined $10,000 by the Louisiana Board of Ethics for the incident. "What [Gary] did with that was wrong," former sheriff Ricky Edwards told me. "Buying from an inmate, that's what was ethically wrong." He insisted, however, that his office "had no clue that [the truck] was even part of evidence [in the Kristen Gary Lopez case]. That didn't come out until way after the fact."

In fact, according to their own reports, investigators knew

that Siler was one of the last people to see Kristen Gary Lopez alive, and that her truck was a crucial piece of the case. As Paula Guillory, a former sheriff's deputy (and Terrie Guillory's ex-wife), confirmed to me, "We knew that Connie Siler's vehicle was probably involved."

According to the ethics board report, Terrie Guillory assisted Warren Gary in making arrangements for Gary to acquire the Siler truck.

Because of Warren Gary's purchase of the truck, the Kristen Gary Lopez case may have lost a key piece of physical evidence. And because Conner refused to flip on her uncle Frankie, and Tracee Chaisson had changed her story repeatedly, the charges against all of them were dropped.

Put simply, the statements from the two female inmates portrayed the Sheriff's Office as willingly disposing of evidence against Frankie in a murder case. Yet the sergeant who took the statements (Ewing) was forced out of his job, and the allegations were never pursued. Ewing's fate was eerily similar to that of Jefferson Davis Parish jail nurse Nina Ravey. Both lost their jobs after reporting alleged misconduct involving Jefferson Davis Parish law enforcement officers.

Warren Gary, on the other hand, was soon promoted by Sheriff Edwards—to run the evidence room. "I don't think it was a bad decision," Edwards told me. "I understand how some people would question that, but no, I don't think it was a bad decision. . . . He is very thorough and very knowledgeable, and that's the decision I made at the time."[9]

Edwards had initially ignored my repeated calls for comment, but after I submitted a public records request for the personnel file of one of his deputies, he met me at the courthouse. I interviewed him there.

Bizzarely, Edwards said that he had received the Ewing

tapes, but claimed he didn't know about the witness interviews: "I'm not aware of that. You'd have to provide those witnesses to me. If you have that information, I'd love it. I don't have that information."

Warren Gary left the Sheriff's Office in 2012. He could not be located for further comment. I reached Terrie Guillory by telephone on January 27, 2014. At first, Guillory told me to call the Sheriff's Office if I had any questions about the Jeff Davis 8 case. When I said that I wanted responses regarding several allegations against him, he immediately hung up the phone.

While imperfect, the inmate accounts come close to what I believe occurred based on my own witness interviews, public records that I've obtained, and witness statements provided to the Taskforce. In early March 2007, Kristen Gary Lopez was indeed partying with Frankie, Tracee, and Siler at Frankie's room at the Budget Inn. This is confirmed by hotel records, my own multiple interviews with Frankie, and Tracee's statements to investigators. Late in the evening of March 5 and early into the morning of March 6, Kristen stopped at the Richard family home on McKinley Street, where she begged to be allowed back in to his hotel room.

Kristen continued to party that night with Frankie, Frankie's brother Billy Conner, and Tracee in Conner's camper. High on crack, Frankie angrily demanded Kristen give him a blow job. When Kristen refused, a furious Frankie forced Tracee Chaisson to hold Kristen's head down in a bucket of water, where she suffocated by drowning. This differs from Chaisson's account to law enforcement, where Kristen was drowned in a canal by Frankie. At least one Taskforce witness who was interviewed by both the FBI and the Louisiana State Police corroborates this theory. "They beat Kristen," the witness told investigators. "He [Frankie] beat her really bad. He told Tracee if she didn't finish the job, he was gonna finish her. She claimed she had no choice. She said she drowned her, held her underneath the water." This witness statement is, in turn, supported by the coroner's report: "Death occurring from drug intoxication, asphyxia, and drowning."

In Tracee's wildly inconsistent statements, she claimed that Conner drowned Kristen in a canal. Those claims are contradicted by the numerous witness statements that claim Tracee drowned Kristen in the trailer. Senior law enforcement certainly didn't think Tracee's allegations about Conner were credible: second-degree murder charges against Conner were subsequently dropped. But Tracee was consistent about the motive for Kristen's slaying. She told investigators that Kristen "said no to [Frankie] Richard about sucking his penis and Richard got mad." Frankie—it's not clear who accompanied him—then transported Kristen's lifeless body in Connie Siler's Silverado and dumped her by the Petitjean Canal just off Highway 99, where she was discovered by fisherman James Aucoin. But a former law enforcement source told me that Aucoin wasn't just a passerby but an associate of Frankie's. He also described Aucoin as a repeat sex offender, and, indeed, in November of 2015 Aucoin was booked into the Jefferson Davis Parish jail on seven counts of aggravated rape related to a sexual assault of an eight–year-old girl.[10] As of this writing, the charges against Aucoin are still pending.

Law enforcement's investigation into the Whitnei Dubois killing was even more troubled than the Kristen Gary Lopez case. Witness A, after all, had told Taskforce investigators that Frankie confessed to killing Whitnei with Jamie Trahan. Yet no charges were ever brought against either, despite multiple witness accounts that put both Frankie and Trahan with

Whitnei in the hours before her murder. As with my work on the Gary Lopez case, I've been able to put together an account of Whitnei's last day and construct a strong theory on who killed her based on my own witness interviews, Taskforce witness interviews, and public records.

At approximately 2:00 a.m. on May 12, 2007, Whitnei visited Frankie's house to score drugs. Frankie's mother, Jeanette, directed her to her son Billy Conner's camper, which sat behind the house. She didn't want anyone partying inside her home. Whitnei then walked over to Billy's camper, where she met Frankie, who was waiting for her with drugs in hand.

Instead of getting high in the camper, the pair climbed into a white pickup truck and headed to the desolate country roads where Frankie liked to take women to do drugs and have sex. There, Whitnei smoked crack and then downed Xanax to help ease the comedown (an autopsy toxicology screen confirmed she had both cocaine and Xanax in her system). At about 3:00 a.m., Frankie and Whitnei fought—it's unclear what the dispute was about—and Frankie strangled her inside the truck. He then loaded her body into a fifty-five-gallon barrel filled with formaldehyde. It's a seemingly outlandish theory of the case, but remember, Witness A told Taskforce investigators that Richard had a "fifty-five-gallon drum behind his mama's house" and that there were "chemicals in the drum." Frankie denied having a drum, claiming that other witnesses were "just talking shit." Incredibly, however, he admitted to Taskforce investigators that his associate Michael Prudhomme had purchased embalming fluid—a mixture of formaldehyde, methanol, and other solvents—from a nearby funeral home. Frankie added to Taskforce investigators, in a jaw-droppingly incriminating remark, "Somebody's using some chemicals" on the eight victims. "Billy," Frankie continued, referring to his own brother, "is saying I'm the one killing them girls."

On that mid-May night, Frankie enlisted the help of Jamie Trahan to dump Whitnei's body. The pair transported Whitnei in a DirecTV van that Frankie's niece Hannah Conner drove for work. Trahan and Frankie disposed of the naked corpse near the corner of Bobby and Earl Duhon Roads on the outskirts of Jennings and, later that morning, Trahan "discovered" Whitnei there.

I was able to confirm Hannah Conner's employment with DirecTV—as well as the Richard family's use of her work vehicle in the Jennings drug trade—via a May 17, 2007, interrogation of Conner conducted by Terrie Guillory. In this interview, Conner admitted to law enforcement that she frequently smoked crack cocaine with her father, Billy Conner, and "would go to work and smoke crack between jobs" with DirecTV.[11] I've made repeated attempts to interview Hannah Conner; on February 11, 2014, she sent me a Facebook message explaining that she "want[s] no part of all this publicity going on. I have a son and my baby sister I'm trying to raise and no offense but I really dnt [sic] want my name brought into this any more than [Tracee] Chassion [sic] already has put [into] it," adding that she has nothing "more to say about these atrocities."

I also obtained a statement to Taskforce investigators in which a witness observed Frankie washing a cable van at Ray's Laundry and Cleaners in the hours after Whitnei's death. Ray's is the very same place where Connie Siler's Silverado, the truck used to transport Kristen Gary Lopez's corpse, was cleaned. A separate Taskforce witness says that Frankie gave Michael Prudhomme, who cleaned the aforementioned Silverado, drugs in exchange for helping to clean the van. It's unclear if employees of Ray's were ever interviewed by investigators; in the Jeff Davis 8 DA files and Sheriff's Office and police department reports that I've obtained, nothing indicates that they were interrogated.

After cleaning the DirecTV van, Trahan returned to the Budget Inn, and then at about 5:15 a.m. he drove back to the outskirts of Jennings. According to Witness A, "Whitnei was in the middle of the road." Trahan tried to convince a disbelieving Witness A that the body was just roadkill.

After spotting Whitnei, Trahan went back to the Budget Inn, took a shower, and left, this time without Witness A. At about 7:30 a.m., Trahan called the police to report the body. About an hour and a half later, Trahan enlisted Richard to join him on his visit to the Dubois family, where he offered to pay for Whitnei's funeral. "He found us thanks to Frankie Richard," remembers Mike Dubois's daughter, Brittany Jones. "He went to my dad's house with Frankie in the car. He cried and cried, he described what he saw: 'Whitnei was raped and beaten.' How would he know that she was raped and beaten? And then he offered to put money on the funeral because he says he feels so horrible about what happened. Jamie Trahan has the answers to what happened to Whitnei. I guarantee you."

The year 2007 was undoubtedly the horrible pinnacle of the Jeff Davis 8 case. Nearly every month brought a new and terrifying development, from Kristen and Whitnei's slayings to the rape of Elizabeth Clemens and the ousting of Detective Ewing. The outcomes in the criminal justice system, however, were perhaps even more disturbing. In Kristen's case, charges were dropped against Frankie, Tracee, and Hannah. In Whitnei's case, not a single arrest. It didn't have to be this way. Several witnesses with firsthand accounts of the homicides—such as Witness A—were providing statements, often tape-recorded, to Taskforce investigators. Suspects such as Frankie Richard had thin, easily discredited alibis and even offered information that corroborated incriminating statements against them.

An atmosphere of total unaccountability prevailed on the streets but it appeared more ominously, in law enforcement, too. There were credible reports of tampered and destroyed evidence, unethical cash deals, an epidemic of sexual assaults in the jail, whistle-blowers pilloried. The reckless atmosphere led South Jennings hustlers to believe that they were above the law. "Frankie and them were very bold for a long time," laments Brittany Jones. "It didn't matter what they did. They ruled the neighborhood. They were untouched."

Certain people in power were seemingly protecting Frankie Richard, his associates, and Jennings's sex and drug trades. Beneath the institutional veneer, had an unholy alliance been formed?

CHAPTER 9

"Death on Me": Muggy, Crystal, and Brittney

By 2008, four sex workers in Jennings had been slain. The violence brought a profound, nearly tangible sense of terror to the town's underworld. "Everyone in that little clique thought we were gonna die," Roxanne "Mama" Alexander told me.[1] Roxanne remembers driving through the outskirts of Jennings with Frankie to smoke crack—just the two of them—when Frankie suddenly pulled over to pick up an imposingly large tree limb. "I thought he was gonna start beating on me," Roxanne recalls. "We were smoking and I started getting scared. I said, 'C'mon, Frankie, *let's go.*'" Frankie returned Roxanne to Jennings unharmed that day. But with several of her acquaintances murdered and dumped on the darkest, most isolated edges of town, Roxanne was rightfully scared. Frankie could easily have killed her, and her murder would likely have gone unsolved.

Of all the Jeff Davis 8, Muggy Brown was perhaps the most fearful of her fate. She had told friends and family that she was deeply traumatized—and perhaps forever haunted—

by witnessing the slaying of Ernestine Patterson in 2005. But what made her so vulnerable was her connection to men in power—in the streets and in law enforcement. Muggy had been charged in the rape of investigator Kirk Menard's daughter Rosalyn Breaux, in which one of Ernestine's alleged killers, her cousin Lawrence Nixon, was a codefendant. And Muggy had worked as an informant for several cops and detectives with the Jennings PD and the Sheriff's Office.

The use of informants by law enforcement, as Loyola Law School professor Alexandra Natapoff testified before a 2007 congressional hearing, creates a "culture of secrecy, rule breaking, and disregard for law and the truth."[2] Informants are often permitted to commit crimes in exchange for information about their drug connections. Law enforcement relies on the say-so of snitches to obtain search warrants and conduct raids, often with disastrous results (Leonard Crochet's death is just one example). In 2006, undercover police mistakenly killed an elderly African-American woman, Kathryn Johnston, in her northwest Atlanta home while acting on a tip from an informant. In May 2014, Jason Westcott was shot to death by police at his Tampa, Florida, home during a drug raid based on an informant's tip. The informant, Ronnie "Bodie" Coogle, later admitted to the *Tampa Bay Times* that he lied about suspects and conspired to falsify drug deals.[3] "In these communities," Natapoff told Congress, "snitching is a fact of life."

Snitching is certainly a fact of life in South Jennings. All of the Jeff Davis 8 were informants for local law enforcement, and most were recruited by the deputy Paula Guillory, ex-wife of Warden Terrie Guillory. The parish had a decades-long history of deadly incidents involving snitches. On February 14, 1998, a Jennings PD informant named Sheila

Comeaux was brutally beaten and left for dead outside Fondel's funeral home on South Main Street.[4] She remained in a coma for about a year before ultimately succumbing to her injuries. Like the Jeff Davis 8 killings, Comeaux's murder remains unsolved. According to Sheila Comeaux's sister-in-law Marie, Comeaux was severely beaten with a two-by-four when her killers realized she was wired by the Jennings Police Department for a drug buy. Marie insists that Loretta, victim number one, was with her sister-in-law that day and compares her fate to that of the Jeff Davis 8. "They've done nothing," Comeaux says bitterly, "just like the other girls."[5]

The street-savvy Muggy Brown, who was also close friends with Marie Comeaux, was well aware of just how perilous snitching could be, but to the chagrin of her family members, she provided law enforcement with a steady stream of street intelligence. In the spring of 2008, Muggy shocked her older sister Gail by calmly informing her that she was working with a cop on a murder case. "She said she was investigating a murder with a cop," Gail told me. "The cop wanted to give her five hundred dollars to tell what happened."[6]

It is unclear what murder case Muggy was working on, but there's no doubt that she talked to the Sheriff's Office about the Jeff Davis 8 murders. In 2005, Muggy was interrogated by investigators in the Ernestine Patterson homicide, and a witness told Taskforce investigators that Muggy and her boyfriend Stymie Washington spotted Loretta Chaisson's body floating in the Grand Marais Canal days before Welsh fisherman Jerry Jackson discovered her there in May of 2005. "The cops know these girls are on drugs," Gail says, "so they use them for information. They were taken care of by cops [in exchange for their cooperation]. They'll give you all the dope you need."

As unforgiving as the streets of South Jennings could be for Muggy, she faced tensions at home, too. In the spring of 2008, Muggy was caring for her then three-year-old son, Jaheim, by herself. She was never able to determine who had fathered him. Her childhood, too, had been similarly fractured. "Her mother, Gloria, was in prison when she [Muggy] was just a baby," Muggy's grandmother Bessie told me, "so I raised her since she was just a year and six months old."[7] Muggy fought with her boyfriend constantly, sometimes physically, and as Memorial Day 2008 approached, Gail and Bessie Brown hoped that the holiday would bring more peaceful times.

But unbeknownst to her family, Muggy Brown was in the crosshairs of some of the most dangerous South Jennings street players. On May 24, 2008, Brown's boyfriend Stymie was partying at the Budget Inn when hustler Ervin "Big Mack" Edwards kicked in the door. Big Mack was furious because he'd just been robbed of $3,000. Stymie claimed Muggy had done it. Big Mack vowed to hunt her down. By the next day, Muggy had learned that she was a wanted woman. "I feel like I got death on me," she confessed to a friend. This was a familiar refrain for Muggy—especially when she smoked crack cocaine—so her friend replied dismissively, "You must be smoking that shit." Muggy composed herself as best she could. "I ain't smoking, but I'll tell you one goddamn thing: if anybody kills me, it'll be Stymie." Muggy paused. "And I'll put up a fight."

For much of May of 2008, Muggy was a ghostly presence at the family home on Wilbert D. Rochelle Avenue. To those close to her, she seemed withdrawn, distracted, and unhappy. She barely engaged with her grandmother Bessie, who had been Muggy's son's caregiver and longtime confidante. But on Monday, May 26—Memorial Day—she showed up for the family's annual reunion-style barbecue, where a spread of hamburgers, hot dogs, and potato salad had just been laid out in the small backyard of Bessie's home. Just after eleven that night, Muggy, who seemed overcome with emotion, approached her grandmother in her tiny, cramped bedroom. She got on her knees and proclaimed, "I love you, there's nothing I wouldn't do for you and Jaheim." Bessie was touched and unnerved; it seemed like a good-bye. Moments later, Muggy went to the living room, packed a red bag with clothing, and told Bessie that she was going to do laundry. The conversation struck Bessie as bizarre—the family has a washer and dryer in its house—but she didn't stop Brown from leaving. "She walked out my house that day," Bessie remembers, "and that's the last time I saw her."

Early in the morning of May 27, 2008, Bessie did make contact with her granddaughter, but only by phone and from a blocked number. "I'm okay," Muggy assured her, and then, referring to her boyfriend, added, "Don't tell Stymie I called." That afternoon, Muggy clambered into a red truck with Tracee Chaisson and Ricardo "Tiger" Williams, a Frankie Richard associate. Unbeknownst to her family, Muggy had purchased a bus ticket to Washington, DC, where one of her brothers lived. That afternoon, accompanied by Tracee and Tiger, Muggy said a few tearful good-byes. She was unsure when she would return to Jennings; the rising tensions with her boyfriend and with her handlers in local law enforcement made it impossible to stay.

My theory of what happened next, based on my own witness interviews and review of investigative reports related to the case, is that Muggy got into a dispute with Tiger in the red truck. Tiger slashed her throat multiple times with a knife and then called upon Big Mack, the South Jennings street hustler who had been looking for Muggy, to dump the body.

Big Mack discarded her off the side of a desolate, dirt-caked stretch of East Racca Road near a decommissioned police firing range on the border of the Jennings city limits. No one—including Stymie—has ever been charged in Muggy's murder, but she repeatedly told friends and relatives, "If anybody kills me, it'll be Stymie." Big Mack's role in her death was corroborated by a Taskforce witness.

Another Taskforce witness—whom I'll identify only as Witness B—told investigators that Tyson Mouton, a South Jennings hustler and Frankie Richard associate with a rap sheet that included charges of cocaine distribution and battery, helped Big Mack dispose of Muggy's body. Witness B recalls riding in a "big older-model car" with Tyson shortly after the murder and being overwhelmed by something "that smelled like rotten meat." Witness B was familiar with the scent of decaying flesh because she had a wild-game freezer at home. One time "the kids left the wild-game freezer open and my husband had just killed four deer," she remembered. "All of that meat went bad. The smell was just atrocious. That's the same smell that was in the car Tyson was driving." Witness B told investigators that Tyson was also close with the Richard family. Indeed, she recalled a day when Tyson walked her over to Frankie's house to purchase drugs. "Tyson took me to that house," Witness B said. "The guy gave me the creeps and the house gave me the creeps."

Intriguingly, Witness B's information was corroborated by none other than Frankie Richard. "Stymie is the one that brought Muggy to meet Mack and Tyson," Richard told Taskforce investigators in a September 2008 interview.

As Muggy lay dead on East Racca Road, a South Jennings sex worker poured bleach on Muggy's body in an attempt to destroy physical evidence. Later, a group of women that included a sex worker known only as Potato cleaned the green Cadillac that Big Mack had used to transport Muggy's body. Indeed, one witness told Taskforce investigators that Potato and several others in Jennings were part of a "cleanup crew" for the killers of the Jeff Davis 8.

In the early-morning hours of Thursday, May 29, Bessie Brown received a call from a family member that her granddaughter had gone missing. Then, much later that night, the Browns got the news that they had long feared. Unlike the other Jeff Davis 8 victims, Muggy was found fully clothed: she was wearing a peach-colored tank top, blue denim shorts, a purple bra, purple panties, and an anklet with colored beads. Her cause of death, unlike with the others, was easy to determine: homicide. Multiple incised wounds to the head and neck, three cuts behind her right ear, and approximately seven cuts across the front of her neck. Muggy's body was discovered not by a fisherman or a passerby, but by the very Jennings police lieutenant for whom she worked as an informant: Michael Janise.[8] As the Brown family made funeral arrangements, law enforcement informed them that Lieutenant Janise would be investigating the murder. The family were also told they could not view Muggy's body, which infuriated them further. Nearly all of the Jeff Davis 8 family members told me that they, too, were prevented from making a positive identification of their loved one.

Then, just before Muggy's funeral in June of 2008, Jefferson Davis Parish coroner Richard Dupont told the Browns that he suspected law enforcement was involved in Muggy's murder. He didn't provide specific names. He feared retribution from law enforcement. He told Muggy's family that he believed he was being followed by deputies from the Jefferson Davis Parish Sheriff's Office. Dupont also often flat-out said that he knew more about the murders, according to Scott Lewis, formerly of the *Jennings Daily News*: "He would never speak, though, out of fear. He said maybe he would one day. And then he died of cancer."[9]

At Muggy's funeral, when pallbearers solemnly carried the casket down the church steps and into a waiting hearse, they noticed something strange and alerted Bessie Brown: the casket containing Muggy, who was just five foot three and 123 pounds, seemed to weigh hundreds of pounds.

"During the funeral," Bessie Brown told me, wiping tears from her eyes, "there were seven men carrying the casket, and they said it weighed three hundred pounds." That inexplicable moment, making Bessie wonder if her granddaughter was really in the casket, haunts her and makes mourning, even years later, difficult. Sometimes, Bessie confessed to me, she thinks that Muggy is still alive somewhere in southwest Louisiana. But then her family and friends bring Bessie back to the inescapable, horrible fact that Muggy's body was found on the road that night, and that, unlike with the other Jeff Davis 8 victims, the cause of death was unmistakably clear. A pretty headstone at Muggy's grave site, adorned with a pair of angels, reading LACONIA S. BROWN "MUGGY" JANUARY 25, 1985–MAY 27, 2008 LOVING MOTHER NEVER FORGOTTEN, provides Bessie with some relief as well as a place to reflect. But it's ultimately of little comfort to her, as she is now raising Brown's son, Jaheim, just as she raised Muggy. Bessie is also now coping with Jaheim's rising waves of grief. "The police killed my mama," Jaheim insists, making a throat-slitting motion across his neck.

Muggy's murder created a seismic fissure in the Jeff Davis 8 milieu. There had been five victims in three years. Brown was perhaps the toughest of the Jeff Davis 8. She always carried a knife with her and was a feared street fighter. As one of her family members told the Taskforce, "Whoever killed Laconia was good." Crime scene photos of Muggy show not just a heavily decomposed, nearly skeletal corpse, but bulging eyes that seemed frozen in fear. That fear infected her peers. Players in Jennings's drugs-and-sex scene such as Roxanne "Mama" Alexander began to prepare their Jefferson Davis Parish escape.

In the late spring and early summer of 2008, the surviving members of the Jeff Davis 8 milieu moved from Roxanne's home on North Craig Street to a ramshackle (and since abandoned) residence at 610 South Andrew Street. The decrepit, old clapboard home, which had an oversize backyard but was within whispering distance of neighbors, became a refuge for Jennings sex workers. "I saw Muggy there about two weeks before she died," a woman who lived next door told me (she spoke to me on the condition that she remain anonymous, out of concern for her safety).[10] "She was there with Brittney [victim number seven] and several others." The neighbor told me she was struck by Muggy's presence because she'd also seen another Jeff Davis 8 victim, Kristen Gary Lopez, there several times in 2006 and 2007. "Kristen was at the house so many times in 2006 and 2007," the neighbor told me, "most of the times with Tracee Chaisson. I last saw her there in late February of 2007 a few weeks before she died. It was an early morning and she was wearing a jacket but had shorts and no shoes on. She walked right by my front door and made her way to Highway 1126." The South Andrew Street neighbor had seen three women who would become murder victims, and one (Tracee Chaisson) who was charged in a killing. As the hot summer of 2008 began, the neighbor resolved to watch the home more closely.

ETHAN BROWN

With the toughest of Jennings's sex workers vanquished, the few remaining were even more vulnerable. At five foot eleven, 170 pounds, Crystal Benoit Zeno cut an imposing figure compared to her diminutive peers. But with her trusting demeanor and devout Christian background, Crystal was totally adrift in the violent and predatory South Jennings streets. She seemed unaware of the dangers posed by Frankie Richard—even though Frankie was a suspect in at least two murders.

Crystal shared much with the other slain women, however. She struggled with prescription-drug addiction and counted on minimum-wage jobs—she worked at a Sonic franchise in Lake Arthur—for a paycheck. And like many of the murdered sex workers in Jefferson Davis Parish, Crystal battled severe mental illness. At age twelve, she was diagnosed as bipolar, and for years her mother, Sarah Benoit, struggled to get her treatment. By age fifteen, Crystal was so alienated that she ran away from home—and didn't return until three years later.

Crystal was ill equipped to handle the realities of the street. In her twenties she had sex with Roxanne Alexander's boyfriend, which earned her Roxanne's long-term wrath and forced Crystal to fend for herself. Roxanne admitted to Taskforce investigators that "she beat her up and told her to stay away from her house." Tired of her nomadic existence, Crystal moved into the home of a notoriously strange and abusive client. One Jennings sex worker told Taskforce investigators that the man liked to shove objects into her anus. Crystal, unsurprisingly, didn't last long at the client's home. By the summer of 2008, her crack addiction had grown severe. A client actually complained to Taskforce investigators that "all she wanted to do was get high."

In July of 2008, Crystal and Brittney Gary—Kristen Gary Lopez's cousin—were recruited by a client to have group sex at a home in Andrus Cove, a desolate area near Jennings. When the pair arrived, the client requested they have sex with each other. They refused. To pacify the client, they took turns having sex with him, and when it was over, Brittney left in tears. According to a witness, the wife of the client "gave [Crystal] two black eyes" the next day.

That same July, Crystal partied too hard at the South Andrew Street safe house and passed out in the stultifying heat. "I saw her there in mid-July, in the backyard," the neighbor told me. "They seemed to be having a party and they looked like they were on drugs. At one point Crystal was lying on the ground, dazed. Two black men had to help her up off the ground."

The most terrifying and violent incident for Crystal occurred in late July when she was partying with a group of men at 630 Second Street in Jennings.[11] An intoxicated Crystal was loudly lamenting the fate of the murdered sex workers when a male friend, sensing that she was putting herself in danger, ushered her into a pickup that was parked outside. Unbeknownst to Crystal, Kenneth Patrick Drake, a forty-four-year-old from Welsh, had followed her outside. As she and her companion talked inside the truck, Drake, who had a history of assaulting women, angrily approached the pair. He was armed with a metal pipe, which he'd hidden behind his back. According to an incident report, Crystal told Drake to leave them alone because she was talking about "personal things." Undeterred, Drake swung the pipe at the truck, which shattered the driver's-side window and struck Crystal in the head. Injured and terrified, Crystal ran back inside and called Warden Terrie Guillory, for whom she worked as an informant. Crystal's work for Terrie is part of a long history of his engaging in work far outside the wheelhouse of a warden. His being called to the scene of the Steven Gunter standoff in 2007, and then killing Gunter, is perhaps the most prominent example of this. Sheriff's Office deputies arrived moments later and took Drake into custody. He was charged with aggravated battery, though the charges were later reduced to simple battery. (On August 25, 2012, Drake died at the Jennings American Legion Hospital, at age forty-nine—it's not clear what led to his passing).[12]

Drake's attack led Crystal, ironically and tragically, to seek refuge with Frankie Richard. Frankie's sister Tabatha told Taskforce investigators that Crystal stayed at their home for "approximately a month." By August 2008, Crystal was frequently shuttling between South Andrew Street and the Richards'. Then, at the end of August, she disappeared.

Crystal frequently spoke about her fears of becoming the next victim. "We talked about it often," her mother, Sarah Benoit, told local TV news outlet KPLC. "We knew she knew Kristen, we knew she knew Loretta. She said she knew Ernestine. She knew Muggy. . . . She was like, 'What if I'm next?' She always said, 'What if I'm next?' "[13] (I attempted to interview Sarah Benoit at her Lake Arthur home on July 11, 2011. She refused to talk to me, explaining that it had been three years since her daughter's murder and they had already done enough media, including the *New York Times*. I spoke with Benoit again in the fall of 2015—she agreed to an interview but then never returned any of my phone calls.)

So what happened? Who killed Crystal? Based on my own witness interviews, public records, and Taskforce witness interrogations, I've pieced together a theory. On August 23, 2008, Crystal celebrated her close friend and roommate

Brittney Gary's seventeenth birthday at South Andrew Street. "You don't know who you can trust," Crystal told Brittney. "They," Crystal continued, a reference to the Jeff Davis 8 killers, "can be your friend." Crystal then told Brittney she knew who had killed Muggy. The statement killed the mood, but the pallor was sadly appropriate. Crystal and Brittney were about to become victims six and seven. In the days after Brittney's birthday celebration, Crystal partied at Billy Conner's trailer and stayed with a client on Jefferson Street.

Finally, on August 29, Crystal rendezvoused with a john at the Budget Inn. At approximately 5:00 p.m. that day, Crystal, who was dressed in a turquoise tank top and blue capri pants and sported tiny stud earrings and a heart-shaped necklace, left the motel on foot, headed toward a Phillips 66 gas station. Phillips 66 is adjacent to the railroad tracks that divide North and South Jennings, so it's a near-daily stop for everyone. The Phillips 66 is, however, a roughly three-mile walk from the Budget Inn. Crystal was plodding along slowly, smoking Newport 100s, when she spotted a stranger in a parked car. She asked to borrow it, but the stranger refused. When she finally reached the Phillips 66, she used a pay phone to call Warden Terrie Guillory, just as she had done after the metal-pipe attack. It's unclear what Crystal told Guillory. But this was the last time she was seen alive.

As she left the gas station, Crystal was picked up by a group of Frankie Richard's "hands-on" men—one of whom was a street heavy known only as Tattoo—in a white truck. The truck drove south on Highway LA 26, where, on the far outskirts of Jennings, the road intersects with Highway 1126. There, the group made a left and drove deep into the country, toward Lacour Road, where pavement becomes rough gravel and essentials such as gas stations are miles away. On Lacour

Road, Tattoo and his associates marched Crystal deep into the woods, strangled her, and left her lifeless on the ground.

Unbeknownst to Crystal's killers, they were not alone that night. As they returned to their truck, they ran straight into Russell Carrier, a forty-three-year-old Lafayette man who was walking by. Though Carrier didn't reside in Jennings, he was often in Jefferson Davis Parish visiting his sister, Barb Ann Deshotel (the close friend of Loretta Chaisson's, whom Loretta was staying with at the time of her murder back in 2005).

Carrier later confessed to his family that he spotted a group of African-American men leaving the woods by Lacour Road. He recognized all of them.

"He told me that he saw some black guys coming out of the woods," Deshotel said. "They had a white vehicle"—the same color of the vehicle that witnesses said Crystal's killers rode in—"and he knew them very well. He would do mechanical work for them and their friends. And they would trade him crack for the work."[14]

Carrier told local law enforcement what he'd seen—Frankie Richard associate Eugene "Dog" Ivory (Richard's codefendant in the 2007 rape of Elizabeth Clemens), Tyson Mouton (named as another possible suspect in the Kristen Gary Lopez homicide and fingered for dumping Muggy Brown's body), and Ricardo "Tiger" Williams, who was suspected of killing Muggy in a red truck. "From my understanding, that white car is connected to a crack dealer named Big Al," Deshotel continued, "and Tyson Mouton works with Big Al." There is no evidence in any of the investigative documents I've reviewed that anyone in local law enforcement—in the DA's office, the Sheriff's Office, or the Taskforce—acted on Carrier's tip.

Even though the string of murdered sex workers in Jennings stretched back to 2005, Crystal's disappearance in late August of 2008 earned scant attention from law enforcement. The *Jennings Daily News* took notice. They published a scathing unsigned editorial headlined "Six" that lambasted both the Sheriff's Office and the parish itself for its classist apathy.

Only the streets, and those closest to Crystal—her mother, Sarah Benoit, and her husband, Stanley Lee Zeno—seemed to care that she was gone. Finally, at approximately 3:00 p.m. on September 11, 2008—nearly two weeks after her disappearance—a group of hunters discovered Crystal's naked body on a levee near a dry irrigation canal in the densely wooded area off Lacour Road. Her body was nearly skeletal. In one crime scene photograph, she lies frozen in terror against the thick knotty vines shrouding the sharp incline of a levee. Her left arm is extended far past her body, as if she's trying to reach for help.

Help arrived far too late. Investigators draped yellow crime scene tape across Lacour Road and the entry point into the woods. They ferried Crystal to the morgue, where her death was quickly determined a homicide. She was the sixth sex worker to be slain in Jefferson Davis Parish in just three and a half years.

Terrie Guillory traveled to the Zenos' home in Lake Arthur to deliver the bad news. According to Crystal's mother, Sarah Benoit, he told her: "They found the body and it's Crystal's body," adding bizarrely, "I didn't kill her but I know that it's her." Benoit asked Guillory how he was able to identify such a severely decomposed corpse, and Guillory said, "There's a tattoo on an intimate area of her body," to which a flummoxed Benoit replied, "The only way you could tell that is if you had sex with her." Guillory was silent and then quickly left the Zeno home.

Beyond the exceedingly strange comment "I didn't kill her," the fact that Guillory had identified Crystal's body was itself suspicious. After all, the corpse was so decomposed that it took nearly two months for officials to confirm her identity. And Guillory's visit with Crystal's mother eerily echoes his encounter with Barb Ann Deshotel the day Loretta was discovered. Back then, in 2005, Guillory said that she was missing even though neither friends nor family had reported her so.

Crystal's slaying and the circumstances surrounding the discovery of her body had a particularly devastating effect on her housemate and friend Brittney Gary. Brittney had watched her tiny milieu in South Jennings get wiped off the map.

Unlike the other victims, Brittney was more typical teenager than experienced sex worker. She loved sparkly accoutrements and decked her fingers with rings—wedding rings worn by her grandparents, a heart-shaped ring with faux diamonds. She painted her toenails bright red, and they gleamed through the straps of her rhinestone-studded flip-flops.

But beneath Brittney's girlishness lay the same family dysfunction that had haunted the other slain women. After her parents' divorce, Brittney and her brother, BJ, and her sisters, Velvet and Crystal, lived a nomadic existence. At first, their mother, Teresa, had moved them to the small town of Sebring, Florida, where the Garys had family. But Teresa, who worked as a store manager at a local Wendy's, struggled to raise the kids on her service-industry salary. She moved everyone back to Jennings about a year later. In Jennings, Teresa seemed unable to provide for the kids at all. Just after New Year's, in early 2006, Brittney ran away from home. On January 24, 2006, when their father, Pappy, stopped by Teresa's home, she told him she couldn't locate their kids. The incident report paints a devastating portrait of alleged child neglect:

> I spoke with Bryan Gary at JDSO [Jefferson Davis Parish Sheriff's Office] in reference to child neglect. Bryan said he dropped his children off to ex wife Teresa Gary for visitation. Bryan said he has custody of the children but every time he goes to pick up the children, Teresa says she does not know where they are. Bryan has filed reports with the New Iberia OCS (a division of Louisiana's Department of Children's and Family Services) and Jennings OCS.[15]

After such incidents, Brittney's older sister Velvet told me, "My dad came and took me and my sister from my mom."[16] Living with their father didn't last long, either. Velvet moved to Slidell, Louisiana, about an hour's drive north of New Orleans, to obtain her GED. Brittney, meanwhile, followed her mother, who had entered into a relationship with a woman named Katie Mott, to Houston. But Brittney was lonely, bored, and friendless in Houston, so she urged her mother to move back to Jennings. Mother and daughter eventually settled on Lufkin, Texas, where Brittney's boyfriend from Jennings had family. But Lufkin was still nowhere near Jefferson Davis Parish. In 2007, Brittney and Teresa Gary began staying with friends and family back home, mostly on weekends. Though Brittney was only sixteen, she experimented with drugs and dated a string of South Jennings drug dealers, including the Hobart Street hustler David "Bowlegs" Deshotel.

By early 2008, Brittney and her mother were living together

in an apartment on South Doyle Street and occasionally crashing together at the South Andrew Street home where nearly all of the Jeff Davis 8 tricked. "She was *deep* in the streets," her sister Velvet Gary told me. In the fall months after Crystal's murder, Brittney became heavily addicted to crack. She had experimented with the drug at the South Andrew Street house while partying with her fellow sex workers of the Jeff Davis 8. The drugs and her mourning over Crystal made her behavior increasingly erratic. She also told her sister that she was petrified of the police. "One weekend my sister was real shooken up," Velvet told me. "I was like, 'Brittney, what's wrong with you?' 'I can't tell you.' 'Are you scared of somebody in Jennings?' She said, 'I don't trust the police.'" One afternoon, Brittney walked to Whitnei Dubois's niece's home and screamed from the front yard that "Uncle Frankie"—Frankie Richard—had murdered Whitnei. Brittney's periodic and dangerous outbursts preceded moments of deep reclusiveness. Her paranoia is a hallmark of severe multidrug use, but given her tragic end, her fears appear to have been justified. By mid-fall 2008, she quietly divided her time between her homes on South Andrew and South Doyle Streets, venturing elsewhere in town only to run errands.

At 5:35 p.m. on November 2, 2008, Brittney ran just such an errand.[17] She walked from the South Doyle Street home toward the Family Dollar Store on the north side of town to purchase cell phone minutes and a new pair of jeans. Surveillance footage from the Family Dollar that evening shows Brittney—her distinctive olive skin, thick bushy eyebrows, and hair tightened in a bun—entering the store at 6:18, checking out at the register at 6:21, and exiting the store at 6:22. This would be the last-known sighting of Brittney, who was wearing a blue shirt and khaki pants. When she didn't return home that night, Teresa stayed up well past dawn, locked with worry. On November 3, an exhausted Teresa reported Brittney missing, noting her daughter's distinctive jewelry—"Teresa said Brittney was wearing rings on almost all of her fingers," according to a Taskforce investigative report—and had a pair of tattoos (the words CRAZY BEAUTI- FUL inked on her right breast and TERESA with a rose and a tribal Indian sign on her left breast).

Brittney's uncle Butch assembled a search team. "I had no support from law enforcement whatsoever," Butch told me. "I'd talked to Ricky Edwards, and he said, 'I have nothing pointing in this direction to justify having officers out there with you. All we know is that she is missing.' "[18] Butch was bewildered and indignant. His niece was directly connected to past victims. Her disappearance fit the pattern. It's hard to blame Butch: when he assembled the search team to look for his niece during the fall of 2008, *six* sex workers had been slain in Jefferson Davis Parish, at least two of whom, cousin Kris- ten Gary Lopez, and housemate Crystal Benoit Zeno, were deeply connected to his niece. So Sheriff Edwards's notion that the circumstances did not "justify" Sheriff's Office resources was simply absurd. Even the search team that Butch assembled was illustrative of the bonds shared by the victims: one of its members was Melissa Daigle, Kristen's still-grieving mother. "We left here looking for Brittney's body. We all left on four- wheelers," Melissa Daigle told me in July of 2011 when I vis- ited her at her home. [19] Photos of her daughter covered the mantelpiece, and potted plants from her funeral bloomed along the driveway. Daigle has kept them alive since 2007.

Every morning that November, the search team assem- bled at the Jennings Fairgrounds near the corner of South Lake Arthur Avenue and Scott Street. From there, they searched the rice fields, crawfish ponds, and canals that surrounded Jennings. "We searched for Brittney from eight a.m. to four p.m.," Butch told me, "every single day. Depending on the day, there could be anywhere from ten to thirty of us. We had family, friends, out-of-towners. One man came from as far away as DeRidder [a Louisiana town about eighty miles northwest of Jennings]."

By the end of the first full week of searches, the team had yet to find a single clue regarding Brittney's whereabouts, let alone Brittney herself. Just before 8:00 a.m. on November 15, 2008, the search team assembled yet again at the Jennings Fairgrounds. It had been thirteen days since Brittney disappeared, and little optimism remained. But that morning a new volunteer, Jimmy D. LeBlanc, from Lake Charles, had joined the team.[20] On this unusually cool morning—the temperature hovered around fifty degrees—when LeBlanc had woken up, he "prayed to God that he would find Brittney . . . and contacted his church and asked them to pray for him." After joining his fellow volunteers, LeBlanc drove—as the search team had done for many days—down the back roads of Jennings, paying close attention to the nearby ditches and drainage canals, which had served as the dumping grounds for the other victims. When LeBlanc turned onto Keystone Road, he stopped his truck and began to walk off the roadside. The tall grass, vast and expansive, seemed to stretch to the horizon. LeBlanc spotted, nearly submerged, what appeared to be a dead animal. But as he moved closer, he saw a pair of human legs. Frightened, he ran back to his truck and called 911; it was 12:30 p.m. and the search team had been out for only a few hours. Around 1:00 p.m. the Sheriff's Office arrived at the scene and filed an incident report:

On November 15, 2008, at approximately 1300 hrs, Detective Jason Chretien received a phone call from JDSO dispatch. JDSO dispatch advised that they received a call from a man crying stating that he had found a body. The man who was later identified as Jimmy LeBlanc gave his location of where he was located. Detective Chretien went and met with LeBlanc at this location which was Keystone Road south of Highway 1126. Upon Detective Chretien's arrival Detective Romero was already present on Keystone Road. Detective Romero made confirmation of what LeBlanc had found which was a body.[21]

Brittney was lying facedown in tall grass approximately ten feet east of Keystone Road; she was completely naked and the only jewelry remaining on her body was a gray beaded bracelet around her right ankle. Uncle Butch Gary rushed to the scene, but investigators quickly turned him away. "Whenever I finally got there, the Sheriff's Department was already there," Butch told me, "and they wouldn't let anybody around. They said, 'You really don't want to see this.'" Brittney's older sister, Velvet, however, was later allowed to see the body. "She was in a fetal position when they found her," Velvet remembers. "And when we saw the body, I wanted to see her hair, which was long and very curly. She didn't have any hair, that's how decomposed she was."

Like Crystal Benoit Zeno, Brittney had been dead for weeks by the time she was discovered. Thus, the Coroner's Office struggled to determine a cause of death. Brittney likely died from asphyxia, but there was no evidence of external injury. As with all of the other Jeff Davis 8 victims, toxicology revealed drugs: cocaine and benzoylecgonine, in Brittney's system.

A lack of suspects dogged the Brittney Gary case from the beginning. "We do have a couple of people who have seen some activity," a far-from-assured Sheriff Edwards told the media soon after Brittney's body was found. "We're following up on that and trying to get that information, trying to get that evidence, so we can follow up on that."[22]

Inexplicably, Sheriff Edwards was hesitant to connect Brittney to the other slain sex workers: "I'm not a fool to believe that they are not connected, but I don't have the evidence to connect it."

Brittney was linked to several of the victims and suspects—she was cousins with Kristen, came up on the streets under the tutelage of Muggy Brown, hustled with Frankie Richard, and tricked at South Andrew Street with Crystal Benoit Zeno. Her mother was also deeply enmeshed in the Richard clan. She took care of Frankie's brother Billy when he was recovering from colon cancer. When Teresa distributed more than seven hundred missing person flyers with her daughter's photograph in November of 2008, she listed a phone number belonging to Richard's niece Hannah Conner, who had been charged—and then released—in the murder of Brittney's cousin Kristen. In an interview with Taskforce investigators, Teresa admitted that Conner "was a close friend" and that she put Conner's contact information on the flyer because she "did not want law enforcement flooded with erroneous calls."

Teresa Gary's explanation of her relationship to the Richards was incomplete. Several witnesses told Taskforce investigators that Teresa prostituted Brittney at South Andrew Street. Teresa and Frankie Richard were in fact criminal associates. In the months to come, one of their many joint hustles would attract the attention of not just the Sheriff's Office but the Taskforce as well.

By now, with seven victims in a little more than three years, the failures of the Sheriff's Office and the Taskforce had become notorious. On November 19, 2008, then Louisiana governor Bobby Jindal addressed the public's increasing discomfort surrounding the case: "It is important for our families to be safe. It shows you none of us are immune, every part of the country. It's not just the big cities; even more rural communities are seeing more violent crime. State Police are working with the Sheriff's Office to make sure if there is anything they need from the state, they get that as they work to solve these cases."[23]

Jindal's dissatisfaction fixed nothing. Just like the murders of the slain sex workers before her, Brittney's also remains unsolved. But witness interviews, Taskforce interrogations, and public records paint a vivid picture of what I have concluded likely happened.

After Brittney left the Family Dollar, Sheriff's deputy Danny Barry picked her up and brought her back to his trailer in Lake Arthur for sex. According to multiple Taskforce witnesses, Barry patronized South Jennings sex workers nearly daily. "Deputy Danny Barry would ride around on the south side with his wife," one witness told Taskforce investigators, "and they would try to pick up girls. . . . [Barry's vehicle was] a small blue sports car. . . . Barry would drop off his wife . . . and she would get the girls. The couple would spike a drink and then take the girls back to the Barrys' house." One witness even told Taskforce investigators, "Danny Barry had a room in his trailer that had chains hanging from the ceiling . . ." and that ". . . a person could not see in or out of the room." Another sex worker claimed Barry had "a trailer with plastic wrap all over the ceilings and floors and walls." In the Taskforce documents that I have obtained, at least nine Taskforce witnesses name Barry as a suspect in the killings.

Brittney was well aware of Barry and his penchant for rough sex. When Brittney had confided in her sister months earlier that she was petrified of Jennings law enforcement, her friends and family believe that she was referring to Deputy Barry.

According to a law enforcement source close to the case, Brittney partied with Barry—they smoked crack and drank hard liquor together nearly round the clock—in his Lake Arthur trailer for about two days. Then on November 4, Barry strangled her—it's unclear what prompted the attack—and dumped her body off Keystone Road (the coroner pinpoints Brittney's date of death as November 4 as well). At least three Taskforce witnesses told investigators that they observed suspicious activity on Keystone Road in the days before Brittney's corpse was discovered; two of those witnesses said that on November 9 they observed a truck parked on the east side of the road (where Brittney was found) with two white male occupants. One of the men was standing on the roadside. The witnesses said that the men had the confident air of authority about them and could have been police.

Barry may not have acted alone in the Brittney Gary slaying. A close, longtime associate of Frankie Richard's, whom I'll call Witness C, told Taskforce investigators that Barry worked with Frankie to carry out Brittney's murder. Witness C said that Barry and Frankie smoked crack together, and that Barry "needed to cover up something. That's how it started going bad." Similarly, according to Witness C, Frankie confessed to him that "the little girl [Brittney] knew too much." Witness C insisted that "Frankie carried the shit [Brittney's murder] out." In multiple interviews with me spanning 2011 to 2014, Frankie has strenuously denied any involvement in *any* of the Jeff Davis 8 murders. But in July 2011, while we were talking, Frankie fingered Barry as a prime suspect in the sex worker slayings. "All these girls or most of these girls was found within a three-mile radius of Danny Barry's house," Frankie told me.[24] "Since he been dead"—Barry died of cancer in August 2010—"nobody died. All these motherfuckers on the sheriff's department are some crooked sons of bitches. Danny Barry was married to a black girl and she smoked crack. Danny Barry go to work and his old lady would smoke crack and trick to make money to smoke her crack. When Danny Barry get off work, he would go huntin' and say to these girls, 'Look, I'll give you twenty dollars if you tell me where my old lady is.' They would take the money and send him on a wild goose chase. When he would find his old lady, he would get one of those girls to trick with him and he would watch. It's not the same person killing those girls. But I think it's the same person behind all of it. Somebody with authority that had something on somebody who instead of locking somebody up got them to take care of somebody." Much of Frankie's remarks about Barry are clearly made out of self-interest; Frankie would obviously like nothing more than a dead man to be held responsible for the murders that he has long been suspected of committing. But Frankie's specifics about Barry's drug use and his patronizing of South Jennings sex workers are corroborated by numerous Taskforce witness interviews.

Witness C's allegations against Frankie are also credible. Witness C is a confidant of Frankie's, a close business associate and friend. Witness C told Taskforce investigators that he tried on multiple occasions to *stop* Richard from confessing, but that he persisted. "Frankie, I don't wanna know this shit," Witness C said. "Do your confessing to God. *I don't want to know this shit.*" Witness C said that Frankie insisted on talking to him about the Jeff Davis 8 murders and admitted to killing "four of 'em" and that "he woulda done hard time with four of 'em." Witness C was apparently referring to victims Brittney, Crystal, Whitnei, and Kristen. Critically, Witness C corroborated details of the Whitnei Dubois murder, specifically that Richard had a fifty-five-gallon drum behind his house, as well as formaldehyde, that he used to store and perhaps preserve Whitnei's body. "I didn't know he was rocking like this," Witness C told Taskforce investigators. "It's some wicked shit. Frankie is a monster. He got this place he go black in, man."

By the end of 2008, there were credible suspects in most (if not all) of the slayings of the seven women in Jefferson Davis Parish. It should have been clear to the Sheriff's Office that the victims were inextricably linked—by blood, by sex work, by the places they lived together, sometimes even as a material witnesses to the murder of a fellow victim. But when Sheriff Edwards, who looked uncomfortable in a tan dress shirt and a dark navy-blue blazer, held a televised press conference on December 18, 2008, in front of the redbrick courthouse on North State Street in Jennings, he said that he couldn't connect the killings: "The facts that we currently have do not allow me at this time to say with certainty that these cases are all linked."[25]

Instead, Sheriff Edwards dwelled on the serial killer theory, even though there were separate suspects in the cases (excluding Frankie Richard, who was linked to multiple homicides). "You have all asked whether or not this is a serial killer," Sheriff Edwards told the crowd, which included community members and relatives of the victims. "I caution you that the term *serial killer* is complicated and conjures images based on Hollywood shows of a frightening-looking maniac. However, most of the time, the offender or offenders in a serial case end up looking as normal as you and me, the typical guy next door." Then, bizarrely, Sheriff Edwards spent the remainder of the press conference ticking off the characteristics of serial killers: "Do you know someone who is superficially glib and charming? Self-confident? Appears nonthreatening initially? Physically strong—not to be confused with someone who works out every day at the gym? Frequents the area where the girls go missing from? Quick to anger especially if rejected? Lures girls with alcohol and drugs? May have a formal criminal record involving assaultive behavior with a knife and may include burglary? May not necessarily have a violent criminal history?"

At the press conference, reporters as well as friends and family of the victims voiced their skepticism and frustration. Scott Lewis of the *Jennings Daily News* asked why it had taken *seven* victims to form the Taskforce. "Why haven't in two years we been contacted by law enforcement?" shouted one of the victim's family members, off camera. (I've heard similar complaints of lack of law enforcement contact from friends and family members of nearly all of the victims.) "Since we found her, we haven't talked to anybody," Brittney Gary's uncle Butch told me. "They say on the news they're staying in touch and they're making progress, but I haven't heard from anybody. I never heard one word. I think they're just making themselves look good in the press." One family member at Sheriff Edwards's December presser was unrelenting in her criticism: "This is not being done the way it is supposed to be done. These girls are not gonna get justice until someone from outside steps in."

Her concern was understandable and widely shared. Allegations of misconduct and conflicts of interest were rife in the Jeff Davis 8 case from the beginning. Warren Gary was alleged to have destroyed key physical evidence in one of the murders (Kristen's) when he bought and resold Connie Siler's Silverado. Taskforce witnesses said that Terrie Guillory had sex with some of the victims and that they suspected that Deputy Danny Barry was involved in at least one of the murders. And whistle-blowers—nurse Nina Ravey, Sergeant Jesse Ewing—had their lives destroyed.

The Taskforce, composed of the upper ranks of local, state, and federal law enforcement, was supposed to resolve this conflict. Instead, just like the Violent Crimes Task Force (VCTF) in Calcasieu Parish in the 1990s, which was tasked with investigating two separate murder cases in which the sheriff's son was implicated, the Jeff Davis 8 Taskforce remained a near case study in conflict of interest. In a 2009 letter about the Taskforce from then FBI director Robert S. Mueller, he wrote that the multiagency team was in fact "led by the Jefferson Davis Parish Sheriff's Office."[26]

The Jeff Davis 8 Taskforce and the VCTF even shared a lead investigator: Calcasieu Parish Sheriff's Office detective Ramby Cormier. Cormier has since moved to the Jeff Davis Sheriff's Office, where he works as a detective. He told me that the "Sheriff's Office is kind of the lead" on the Taskforce.[27] This orientation is deeply troubling, given that the employees of the Sheriff's Office have been implicated in the same murders that office is tasked with investigating. Cormier has long bristled at the notion that the Taskforce is a case study in conflict of interest. "If you can convince the feds to take it over, then you should do that," Cormier told a Taskforce witness in the spring of 2015 who raised the issue of the Taskforce's conflicts. "But they've been involved. . . . If he [Sheriff Ricky Edwards] had wanted to cover something up, he wouldn't have other agencies coming in."*

---

*I was present during Detective Ramby Cormier's interview of this Taskforce witness. The witness—whose identity I will not disclose due to concerns about his safety—requested that I, in my capacity as a licensed private investigator, accompany him to an April 2015 meeting with Cormier of the Jefferson Davis Parish Sheriff's Office. The witness was concerned about being interviewed by Cormier alone because he previously had negative experiences with the Taskforce, including being swabbed for his DNA by FBI agent Andrew Gavurnik. I agreed to accompany the witness to the meeting at no cost—both because I wanted to help a frightened and reluctant witness and, more important, I felt that any exchange of funds between the witness and me would represent a potential conflict of interest because of my work on the Jeff Davis 8 case. During the interview, which was conducted at the Jefferson Davis Parish Sheriff's Office Criminal Investigations Division at 506 Roberts Avenue in Jennings, I introduced myself to Detective Cormier and Detective Kimberly Juneau as a private investigator retained by the witness to accompany him to the interview and corroborate all details of the interview.

CHAPTER 10

The Undoing

On an unusually chilly day in mid-December 2008, Frankie Richard called Jarett Dobson, an investigator with the Louisiana State Police. Dobson had joined the Taskforce after serving on the team that investigated the 2005 police killing of Leonard Crochet. He'd also interrogated jail nurse and whistleblower Nina Ravey. Frankie wanted to talk about the unsolved murders; he made the call from the Freedom Baptist Church in Logansport, where he was hunkered down in an inpatient drug rehabilitation program. It was a moment of drying out, far from the temptations back home.

The church sits on a narrow, desolate stretch of Highway 5, surrounded by tall pine trees, nearly two hundred miles northwest of Jefferson Davis Parish. When Dobson arrived, Frankie immediately began talking about the slayings. He said that fellow rehab patient Michael Prudhomme—boyfriend of Jennings sex worker Necole Guillory, who months later would become the eighth and final victim—had cleaned the Chevy Silverado that investigators believed was used to dispose of Kristen's body. Frankie also confessed that his sister Tabatha was with Loretta Chaisson just before she died, though he insisted that Loretta had suffered a seizure and then "people got scared and dumped [her] into the canal" (there's no evidence to corroborate this). Then he ticked off an extensive list of corrupt members of local law enforcement (including Deputy Danny Barry) who he claimed paid for sex with the murdered women and were also involved in their violent demise.

Though Frankie was—and still is—a strong suspect in at least two of the Jeff Davis 8 murders (Whitnei and Kristen), he had a long history of cooperating with law enforcement. Indeed, Frankie was debriefed by the Taskforce on at least four separate occasions in 2008 and 2009. While Frankie often made incriminating statements, he always eluded law enforcement's grasp, it appears, because he is savvy at making alliances born of mutual interest. His criminal history is a series of dropped charges in cases ranging from theft to rape and murder. It invites the conclusion that in exchange for information—and, likely, fearing what Frankie knows about their misconduct—local law enforcement provides him cover. His relationships extend to the highest ranks of the Taskforce. I've learned that Frankie was issued a key to the Taskforce office on South Lake Arthur Avenue. Multiple witnesses watched him let himself in, both day and night. The relationship far precedes the Jeff Davis 8 era; a law enforcement witness named Frankie as a coconspirator in the March 2, 1990, theft of nearly three hundred pounds of marijuana from the Sheriff's Office. The other conspirator was a deputy.[1]

Frankie has been dubbed the Cajun Country Charles Manson. His grizzled look—flowing brown hair and wild, unkempt beard—and his circle of women make the comparison visually apt. But Frankie's close confederacy with law enforcement is less reminiscent of Manson than of Whitey Bulger, the Boston Mob boss who for two decades provided information on murders, drug deals, armed robberies, and fugitives to corrupt FBI agent John Connolly. In exchange for Bulger's cooperation, Connolly protected Bulger from the FBI and tipped him off to snitches in his midst, some of whom later wound up murdered.[2] The feds essentially protected Bulger's sprawling criminal enterprise until he was tried and convicted in federal court in 2013.[3]

A small-town street heavy such as Frankie Richard has none of the stature or influence of a big-city Mob boss. But Frankie's troubling relationship with law enforcement is symptomatic of a larger trend. A recent FBI report, for example, concluded that the agency gave its informants permission to break the law at least 5,658 times in one year.[4] "Not only do informants' past crimes go unpunished," says Loyola Law School professor Alexandra Natapoff, "authorities routinely tolerate the commission of new crimes—authorized and unauthorized—as part of the cost of maintaining an active informant."[5]

Frankie was far from the only suspect in the Jeff Davis 8 case to be treated with kid gloves by the Taskforce. When investigators finally interviewed Deputy Danny Barry on February 25, 2009, they asked him a string of simple, relatively non-adversarial questions. He was never confronted with the myriad allegations that he, along with Warden Guillory, prostituted female inmates from the parish jail or that he was seen picking up victim Brittney Gary in his vehicle—a failure that is particularly shocking because a high-ranking FBI agent from Lake Charles assisted in conducting the interview. Even worse, the first Taskforce interrogation of Barry would be the last because he passed away in 2010.

While Taskforce interrogations in an ongoing case were

hidden from public scrutiny, in the spring of 2009 a member of the Taskforce made a very public mistake. That May, Jennings saw a series of home burglaries, in which high-powered weapons, rare coins, and expensive jewelry were stolen and then sold at a local pawnshop. Among the stolen items were a Colt .380 and two diamond rings valued at $4,300 and $3,300. On May 21, 2009, the Sheriff's Office initiated an investigation, spearheaded by Deputy Paula Guillory, a key member of the Taskforce and ex-wife of Terrie Guillory.[6]

Paula Guillory quickly made headway because the burglars were caught on surveillance at Chad's Pawn Shop. One of the thieves was longtime Frankie Richard associate Michael Prudhomme. When Deputy Guillory interrogated Prudhomme, he admitted that he was "riding strong" with Frankie Richard and Teresa Gary, the mother of Jeff Davis 8 victim Brittney. Prudhomme also told investigators that he was staying at the South Andrew Street home where most of the Jeff Davis 8 victims had resided. The theft ring was a microcosm of the drugs-and-sex milieu in South Jennings, and as Deputy Guillory investigated further, she found that both Richard and Teresa Gary were indeed involved in it. Richard admitted to investigators that another player in his organization "gave two of the [stolen] diamond rings to Teresa Gary."

On May 26, 2009, arrest warrants were issued for Richard, Teresa Gary, and several other players in the theft ring.[7] Investigators believed the stolen goods were being held at the Richard family home at 811 McKinley Street. Authorities raided the properties on May 28, 2009. Nearly everyone involved—Paula Guillory, Ramby Cormier, and Jarrett Dobson—also served on the Taskforce. During the raid, investigators recovered old-coin collections and jewelry as well as drugs and approximately $3,500 in cash stored in a freezer. Both Frankie and his elderly mother, Jeanette LeBlanc, were taken into custody, and Paula Guillory turned over nearly sixty bags of evidence to the Sheriff's evidence custodian, Warren Gary. Gary, of course, had been accused of helping to dispose of evidence (the Silverado) in the Kristen Gary Lopez homicide. Yet despite such misconduct, Gary was tasked with cataloging and storing evidence in a brand-*new* and potentially significant criminal case against Frankie.

Just as in the Kristen Gary Lopez case, evidence problems arose in the theft investigation. When Warren Gary reviewed evidence bags 58 to 61, he said that the cash ($3,500, $130, $71, and $90) was missing.[8] So, on July 7, 2009, the Sheriff's Office initiated an internal investigation, which was turned over to the Vermilion Parish to help avoid any potential conflicts of interest.

The following day, Paula Guillory was suspended and sent home from work. I've obtained a copy of her personnel file. Paula's fellow deputies accused her of an array of misdeeds, from evidence pilfering to involvement in the drug trade. Derrick Miller, a detective with the Sheriff's Office who had previously worked for the Jennings police, said that "prior to her being hired, they never had anything come up missing from the office," and that he did "not trust her because there is information that leaked and knows that it came from her." Miller didn't specify the nature of the leaks—or to whom she leaked. But any allegation that Paula Guillory was improperly disclosing information is deeply troubling because she was a core member of the Taskforce. Others who worked with Paula slammed her poor work habits, alleged that she often left evidence unsecured, and claimed that her children were involved in the Jennings drug trade. "All of her cases are being reassigned because she never did anything with them," Detective Miller told investigators. On August 11, 2009, Paula Guillory was fired.[9]

Paula Guillory denies any wrongdoing in the theft raid. She told me that she even offered to take a polygraph test. "I never even gave my own side of the story," she says.[10] What happened to the evidence seized in the raid may be disputed, but the vanished cash marked the third time that a significant case against Frankie Richard collapsed (the first being second-degree murder charges in the Kristen Gary Lopez case, the second being the Elizabeth Clemens rape case). "I'm not mad at that," Frankie told me when I asked him about the missing evidence. "In fact I thank her for doing that. If she had handled her business right, my mama would still be in jail."[11] Paula Guillory says this sentiment infuriates her. "I believe *he* should be in jail," she said.

But allegations of misconduct by the disgraced former deputy go far beyond evidence mishandling. I've interviewed several witnesses who claim that at around the time of the collapsed theft case, they saw Paula Guillory socializing with Frankie Richard at both his McKinley Street home and at South Andrew Street during the summer of 2009, when the raid took place. One South Andrew Street resident, who asked not to be identified out of concern for her safety, spotted Paula Guillory at her neighbor's home "constantly" after Muggy Brown was murdered. These witness accounts are corroborated by private investigator Kirk Menard, who says he surveilled both Paula Guillory and her then husband, Terrie, hanging out at South Andrew Street. Around the same time, Menard—joined by Mike Dubois's daughter Brittany Jones, who'd obtained a private investigator's license out of frustration with local law enforcement's handling of the unsolved murders—videotaped the Guillorys socializing with Frankie Richard at McKinley Street. "The month before the bust," Jones told me, "I saw Paula and Terrie separately at Frankie's house. Frankie and them would be sitting on the porch. They'd be standing on the porch talking with him. They wouldn't stay very long, but they were there."[12] When I visited with Frankie one day in the spring of 2012, I asked him if he ever socialized with either Terrie or Paula Guillory. "They don't hang out at this house," he told me, before clarifying: "They never hung out at this house unless they came for police business or unless they was coming to buy crack in the middle of the night from somebody else. I didn't sell it. I smoked it." When I confronted Paula Guillory with these allegations, she replied, "That's news to me. I've heard many rumors. That me and [Terrie] were serial killers." Guillory added, more generally, that Jennings residents who've observed Taskforce investigators at the homes of suspects wrongly "assume investigators are there because they are corrupt."

By the summer of 2009, Jennings was still staring down seven unsolved murders. A charitable explanation for the Taskforce's failures would be incompetence. But that theory ignores the Taskforce's close relationship to one of its prime suspects, Frankie Richard. Jennings residents, especially those in South Jennings, remained frightened and distrustful of law enforcement, and their fears were justified. In late November of 2008, a Jennings sex worker told Taskforce investigators that one of her clients had just picked up Necole Guillory, a cousin of Terrie Guillory's, and "she felt that she might be the next victim." This highly specific tip received no follow-up by the Taskforce—a lapse that may have proved fatal.

Private investigator Kirk Menard also openly worried about Necole's fate. Earlier that summer, Menard had cultivated a source who closely watched the base of operations at South Andrew Street. On July 13, 2009, the source reported that a large group of sex workers were gathering at the house. Menard gunned his battered Ford Escape toward South Jennings. But when he arrived, he saw just one sex worker, a white woman in her twenties, sitting on the front steps. "It took only eight minutes of surveillance to get that," Menard remembers. As he focused his camcorder on the woman, she rose from the front steps and walked up and down South Andrew Street three times, brushing her long brown hair as she walked. Satisfied that he'd captured her on tape, Menard drove over to Brittany Jones's house to show her the footage. "That's Necole," she told Menard that day. "She's in the lifestyle."

Necole Jean Guillory, twenty-six, was not merely "in the lifestyle" of sex work in Jennings; she was at the very center of it. "Necole knew a whole lot," Frankie Richard admitted to me, "about a whole lot."

Indeed in 2005, Necole told friends and family that she, along with Muggy, had witnessed Loretta's being smothered to death by Muggy's boyfriend Stymie at the Boudreaux Inn. "Necole was extremely paranoid since the murder of Loretta," a former law enforcement source told me. "She locked all her doors and windows, and if she fought with you, she came at you with a knife."

Her boyfriend, Michael Prudhomme, and she were at the center of the Jeff Davis Parish jail's sex ring. Prudhomme told Taskforce investigators that Warden Guillory offered to release him from jail in exchange for sex with Necole. Prudhomme also said that Warden Guillory informed Necole's sister Jessica that "if she [Necole] would have sex with him, he would get him [Prudhomme] out of jail." According to a Taskforce investigative report that I've obtained, "Prud-homme . . . stated that Necole had told him that she had sex with Warden Guillory so he would let *her* out of jail." It's unclear when Necole may have had sex with Warden Guillory, but Prudhomme alleged, on record, that Necole would routinely gain her freedom when she was locked up for her many arrests (at least eight according to Jefferson Davis Parish court records) by having sex with Warden Guillory.

Prudhomme also said he helped clean out the Silverado truck used to transport Kristen Gary Lopez's body. Here's Prudhomme's statement from the Taskforce file:

> Prudhomme told investigators that shortly before Gary-Lopez's body was found, he was approached by Randall "Boy" Tyler and asked to clean out Connie Siler's truck. Prudhomme said there was a little blood inside the truck in the front and rear seat of the truck. Prudhomme told investigators that Jessica Guillory [Necole Guillory's sister] was with him when he cleaned the truck.

Randall "Boy" Tyler is a Jennings hustler with a towering rap sheet. His offenses range from carjacking to cocaine dealing. He is also closely tied to Frankie Richard; indeed, he's known in town as one of Frankie's "hands-on men." So Prud-homme's implicating Tyler should have been a huge break for investigators working a murder case in which Frankie Richard was the prime suspect. Nothing in the Sheriff Office's and DA's records I've reviewed indicates that Siler's truck was ever examined for blood, hair, or other types of physical evidence. Such an examination may have been impossible because the Silverado had been cleaned and sold to Warren

Gary, the chief investigator. But multiple witnesses had corroborated Prudhomme's confessions. If Prudhomme's own admissions weren't enough, Witness A—the highly credible, firsthand witness in the Whitnei Dubois slaying—echoed Prudhomme's confessions. "[Prudhomme] thinks he cleaned one of the vehicles used to kill one of the girls," relayed Witness A. Quoting Prudhomme: "I think that I cleaned a vehicle for Frankie. It was a pickup truck."

Prudhomme and Necole were not just lovers but criminal associates, too. In August 2001, they stole a wallet containing $449 in cash from a Jennings man.[13] Several months later, the pair robbed a customer at a Popeyes as he was sitting in his car placing a drive-through order, holding him up at gunpoint and forcing him to hand over $100. Necole told him she was Warden Terrie Guillory's daughter (they are in fact cousins, which makes the allegation that Warden Guillory demanded sexual favors from her in exchange for her release from jail all the more disturbing).[14] This was a bizarre statement to make—why would the perpetrator of an armed robbery suddenly announce who she was?—but it indicated the close working relationship that Necole had with cops and Sheriff's Office deputies, especially Terrie Guillory. Like the other murdered sex workers, Necole worked the South Jennings streets as an informant, though she was much savvier than her fellow Jeff Davis 8 victims. She leveraged her cooperation to get out of a string of serious charges—ranging from theft to drug possession to robbery.

By midsummer 2009, Necole realized she was in too deep. She told her mother, Barbara, who lived in a trailer in nearby Lake Arthur, not to worry about baking a birthday cake because she doubted she'd be alive to blow out the candles. "I had bought some icing and cake for her twenty-sixth birthday," Barbara told me. "She said, 'Mama, it doesn't matter, I'm not gonna be here.' I asked her, 'Just tell me what kind of icing you want on it?' And she said, 'Get what you want, I'm not gonna be here.'"[15] For their safety, Necole had her four children placed with relatives. "She always lived in fear," Barbara remembers. "She was always paranoid. It got to the point where she did not want to go anywhere by herself. I think she could feel that they were closing in on her. She knew, she knew, she knew, and that's why they killed her." Barbara implored her daughter to tell her family whatever she knew about the unsolved homicides. " 'Necole, just tell us,' " Barbara remembers saying. " 'A name. Something. Write a letter and leave it somewhere. Let us know. We can help you.' 'No, Mama. It's too far gone. It's too big. I'd rather y'all not know nothing. That way nothing can happen to y'all.' And she left it like that. You couldn't get anything else out of her."

In mid-August, Necole Guillory disappeared. An elderly acquaintance named Shelby Janise, with whom Necole had long had a combative relationship (in December of 2006, she attacked him with a sledgehammer), was the first to notice she was missing.[16] Shelby had not heard from Necole for several days, and fearing she might have been murdered, he alerted her mother. He had last seen Necole between 7:00 and 7:30 a.m. on Sunday, August 16, climbing into a white van with Jeff Daniels, the father of Jeff Davis 8 victim number two, Ernestine. Daniels later told investigators that he picked up Necole that morning, drove around town with her for about twenty minutes, then dropped her off at Ray's Laundry and Cleaners, the notorious car wash allegedly used to clean the Silverado truck. But he had not seen her again after that.

Barbara immediately went to the Sheriff's Office to file a missing person report. That afternoon, maintenance workers from nearby Acadia Parish were weeding a stretch of highway dominated by adult superstores and boudin shops. There, off I-10 just outside the limits of the town of Egan on the slope of an overpass, they found Necole lying dead in the grass."[17]

Necole was the first victim found outside Jefferson Davis Parish, and unlike the victims before her, her body was found in an extremely visible place. But in just about every other respect she was just like the seven victims who came before her. In the autopsy report, the coroner noted no evidence of external injury, excluding a few minor postmortem cuts on the left side of her face, left eyebrow, and left clavicle. "No trauma seen," the coroner wrote. A toxicology screen found, as with the other Jeff Davis 8 victims, traces of cocaine and pain medication (in Necole's case, tramadol). Similarly, the cause of death was unknown, though asphyxia was deemed "probable."[18]

It is difficult to theorize about who may have murdered Necole Guillory. But a Taskforce witness whom I will call Witness D provided investigators with a highly credible account of her final hours. Witness D is a close relative of Brittney Gary's. She frequented the South Andrew Street home where the Jeff Davis 8 engaged in sex work, and she encountered Necole there at approximately 9:00 p.m. on Sunday, August 16. Necole warned Witness D to be careful out on the streets. Then a South Jennings street hustler nicknamed Croc—Witness D did not know his real name—followed Necole outside, and that was the last time she saw her. Brittney Gary's mother, Teresa, was also at South Andrew Street that night. The coroner noted Necole's date of death was August 17, 2009, so she was likely murdered just hours after leaving South Andrew. In an acknowledgment of how little trust remained between parish residents and the Taskforce,

Witness D told investigators, "We need a whole new police force." She paused, then offered some Southern manners to soften the blow: "Forgive me."

Necole's mother, Barbara, was also consumed with anger and distrust. Instead of grieving, she kept replaying conversations. She returned obsessively to Necole's terrifying claim—"She used to tell us all the time it was the police killing them girls," Barbara remembers. This allegation may have explained why Necole had been so fearful of naming suspects. "She wouldn't tell us because she didn't want to put us in harm's way," Barbara told me. "She'd tell us, 'Mama, the less y'all know, the better off you are.'"

For years it had been easy to see the slain sex workers as simply the victims of, as Sheriff Edwards has repeatedly and dismissively told the media, a "high-risk lifestyle." But with eight murdered in four years in a town of just ten thousand, fear was growing, as was a sense among the Jennings elites that the case was becoming a civic black eye. In the winter of 2009, with public outcry over the murders mounting, Sheriff Edwards ordered all investigators working the Jeff Davis 8 case—including non-law-enforcement such as private investigator Kirk Menard—be swabbed for DNA. Sheriff Edwards assured reporters that the DNA testing was meant to silence "gossip and rumors" about law enforcement's involvement in the killings, a much-needed moment of transparency. But these public comments were patently false; the Sheriff's Office was not implicated in the Jeff Davis 8 case due to "gossip and rumors," but by the Taskforce's very own witnesses. When I interviewed him, Sheriff Edwards refused to comment on the DNA test results, nor have the results ever been made public; this sort of withholding of information is commonplace in open criminal cases.[19]

On October 28, 2009, Sheriff Edwards held a second, higher-profile Taskforce press conference to address the public's concerns, this time in a wood-paneled room in the parish courthouse.[20] "The agencies comprising the Multi-Agency Investigative Team have called you here today to provide you with an update regarding where we are in the investigation," said Sheriff Edwards, who was flanked by the special agent in charge of the FBI's New Orleans office, as well as several sheriffs and police chiefs from surrounding parishes, "to give you facts as we have them, and to announce an increase in the reward that is being offered. We will take no questions today and we thank you for your continued efforts to release factual information, not opinions or gossip."

As photographs of the Jeff Davis 8 were projected onto an imposing flat screen, Sheriff Edwards explained that the reward for information leading to an arrest and successful prosecution was increasing from $35,000 to $85,000. He boasted that "investigators have followed nearly one thousand leads, interviewed approximately five hundred people, and fielded countless telephone calls providing information on these cases." While in 2008 Sheriff Edwards had not been ready to commit to the serial killer theory, he was now seemingly prepared to do so. "It is the collective opinion of all agencies involved in this investigation," he said, "that these murders may have been committed by a common offender."

Soon after Sheriff Edwards held the Taskforce press conference, local NBC affiliate KPLC aired a sprawling, seven-part series on the Jeff Davis 8 called "Unsolved: Mystery in Jeff Davis Parish," in which many of the case's central players appeared on-camera.[21] Frankie Richard, naturally, agreed to an interview and talked to reporters from a chair on his front porch. "I knew all the girls," Richard said proudly. "I was

friends with all of 'em. They all used to come around here."
Frankie denied involvement in any of the Jeff Davis 8 murders and pointed out that he was like kin to many of the victims, particularly Kristen Gary Lopez. "Kristen would call
me Uncle Frankie," he said. Yet Frankie would not confirm
that he was with Kristen, Connie Siler, and Tracee Chaisson
just before Kristen was murdered.

Tracee made her first-ever media appearance, telling the
KPLC reporters that she was close with Kristen, Muggy
Brown, Crystal Benoit Zeno, and Brittney Gary, while
recanting her 2007 statements implicating Frankie in Kristen's
murder. "I lied on Frankie," Tracee said, "and I went back
and told the people [investigators] that I lied." Tracee claimed
that she provided the confession because law enforcement
harassed her: "I was just tired of 'em. I wanted 'em out of my
life." Sounding fearful, she declared, "The truth is, I know
nothing."

Mike Dubois, Whitnei's brother, also appeared in the
KPLC series. In a taped interview he claimed to have "no confidence in the Taskforce or the sheriff's department." About
a week after the series aired, Dubois was driving from Houston to Jennings when he was pulled over by a police officer
in Basile, Louisiana, a tiny town of about eighteen hundred.[22]
Dubois was still recovering from cancer treatments and had
traveled to Houston for doctors' appointments and medication. Police, claiming they were acting on an anonymous
tip, had stopped Dubois on suspicion of drug trafficking.
"Of all the times I was dirty, all the times I was doing some
fucked-up shit, the one day I was actually clean and doing the
right thing, they stopped me," Dubois told me. "First they
told me, 'We're gonna search your car, and if there's no drugs
in your car, we're gonna let you go back to Jennings.' I said

there's only my prescriptions in here, and then a minute later they picked up my prescriptions and cuffed me." The Basile Police Department claimed they recovered dozens of prescription pills from Dubois's car, including thirty Xanax and thirty tramadol. Dubois insisted that he had prescriptions for the medication; he was still recovering from a surgery that removed part of his neck muscle, jugular vein, and thirty-five lymph glands.

But on November 10, 2009, Dubois was nonetheless hit with a raft of drug charges, including possession with the intent to distribute. These sorts of escalated charges are commonplace in drug cases. Straightforward drug possession could be ginned up to "possession with intent to distribute" based on the quantity of drugs and the background of the alleged culprit. The dispute was not whether Dubois possessed the drugs, but whether his possession was illegal. He was subsequently jailed in Basile and later transferred to the Jefferson Davis Parish lockup. At first he was relieved to be closer to home, but then prison officials declared him a "high-profile" inmate and he was shipped to the Cameron Parish jail, about seventy miles from Jennings.

"They knew what they were doing," Dubois told me. "They wanted me where I couldn't get to no lawyers from Jennings to there to see me. They wanted to hide me away." Despite several attempts to bond out, Dubois spent eighteen months incarcerated in Cameron Parish. "They thought they was gonna shut me up," Dubois continues, "but I did telephone interviews from the jail."

Indeed, Dubois made headlines—and garnered support from several of the families of the Jeff Davis 8 victims—thanks to a series of jailhouse interviews. "It was a setup from hell," Barbara Guillory says of Dubois's arrest, "and everybody in town knew that. We're not stupid. If you don't hush, they'll put you in jail."

In one jailhouse interview with KPLC, Dubois lamented, "I think that they are just trying to keep me in to keep me quiet so I'm not back on the news with you all or back in the newspapers putting the pressure on them."[23] When reporter Lee Peck asked, "So you think this [the arrest] is a direct result of speaking out against the investigation?" Dubois bluntly replied, "Yes, I do." Dubois offered a dire prediction for Jeff Davis Parish for 2010 and beyond: "I believe we will have still more murders yet to come."

Dubois's prediction proved prescient. The beginning of 2010 brought a wave of unprecedented violence. This time, however, the victims were not sex workers but South Jennings street hustlers. On January 6, Alan West, a Jennings drug dealer with connections to the Houston wholesale trade, was killed in his driveway. According to law enforcement, the shooter had been hiding over a hundred yards away. Investigators suspected that the killer had traveled all the way from Houston to do the job.[24] The West case remains unsolved.

On February 8, Marsena Alexander, a street associate of Muggy Brown's and Ernestine Patterson's, was shot in the back.[25] Alexander survived but her cousin Kenneth Pelican wouldn't be so lucky. On February 24, Pelican—aka Kenny Boo—was shot to death inside his car, which was parked near the corner of West and Smith Streets in South Jennings.[26] Local law enforcement found Pelican slumped over in the driver's seat. No one has ever been charged in the Pelican killing.

All the escalating violence scared off potential Taskforce witnesses. "I think it pulls the Taskforce away from that investigation," private investigator Menard told KPLC in early 2010, "to work on the shootings and the violence." But local law enforcement's failings were too severe and multitudinous to be explained away by the distraction of new murder cases.

A painful and potent reminder of the lack of closure in the Jeff Davis 8 case came in June of 2010, when Byron Chad Jones was arrested in Lake Arthur for stabbing a woman in the mouth.[27] Jones had previously been indicted on second-degree murder charges in Ernestine's death, but those charges had been dropped. In the Lake Arthur stabbing, Jones was charged with attempted second-degree murder and subsequently convicted; he is currently behind bars at the Dixon Correctional Institute near Baton Rouge. To the families of the Jeff Davis 8, Jones's arrest in a new stabbing was a particularly brutal blow.

By fall 2009, the national media was beginning to descend. A reporter with *Marie Claire* traveled to Jennings to write a long feature about the Jeff Davis 8 and met with everyone from Frankie Richard to Sheriff Edwards (the piece was killed by the magazine and did not run elsewhere). More significant, in early 2010 a long piece about the case appeared on the front page of the National Section of the *New York Times*, headlined "8 Deaths in a Small Town, and Much Unease." "Every few months for the last four and a half years," wrote the *Times'* Southern correspondent Campbell Robertson, "someone driving the back roads here in Jefferson Davis Parish has come across a body."[28] Robertson cataloged the "apparent mistakes" made by investigators, including that of the detective who "had washed and resold the truck" that may have been used to transport Kristen's body.

The destruction of physical evidence in the Jeff Davis 8 case paled in comparison to another, far more disturbing pattern: the slaying of witnesses to murder. Kristen was a witness to the shooting death of Leonard Crochet and was also interrogated in the slaying of Loretta. Muggy Brown witnessed the killing of Ernestine. Necole was present when Loretta was slain.

On October 10, 2010, another witness to the Jeff Davis 8 murders wound up dead. Early that morning, Barb Ann Deshotel was visiting a girlfriend in Jennings when two Jennings police detectives showed up at the house.[29] "What's the matter?" Deshotel cried, stricken with panic. The moment was eerily similar to when her close friend Loretta went missing. The police had shown up at her door unexpectedly that day as well.

The officers told Deshotel her brother was dead: "They said he had committed suicide. I couldn't believe it. Russell never talked about suicide or even attempted suicide. And there was no note, nothing." Earlier that morning, Russell Carrier had been struck and killed by a train. Jennings police chief Todd D'Albor later told the media that "for whatever reason" Carrier had simply lain down on the tracks and was run over.

Russell Carrier had witnessed Frankie Richard's three associates emerge from the woods where Crystal Benoit Zeno's body had been dumped in 2008.

Skeptical of the official account of her brother's death, Deshotel searched the streets for answers. She quickly discovered that her brother was doing drugs with two friends the night of the ninth. Those friends had then dropped off Carrier at the popular South Jennings haunt Tina's Bar. Deshotel believed that this was the last-reported sighting of her brother. But then she discovered that an elderly couple on their way to church had spotted him the next day.

Deshotel's suspicions were confirmed when a detective with the Jennings Police Department named Jean Cooley told her about a tip he'd received from Tracee Chaisson. Cooley was sympathetic to Deshotel about the loss of her brother and spoke freely about the information he'd received from Tracee. Tracee said that Tyson Mouton had allegedly beaten Carrier with a baseball bat, nearly to death, then forced him onto the railroad tracks. Tyson had a clear motive for this. He was one of the men whom Carrier allegedly saw coming out of the woods after Crystal's murder. But Detective Cooley (who passed away in 2014 from cancer) dismissed the tip, telling Deshotel, "It doesn't matter what she has to say. She's lied so many times, so she's not credible." While Tracee did have huge credibility issues, the theory that Tyson Mouton may have killed Carrier was more than plausible. He had every reason to want Carrier dead. In this case, law enforcement should have taken Tracee's statement seriously.

Even more disturbingly, Deshotel's daughter told her mother she received a call from Tyson offering his condolences the morning of the tenth—before anyone in Jennings knew that Carrier had died. "That morning, before any of it was known to the public," Deshotel told me, "Tyson Mouton called my daughter's cell phone and said, 'I'm sorry Russell got killed.'" This call would fit a pattern in the Jeff Davis 8 slayings in which central players offer preemptive attempts at sympathy to victims' families, the most notorious example being Frankie Richard and Jamie Trahan's visit to the Duboises in which Trahan offered to help defray the costs for Whitnei's funeral.

CHAPTER 11

"Frankie Richard's Coming and Hell Is Coming with Him"

It takes a near-supernatural force to move Frankie Richard off his front porch, but by 2010, the increasingly high profile of the Jeff Davis 8 case goaded him not just off his porch, but out of the parish. On a steamy July day in 2011, I pulled up to Frankie's house to meet him. When the front door swung open, I was greeted not by Frankie but by his nephew Billy Conner Jr., who told me that Frankie was no longer living there. Billy invited me in anyway and led me to a low-ceilinged kitchen, where Frankie's sister, Tabatha, his brother, Billy Conner Sr., and his mother, Jeanette LeBlanc, were all seated. Though she is barely over five feet tall and in her midseventies, LeBlanc (called Maw Maw, Southern slang for "grandma") was the room's center of gravity. As LeBlanc scooped gloppy heaps of peanut butter with a pair of oversize spoons, she soothingly promised me that she would find Frankie's cell phone number. In the meantime, she instructed Billy Conner Jr. to find out where Frankie might be. While Billy made several calls from an old rotary phone affixed to the kitchen wall,

LeBlanc proudly boasted that the Richard family had hosted reporters from New York to Switzerland. As she lidded one of the peanut butter jars, she lamented law enforcement corruption, ranting about Paula Guillory's alleged mishandling of the theft-ring raid on their home back in 2009. "She took thirty-five hundred dollars that I'd saved up for braces for one of my children," LeBlanc told me, "about a thousand dollars in rare coins, and two of my pistols!" She let out a hearty laugh and then became serious. "This is a corrupt parish," she said sternly, "but it's the people who run the parish, not the people themselves." Before LeBlanc was able to say much more about the raid, Billy Conner Jr. returned to the kitchen with Frankie's cell phone number scrawled on a piece of notebook paper. I thanked LeBlanc for her help and made my way back outside. On Frankie's front porch, I dialed his cell phone number and he immediately picked up. He nervously explained that he'd fled to Breaux Bridge—nearly fifty miles east of Jennings—and that he was hunkered down in a friend's camper.

At around 5:00 p.m. the next day, I pulled up to a long tan mobile home in a rural section of Breaux Bridge just off I-10. Before I could even put my car in park, Frankie, who was dressed in a gray short-sleeve shirt and jean shorts, ambled to my car to meet me. He appeared frailer than a man in his midfifties, but he struck an imposing presence nonetheless; when we shook hands, his thick fingers seemed to envelope my own. After our greeting, Frankie led me into the camper and shut the door behind us; we sat just inches from each other at a tiny kitchen table squeezed in by the front door. In the almost deathly quiet, the only sound came from a small, boxy air conditioner that rumbled to life every few minutes. "I didn't hurt none of them," Frankie told me of the Jeff

Davis 8 as he leaned back in his chair. "All them girls was my friends."[1] He paused for a breath and then admitted that he's been known as one of the roughest street players in Jennings for decades, "a dope addict, a coke head, meth head, alcoholic, no-good son of a bitch" always up for a fight and willing to commit acts of violence for others.

But Frankie insisted that he swore off violence for good in the early 1990s when his daughter Lauren, now twenty-four, was born. She was not breathing and essentially lifeless after she was delivered at a hospital in Jennings. After forty-five minutes she was medevaced to Ochsner Hospital in New Orleans. Her full recovery—doctors had told Frankie that his daughter would suffer significant brain damage as a result of being deprived of oxygen—convinced Frankie to make a "deal with the Lord." He would never resort to violence except to defend himself or his family. "That right there oughta tell somebody that I wouldn't hurt nobody," Frankie says angrily. "I would not put my hands on somebody, because that's the deal I made with the Lord. I cannot break that deal for no other reason that I can't do it because of my daughter's life."

Frankie spoke to me passionately and with a surprising eloquence about his daughter and his relationship with the Jeff Davis 8 victims. He had grown up with Whitnei's relatives, and Brittney's family had helped his brother Billy Conner Sr. recover from colon cancer. He laments how the murders set Jennings families at odds with one another.

Despite his vows to swear off violence, Frankie has been charged with simple assault, simple battery, aggravated battery, and second-degree battery in the years following the birth of his daughter. And the almost never-ending series of dropped charges against him—Clemens and Kristen in 2007, and the theft case in 2009—can likely be attributed not to Frankie's innocence but law enforcement's incompetence.

There is no doubt, too, that Frankie was one of the last to see both Whitnei and Kristen alive. In our interview, he provided a string of incriminating statements, including an admission that Michael Prudhomme cleaned Connie Siler's truck "before Warren Gary ever got ahold of it." However, he has denied involvement in any of the murders and dismissed allegations—such as transporting dead women in barrels—as ludicrous in both interviews with me and with Taskforce investigators. In a January 2009 interview with the Taskforce, Frankie said the notion that "in the back of the house I had one of them girls in a fifty-five-gallon drum of chemicals . . . [is] a lie."

Perhaps because he sensed that he'd talked too much about the Jeff Davis 8 slayings, Frankie turned defiant. "I'll never go back to Jennings," he told me. "And I was raised right there at my mother's house on McKinley Street." I asked him why he'd never return home. "I been hospitalized for depression, for cocaine, alcohol, just trying to forget that shit," he explained, referring to the accusations against him in the Jeff Davis 8 case. "What I'm trying to do is get away from Jennings and get my head right and put this behind me and my family." Frankie tapped a pack of cigarettes on the kitchen table. "I'm determined to get my head on right. I'm one year clean from meth and a hundred days clean from alcohol and cocaine after forty-two years. That's a long fuckin' time for a motherfucker like me." For a moment, Frankie seemed vulnerable and wounded, but just before I left his camper, he tapped my notepad and tape recorder with a stubby index finger and asked me to take down the following, a paraphrase of a Wyatt Earp quote from the 1993 movie *Tombstone*: "If something ever happens to my kids behind this shit, they can believe one fucking thing: Frankie Richard's coming and hell is coming with him."

In the early-morning hours of July 8, 2011, I was awakened by a phone call from private investigator Kirk Menard, who told me that yet another murder had occurred on the streets of South Jennings. "Bowlegs is dead," Menard said mournfully. David "Bowlegs" Deshotel was a white, heavily tattooed twenty-nine-year-old hustler and onetime boyfriend of two Jeff Davis 8 victims, Necole Guillory and Brittney Gary. Bowlegs was so close with Brittney that when she was reported missing in the fall of 2008, her family thought she might have fled town with him. Necole's mother, Barbara, told me with a smile, "Little Dave and my daughter used to get into a lot of trouble together."

Family members and friends of David Deshotel told me that he earned the Bowlegs nickname as a child when he was diagnosed with the bone-weakening disease Rickets. And in March of 2011, his physical condition worsened significantly when he was shot in the leg, allegedly by a Houston-based rival named Carvell O'Brien.[2] O'Brien turned himself in to the cops and was charged with attempted second-degree murder. It was a rare case of a violent crime being solved in Jennings. But the shooting left Deshotel on crutches. *Bowlegs! Bowlegs! Bowlegs!* South Jennings residents hollered as he hobbled by. When Bowlegs became too exhausted to walk, he'd hoist himself into a clunky wheelchair and roll around the neighborhood. Bowlegs and his wheelchair became such a fixture in South Jennings that I spotted him myself. On the night of July 7, 2011, as I rode down Hobart Street in Menard's battered Ford Escape, Deshotel waved at us from his wheelchair. It was a fleeting encounter, but I instantly remembered him because his red baseball cap and matching sweatpants reminded me of Wayne D., *South Park*'s send-up of Caucasian gangsta.

On the morning of July 8, 2011, just hours after I'd seen him, Bowlegs was shot to death in his tiny single-family home on Hobart Street, which sits in a particularly rough section of South Jennings. The coroner pronounced him dead at the scene. Yet law enforcement left his home unsecured. When I met Menard there that morning, we were both stunned not to find any yellow crime scene tape. Worse, we watched, slack jawed, as burly, shirtless tattooed men—one with a gigantic 337 (the area code for southwestern Louisiana) across his bare back—casually strode in and out of the crime scene. I even saw a few men remove items from the home. The chaotic atmosphere vividly demonstrated the ineptitude of local law enforcement. Unsurprisingly, no one has ever been arrested or charged in the case.

In the wake of Bowlegs's murder, I traveled with Menard to the outskirts of Jennings to follow up on a tip. A female witness had told Menard that during the peak of the Jeff Davis 8 murders in 2008 and 2009, she had done drugs with several of Frankie Richard's associates, including Necole Guillory, at an abandoned home on Martin Roy Road. Inside, she saw drawings of the Jeff Davis 8 scrawled across the walls. It was a seemingly outlandish claim, but because Tracee Chaisson had told investigators that she had done drugs with Frankie in a house on Martin Roy Road just prior to Kristen Gary Lopez's murder, it nonetheless seemed worth checking out. So, Menard, Mike Dubois, and I piled into Menard's car. As we drove down Martin Roy, the atmosphere grew quiet and tense. All of us knew that the Jeff Davis 8 had followed a similar route to the outskirts of Jennings in their final moments.

We reached an abandoned house set back on a large plot

of land. A white camper was sunk into the tall, unkempt grass beside it. Menard spotted a gold Dodge Ram parked on the front of the property, and Dubois said he'd seen Tracee Chaisson riding around town in a truck that resembled it. Just as we clambered out of Menard's truck, an older white man strode across the back of the property. Dubois jogged over to him. He seemed unbothered by Dubois, and the pair engaged in what seemed to be a friendly conversation. A few moments later, the man was joined by a burly, bearded man who, I later learned, was his nephew.

The trio was out of earshot, though I caught what sounded like snippets of French. Menard told me that Dubois was speaking in Cajun French. Dubois, who was smoking the end of a cigarette, started gesturing wildly with his hands. Then he gave the others a handshake and climbed back in the truck. Dubois said no one had been using the abandoned house recently and that it was near collapse, with nothing—certainly not drawings of murdered women—on its walls. "But I seen Frankie and his brother Billy here," the older man told Dubois, "years ago. And I know Frankie been in some homes down the road. A yellow house and one old wooden place that's falling apart."

Menard took pictures of all three properties and then called his witness to tell her the tip had partially panned out. During the phone call, the tipster reiterated that she was certain that drawings of the Jeff Davis 8 were on the walls and that she'd recognized a portrait of Necole because she'd seen her face on the news. Menard was unable to verify the witness's claim because she had allegedly seen the drawing more than a year before our trip—even if the drawing had existed, it was long gone before we checked out the homes.

On the ride back to Jennings, Menard realized that he was

nearly out of gas, so we stopped at an E-Z Mart to fuel up. The low-riding Cadillac parked next to us had an RIP BOW-LEGS banner in its back window, another sign of the endless mourning that had plagued the region for so long. The new murders in the parish—most of which are still unsolved—led to unprecedented pressure on Sheriff Edwards and, finally, a pervasive sentiment in Jennings that he was no longer the right man for the job. "I was approached by a businessman who said, 'Maybe Ricky's not the guy,'" former *Jennings Daily News* reporter Scott Lewis told me. "Other business-men grumbled that he was giving a black eye to the town: 'Maybe it's time for Ricky to step down.'"[3] Suddenly Sher-iff Edwards's vocal business-elite supporters had dwindled, which meant that he was unlikely to last long. It was a pro-found fall for Edwards, who had been sheriff for nearly two decades. Few in the parish were surprised when, in May of 2011, he announced he would not seek reelection.

In the dynastic tradition of southwest Louisiana, Edwards handpicked his successor: Chief Deputy Larry Dupuis. But as the race for sheriff began in the fall of 2011, Dupuis faced off against a surprisingly large number of candidates, among them former detective Jesse Ewing, the whistle-blower who took the notorious witness statements implicating Warren Gary in evidence destruction, and Ivy Woods, a twenty-one-year vet-eran of the Louisiana State Police. In 2006, Woods had seized $3.3 million in cash off I-10, which at the time was the largest illegal drug currency seizure in Louisiana history.[4] The candi-dates held a debate on September 27, 2011, in the Strand The-ater, a soaring art deco building on North Main Street. The discourse was often contentious, though nearly all of the can-didates promised to make the Jeff Davis 8 case a priority. "As your sheriff," Woods told the crowd of Jennings residents, "I will be able to access the files to see what has been done and what needs to be done. Right now, I am unable to look at any files."[5] The next day in the *Lake Charles American Press* the headline read "Unsolved Deaths Priority for Candidates."

As the election approached, Dupuis, Sheriff Edwards's anointed successor, was slipping in the polls, while Woods was gaining momentum. The election reflected voters' indignation with the status quo. Woods gave Dupuis a profound thumping, receiving 70 percent of the votes (6,624) to Dupuis's 22.38 percent (2,114).[6] "We want to look over all the investigations," a jubilant Woods told KPLC that night. "The number one thing we would like to do is regain the trust of the public. There's a gap there and we want to close it and make it more personal."

Even though I watched the election results from afar, in New Orleans, I, too, was thrilled to see change come to the parish. The Edwards era was finally over, bringing with it new hope for resolution in the Jeff Davis 8 case. That December, I called Sheriff-elect Woods to discuss his approach to the Jeff Davis 8 investigation. His wife, Brigit, answered the phone and was friendly when I introduced myself. She gave me Woods's cell phone number, but when I called him there, the number wasn't working. I called Brigit back and she again sounded happy to hear from me, but she claimed she hadn't been able to reach Woods either.

Later that day, as I interviewed Sheriff Edwards at his office, my cell phone rang with an unfamiliar number. I silenced the call. Afterward I checked my voice mail and found a message from Joy Huvall, who identified herself as a member of Woods's transition team.[7] She told me that Woods wouldn't be making any comment on the case until he took office, in July. When I called Huvall back, she told me that Woods didn't want to say anything about the Jeff Davis 8 murders until he could "review all of the evidence." I thanked Huvall for getting in touch; it made a lot of sense that Woods wouldn't want to comment until he took over as sheriff.

Woods's electoral triumph should have instilled a profound sense of fear among the Jeff Davis 8 suspects, particularly Frankie Richard, who had a good thing going with the Edwards administration. But when I arrived at Frankie's house during the spring of 2012, just months after he vowed to never return to Jennings, I found him at ease in his front-porch rocker, shirtless and paunchy as ever. Next to him sat Brandon "Disco" Wise, the street associate who accompanied Frankie and Trahan to the Dubois family home the morning Whitnei's body was found. Though decades of drugging, pimping, and street brawling have severely impaired Frankie's cognitive skills, he was nonetheless acutely aware of just how odd it looked that he was happily back on his porch. He had insisted that the publicity surrounding the Jeff Davis 8 case had forced him into permanent exile, and now he knew he would have to explain the turnabout. He quickly reverted to a tried-and-true strategy, one that he'd deployed when we first met in Breaux Bridge: framing himself as the victim in the Jeff Davis 8 case.

"I can remember a time when Dallas Cormier lived right over here," he said of the former sheriff, who is also a South Jennings native.[8] "They would call me and tell me they have a warrant for me, and I would get a bondsman and post the bond. Now the *whole force* is coming for me." Frankie flashed a conspiratorial smile and asked me if I wanted to hear a story; I said that I'd love to. "One day I was walking down the street and"—he paused for dramatic effect, then clapped his hands loudly to make a gunshot sound—"*pow!* Where it was coming from, I don't know." I asked him if he was serious—was he really targeted in an assassination attempt? "Oh, yeah. If you gonna shoot me, look me in the face when you shoot me, motherfucker." He rubbed his goatee. "Three different times that happened since this shit started with them murders."

Frankie spun incredible tales about his life in Jennings in the Jeff Davis 8 era—the entire Sheriff's Office was after him, he was nearly killed in *three* assassination attempts—but as the sun began to set that day, the Richard home took on a familial, everyday feel. His family ambled up the front steps for dinner, and Frankie's sister Tabatha offered me their mother Jeanette's specialty, crawfish pie. When I politely declined, the frowning, disappointed look on Tabatha's face told me I'd violated a core principle of Southern life, graciously accepting a host's meal. But I was far too aware that at least two of the victims in the Jeff Davis 8 case had spent their final hours here. I imagined sitting down to dinner and then waking up (or perhaps not waking up at all) in a nearby bayou. So instead of eating, I pushed Frankie to wrap up his assassination tale. Who did he think tried to take his life? I asked. "I don't know," Frankie replied, adding with a sly smile, "If I knew, he wouldn't shoot me again."

Even though one criminal case after another against him collapsed, Frankie insisted that the assassination attempts demonstrate he is a wanted man, by everyone from Sheriff Woods to pimps and pill pushers of South Jennings. "They haven't stopped me," Frankie told me, "but of course I don't go nowhere." He pointed to the wooden porch below him. "I stay right here."

Just as Frankie proclaimed himself a victim of police harassment, a procession of beat-up, low-riding Oldsmobiles and Cadillacs rolled by in ominous slow motion. *"FRAN-*

KAY!" a couple of young African-American men yelled out car windows, trying to grab his attention. One man in saggy pants actually clambered out of a Cadillac and bowed to him. *"Hey, FRAN-KAY."* Frankie halfheartedly acknowledged the hustlers with a slight, awkward wave. He was visibly aware that the tributes from South Jennings street hustlers profoundly contradicted the down-and-out image that he was so desperately trying to project to me.

The impromptu salutations also attracted the attention of Frankie's mother, Jeanette, who had been watching the evening news in the living room. "C'mon, Richard," Jeanette said derisively, striding onto the front porch, "cut it short!"

Frankie shifted uncomfortably in his rocker. "They doin' a life history on me," he said meekly, sounding like a chastened child.

Jeanette rolled her eyes. "Oh, Lord." She let out a long sigh.

For the first time that night, Frankie looked nervous. "I'm not telling him everything," he protested.

"Keep some secrets," Jeanette said icily before turning back to the living room.

Jeanette's warning resonated with Frankie's associate Disco, who had until then been quietly monitoring the interview. "You got big nuts," Disco warned me. "You writing on Jennings. And you're *riding* in Jennings. You got big nuts, man." At first Disco's comments seemed little more than a reflection on how crazy I've been to tackle this sprawling case. But then his warnings turned sinister. "You in the crookedest town in Louisiana," he drawled. "New Orleans ain't got shit on us." The gibe against New Orleans was purposeful—Disco clearly wanted me to know the violence in my hometown couldn't even compare to the bloodshed in Jennings.

He finally dropped the potshots and made the danger I'd be facing plain. "If you destroy they business," he said, referring to the crooked cops and deputies in Jefferson Davis Parish, "you be a dead-ass lil' white boy." Disco wiped his nose with his right hand and surveyed the neighborhood. "You a bold-ass little man, dog. Don't get caught in Jeff Davis Parish at night. Make sure you're staying somewhere with security cameras. Watch your fuckin' back, bro."

But such warnings didn't dissuade me from my investigation. Even then, back in 2012, I'd already spent months investigating the Jeff Davis 8 case and had become accustomed to dire predictions about my fate. "Do you like to live?" Necole's mother, Barbara, asked me when I visited her in her trailer in the summer of 2011. "I'd hate to read a newspaper and see your name in it." But Disco had sensed that I wasn't about to be scared off, and his tone transitioned from intimidating to darkly humorous: "It's Jennings, man." He gave me a friendly, almost collegial clap on the shoulder. "Welcome to the Dirty South."

Despite Sheriff Woods's promises, nothing new developed in the Jeff Davis 8 investigation. And he was also breaking his promises of transparency. As instructed, I waited until July 2012 to contact his office. I spoke to Joy Huvall again, who told me dismissively, "Do you have a bald head? The sheriff googled you. He'll call you back."[9] More than four years later, I have not heard back from Sheriff Woods, though I do in fact have a bald head.

The Taskforce, too, continued to operate as an inneffective and conflicted entity. In the spring of 2012, private investigator Kirk Menard referred a pair of female witnesses to the Taskforce. They claimed they were being stalked by Frankie Richard. One even claimed that Frankie had used her father's phone after killing Whitnei. Menard strongly believed that both witnesses were credible. One had highly specific information about the Whitnei Dubois slaying.

The women reported back to Menard that Taskforce investigator Ramby Cormier dismissed them outright, claiming, "Frankie works for me." Furious, Menard wrote the following e-mail to Cormier on May 10, 2012:

To: Ramby Cormier [e-mail address redacted]:

Ramby,

I will give you some information I've received but I will ask that you keep it between us as I keep confidential information between us as well. I've received a phone call from WITNESS A regarding the questioning of FEMALE WITNESS 1 and FEMALE WITNESS 2. FEMALE WITNESS 1 explained to me that you told FEMALE WITNESS 2 not to worry about Frankie because Frankie works for you (her exact words were ["] do not worry about Frankie because he works for me["]) and supposedly for Acadia Parish detective Keith Latiolais. She also mentioned that you stated that she was to be the next victim, which scared her tremendously. She also stated that you stated to FEMALE WITNESS 2 that Mike Dubois was the killer. . . . She also stated that you said "watch who you trust" which is understandable. I found the phone call very strange because you are usually reserved and questioning a witness usually receives information and does not give information. She stated that you told her that she did not need a gun or mace but stated she was confused because of your comment about "she may be the next victim." She did call the FBI and repeat to them about her questioning with you because she was scared when you told her that she will be the next victim or may be the next victim. From what I understand, she reiterated to the FBI about your questioning of her and FEMALE WITNESS 2. In any case, both girls are terrified. She also informed me about Frankie and that he has three cell phones and one is issued to him by the task force. In any case, I felt you should know this information in maintaining my reporting procedures. The only reason I would not want FEMALE WITNESS 1 or FEMALE WITNESS 2 to know that I've informed you of what I was told is because they are already terrified and if they do have any more information, it may scare them into coming forward in the future. Just FYI. Thanks.[10]

Menard had expected to receive a reply from Cormier immediately because this e-mail contained so many explosive allegations, top among them that Frankie Richard had a Taskforce-issued cell phone. But Menard says that years later Cormier has still not responded to this e-mail even after acknowledging a flurry of other tips. Menard insists that both witnesses truthfully recounted their interrogation.

"No, it's not correct," Cormier told me when I asked him about the allegations in the e-mail. "Just because that's what people say, that doesn't mean that's what happened."[11]

The Taskforce and the Sheriff's Office may have been corrupt and ineffective, but on the streets and in the courtrooms of southwest Louisiana an alternative form of justice was being served. On August 25, 2012, Kenneth Patrick Drake, the forty-four-year-old man from Welsh who attacked Jeff Davis 8 victim Crystal Benoit Zeno with a metal pipe, passed away (the circumstances of his death are not clear).[12] A little more than one year later, on November 26, 2013, Ervin "Big Mack" Edwards, one of the men who dumped Muggy's body, died at the West Baton Rouge Parish jail, where he was being held for resisting arrest and disturbing the peace.[13] The thirty-eight-year-old Big Mack had been arrested for fighting with his girlfriend in a gas station parking lot and was placed in an isolation cell. There, Big Mack's family claims, a police officer shocked him with a stun gun, causing his death. (In the spring of 2015, in the midst of a period of high-profile police misconduct such as in the case of Freddie Gray, a Baltimore man who died from severe spinal injuries after being held in police custody, Edwards's case was discussed nationally. #ErvinEdwards even became a hashtag tweeted by celebrities such as Mia Farrow.[14])

That same month, former Jennings police chief Johnny Lassiter, who served as a lieutenant under Chief Todd D'Albor, pleaded guilty to two counts of malfeasance in office.[15] He had pilfered $4,500 in cash, 380 grams of cocaine, several pounds of marijuana, codeine, and 1,800 pills from the evidence room. In June of 2014, he was sentenced to five years' imprisonment and ordered to pay back $4,500 to the city of Jennings.[16] Lassiter is a key figure in both the Jeff Davis 8 case and the KK's Corner killings in Calcasieu Parish. A witness claimed to have observed Lassiter in an unmarked police unit outside KK's in the hours after the triple homicide there in July of 1997. According to an official complaint by Jeff Davis 8 whistle-blower Jesse Ewing, in January 2008, Lassiter pulled a gun on him. Specifically, Ewing reports, Chief Lassiter removed a handgun from a holster, placed the gun on his desk, and pointed its barrel directly at Ewing.[17] "The way I have been firing people," Lassiter allegedly told Ewing, "you never know who is going to want to take my head off." It's unclear if any charges were ever brought against Lassiter in the incident with Ewing.

Still, the fates of these Jeff Davis 8 players did not bring about a resolution in any of the slayings. By the outset of 2014, the eight women were fading even further into history. That spring would mark nine years since Loretta's body was discovered in the Grand Marais Canal.

CHAPTER 12

"The Past Is the Past"

On January 31, 2014, I published a long-form feature head-lined "Who Killed the Jeff Davis 8?" that ran on *Medium* *.com*.[1] The piece reignited interest in the case, garnering cover-age ranging from the *Jennings Daily News* to *Business Insider* to the feminist blog *Jezebel* to *True Detective* creator Nic Piz-zolatto, who called the piece an "important study of police corruption and supposed serial killer in Louisiana."[2]

I'd worked on the piece quietly for years and was stunned by the reception it received, particularly because the case had already been covered by the likes of CNN and the *New York Times*. I was floored, however, by developments on the ground in Jefferson Davis Parish the day my piece was pub-lished. The body of twenty-seven-year-old Lacie Fontenot was found in a shallow ditch in Lake Arthur. "Story on Jeff Davis murders comes out this AM," tweeted Campbell Rob-ertson of the *New York Times*. "Another body is found this PM."[3] Like the Jeff Davis 8, Fontenot had been missing for days before she was discovered. "We have been talking to a few people," Lake Arthur police chief Cheryl Vincent had told the media, "and nobody has seen her in four or five days."[4]

Fontenot, who had long red hair and a pale freckled face, was found in a location much like the shallow water where the murdered sex workers were discarded: a foot of water in a ditch in a wooded area on Lake Arthur's west side. Like the Jeff Davis 8, Fontenot struggled with substance abuse and shared a comparable criminal history. In 2006, she allegedly stabbed a sixty-three-year-old Lake Arthur man during an argument and faced second-degree murder charges, which a grand jury ultimately dismissed.[5] Despite the many striking and undeniable similarities between the Jeff Davis 8 and Fontenot, the Lake Arthur police chief instantly dismissed any connection to the cases. Later, the coroner determined that Fontenot's cause of death was drowning as a result of hypothermia. Yet the coroner's ruling does not take into account the circumstances surrounding Fontenot's death—namely her role in the brutal Jefferson Davis Parish sex-and-drug trade.

Fontenot, incredibly, was the *second* possible ninth victim. In 2012, a relative of slain drug addict Leonard Crochet, who asked that she remain anonymous out of concerns for her safety, was leaving Tina's Bar, the South Jennings haunt frequented by the Jeff Davis 8, when she claimed that Tracee Chaisson approached her in the parking lot. "When I was walking out with my ride," the Crochet family member told me when we spoke several weeks later on the front porch of her home, which is just down the street from the Richards', "she was screaming out the car with some black people, *'You're gonna be number nine.'*"

Crochet told me she reported the incident to Taskforce investigator Ramby Cormier. She cleared her throat nervously and said, "I could tell you more, but I'm scared. I'm scared for my own life." The Jeff Davis 8 killings, she said, "started right after" her relative Leonard was killed. *"Right after.* All them girls were in there at one point. They were all in there for two days in and out."[6]

And while Fontenot, like Crochet before her, was not the ninth victim, I unearthed myriad personal connections between her and the Jeff Davis 8. In the months before her death, Fontenot dated Bootsy Lewis, the father of Whitnei's daughter and Loretta Chaisson's brother-in-law. I also discovered that one of the last people to see Fontenot alive was Eugene "Dog" Ivory, a strong suspect in the slaying of Crystal Benoit Zeno. "Just before she turned up missing, she tried to get ahold of Dog," a source close to Fontenot told me. "She'd asked for Dog's phone number and met up with him. One of Lacie's friends said that the last time she heard from Lacie was when she was connecting with Dog."

I wasn't the only one skeptical of local law enforcement's handling of Fontenot's death, specifically their dismissal of any links to the Jeff Davis 8. "We're distrustful," a member of Fontenot's family, who asked to remain anonymous, told me in February of 2014. "We don't think the timing of your article is a coincidence. I was sent a link to your article that morning, and Lacie was found that afternoon." The Fontenot family member rightly noted that the coroner's determination "doesn't explain how she was dumped in the woods."

On February 9, 2014, the *Jennings Daily News* ran three separate articles, quoting sources from the Sheriff's Office, from the DA, and from the Jennings PD, all denouncing my work. I was cast as the out-of-town reporter who was "causing further pain to the victims' loved ones and potentially harming investigative efforts."[7] The editors of the *Jennings Daily News* parroted the police brass with a subhead that read, absurdly, "Brown . . . created more problems." The newspaper also ran an unsigned editorial on the same day, claiming that my article "leads the reader to point fingers, question authorities, and worst of all, force the families of the victims to relive the nightmare once again."

The *Jennings Daily News* is a small paper for a small town; its attack on me took up most of the day's real estate. While investigators talking to the paper claimed that my piece contained "misinformation" and "numerous inaccuracies," they also consistently "declined to be specific on details" regarding what those supposed inaccuracies might have been.

The most ludicrous charge leveled against me by Jennings law enforcement was the implication that they never shared public records with me. "I'm not sure how some of the information was obtained," parish DA Michael Cassidy told the *Jennings Daily News*. Cassidy should know how I obtained records in my investigation: I made requests directly to his office under Louisiana's Public Records Act and received written responses from one of Cassidy's own prosecutors, Assistant DA Kevin Millican, who also serves as the city attorney for Jennings. Indeed, I received *thousands* of pages of records from Millican alone. In a September 28, 2011, e-mail message, for example, Millican wrote to me, "At this point I have made 539 copies for the City of Jennings Police Department (JPD) files. I have all the District Attorney's files and expect the total copies to exceed 1000 pages."[8] The dump of public records directly from Millican was so enormous that in the same e-mail he warned me that his office's copying charge of fifty cents per page was going to result in "cost[s] that jump quickly."

So when I published a short follow-up story for *Medium* called "My Investigation into the Jeff Davis 8 Murders" in which I detailed the thousands of pages of records that I'd obtained from the Louisiana State Police, the DA's office, the Sheriff's Office, and the Jennings PD, they were forced to acknowledge that they had indeed turned over records to me to comply with Louisiana's Public Records Act. "We don't necessarily like giving out these records," Michael Cassidy then told the *Jennings Daily News* in a piece titled "Murder Investigation Documents Released under Public Records Law," "at the same time, though, we have to comply with the law."

I was never given an opportunity to comment for any of the pieces the *Jennings Daily News* ran about me, even though its reporters and editors had my e-mail address and phone number as well as the contact information for my agent and my editor at *Medium*.

While the DA was forced to walk back his claims about how I procured my documents, Sheriff Woods posted an extraordinary message about me on the Jefferson Davis Parish Sheriff's Office website:

Recently our office has come under fire by an investigative reporter from New Orleans and an author of fiction stories. They have written some very negative articles involving the Jeff Davis Sheriff's Office, including the Multi-agency Investigative Team (MAIT) formed under former Sheriff Ricky Edwards on the eight deaths that occurred in our area from 2005 to 2009. They have drudged up investigations and incidents, some going back thirty years, insinuating corruption in our Sheriff's Office. Well, I don't dispute the Sheriff's Office has had problems, but the past is the past.

When you elected me as your sheriff in 2011, I promised to bring professionalism to the department, which included having integrity that is beyond reproach, and gaining the respect and trust of our citizens. We have worked hard at this and will continue to do so. Having said that, I would like to say I resent out-of-town journalists trying to paint our parish with a broad brush that insinuates we are corrupt.

As your sheriff, I want to insure the victim's families and the public that we are continuing to work on these eight investigations. I have the utmost confidence in the people I have assigned and the members of the MAIT from other agencies. They will continue the investigations into these deaths until all leads are exhausted. I also would like to make it clear that the MAIT and the law enforcement personnel working these investigations are not hiding anything. We are doing everything possible to solve these cases. It is unfortunate out-of-town journalists are taking information and twisting it to support a fictional conspiracy theory to gain followers and sell a story.[9]

Just as he had done in the past, Sheriff Woods failed to cite even a single error in my piece, preferring instead to attack me personally (he referred to my being from out of town three times in the short message, I live in New Orleans). He also described me, falsely, as an "author of fiction stories," unless that reference was mistakenly meant to be about Nic Pizzolatto, the novelist and creator of *True Detective*. Bizarrely, the notion that I was either involved in the creation of the HBO hit series or connected to its showrunner gained traction during the race for Jefferson Davis Parish district attorney in the spring of 2014. A rumor surfaced that DA hopeful Ric Oustalet, a criminal defense attorney whose family once ran the Zigler hotel, covertly worked with me on my article in an attempt to discredit the incumbent Michael Cassidy, and that I pursued my investigation to piggyback off the success of *True Detective*. "As this article states," Oustalet wrote on his Facebook page on March 28, 2014, referring to a *New York Observer* piece that compared my *Medium* piece to *True Detective*, "the story was researched several years ago and the publishing of the article was part of a marketing push to sell the story based on an increased interest generated by the HBO Series 'True Detective.' I can assure you that I have no involvement with the author of this article. However, the recent statements by the DA beg the question: If he has to fabricate lies about the person behind the article . . . what is he afraid of???"[10] I posted a public response to Oustalet on his Facebook page, noting, "Ric did not pay me for my article" and that I began work on the Jeff Davis 8 case years before *True Detective* premiered on HBO.

It was no surprise that the sheriff, DA, and police chief were unhappy with my *Medium* piece. It garnered so much attention that then Louisiana attorney general Buddy Caldwell was forced to respond to it even though he rehashed the discredited serial killer theory of the Jeff Davis 8 case. "Every one of us is really interested in getting the case solved," Caldwell told KPLC on February 6, 2014. "And as you may well know, serial killers are all around the country, and if they were easy to solve, it should've been done. In my view it's very likely that the person who was doing this has either moved out of the area or is now in prison."[11]

Even the attorney general was sticking to the serial killer theory to the bitter end.

What shocked me most about this media backlash was the role played by the *Jennings Daily News*. I never expected the newspaper would publish allegations about me and my work, because its editors not only praised the *Medium* piece but asked me, my agent, and my editor for permission to republish it. "You certainly have Jeff Davis Parish talking today,"

Sheila Smith of the *Jennings Daily News* wrote to me on January 31, 2014, "which is a good thing. My editor and I are hoping to have your permission to reprint the Jeff Davis 8 article in our newspaper, with all credit given to you, as well as Medium.com if necessary."[12] I responded to Smith in an e-mail that I was "pleased and humbled" that they were interested in my story, and in subsequent communications with Smith among me, my agent, and *Medium* we agreed to allow the newspaper to republish the piece.

Later that day, however, Smith e-mailed me to tell me the newspaper's vice president didn't want the story to run in the paper: "His opinion is that our newspaper cannot verify all of Ethan's sources, mainly case files, and victims' families have already contacted us claiming some of the information is wrong. The staff here, however, believes Ethan did an incredible job of obtaining information and files and we hope residents continue to share the story for the public to see. We also believe that Ethan has brought this case to the forefront again and now local officials will have tough questions to answer."

I would have happily shared the case files, and the only specific complaint I received from victims' families was from the family of Leonard Crochet, who said that I had wrongly implicated Crochet in the drug business run by Harvey "Bird Dog" Burleigh in Jennings. I seriously considered that criticism and believe that my account of Crochet in this book more accurately reflects Crochet as a drug addict and not a drug business player. The *Jennings Daily News* may, of course, have chosen not to republish my *Medium* piece regardless. But what was so disturbing about my experience with the paper was the way they supported my casework one day and castigated it the next, all without any effort—by phone or e-mail—to contact me for comment. It's a basic tenant of journalistic fairness that

I afforded them. On March 31, 2015, I called Sheila Smith in hopes of having her explain to me how the newspaper's position changed so quickly, and why law enforcement was given a platform to attack me. Smith never called me back.

The blowback in Jefferson Davis Parish about my work was unpleasant and sometimes scary. One of my contacts in southwest Louisiana who is deeply connected to the case told me, "I've already heard more than once that you'll never get that book out. You can take that however you want to. But is that book worth your life?" I stayed away from the parish for months after the *Medium* piece, and a former Jennings law enforcement official warned me, "As soon as you hit town, they know you're there." But whatever challenges I faced in reporting on the Jeff Davis 8 case paled in comparison to the attacks on the parish's citizens and whistle-blowers alike. I learned that after my *Medium* piece was published, a Jennings drug dealer and sometime rapper named Christopher Trent, who made a mixtape calling out Jennings police officers by name, threatened a former Jennings sex worker who he believed had talked to me (Trent was mistaken; I didn't interview her for the *Medium* piece). "Loose lips," Trent told the Jennings woman, "sink ships." I planned on confronting Trent about his harassment, but in March 2015 he was shot to death at a travel plaza in Rayne, Louisiana, about twenty-five miles from Jennings.[13] (On April 29, 2015, police in Rayne arrested two Lafayette men in the Trent homicide.[14]) And Jennings police detective Jesse Ewing and jail nurse Nina Ravey had their careers shattered and faced criminal charges after they passed on reports of law enforcement misconduct. Ewing and Ravey will continue to live with the consequences of seeking the truth about the Jeff Davis 8 long after the attacks on me have faded into the parish's memory.

CHAPTER 13

Coda: Boustany and the Boudreaux Inn

I had long been told by everyone from sex workers to law enforcement that the Boudreaux Inn, the very hub of the Jeff Davis 8 milieu, was operated by politically powerful men. But there was no indication—in my witness interviews, Taskforce documents, police reports, or anywhere else—just who those men were.

Then, on September 2, 2014, I got a huge break: I received a tip that a southwest Louisiana political heavyweight known as "Big G" ran the Boudreaux Inn. The tipster didn't know Big G's real name, and I feared that such a generic nickname could be used by dozens or even hundreds of people in Louisiana.

But I quickly found a southwest Louisiana–based Big G in an unlikely place: on April 26, 2013, he'd been honored by Rayne country radio station Bayou 106.7 as the "Bayou Buddy of the Day." An entry on the station's Facebook page that day read: "Our Bayou Buddy of the day is Martin Guillory 'Big G' of Branch." Branch is about thirty miles from Jennings, but this Big G's last name—Guillory—is obviously very common in southwest Louisiana.

Because Big G was a businessman, it made sense to start by searching Louisiana LLC registrations via the Louisiana Secretary of State's website. There, I found a Martin P. Guillory of Church Point, Louisiana, a town about five miles from Branch. This Martin Guillory was a partner in an LLC called Tri-Tech LLC. After I conducted further business searches, I discovered that Guillory also maintained a company called Big G's Kans, out of Rayne. It was clear then that Martin P. Guillory was Big G, perhaps the Big G of the Boudreaux Inn. But who was Martin P. Guillory?

Martin P. Guillory is a field representative for Louisiana congressman Charles Boustany. I flashed back to a phone call, years earlier, from Frankie Richard. "Charles Boustany," Frankie Richard told me on June 25, 2012, "you need to investigate him."[1] Back then, I only knew Boustany was a representative for Louisiana's Seventh Congressional District. I had no idea what to make of the tip. I also had little reason to trust Frankie, who is especially fond of espousing case theories that somehow always exclude himself. But Frankie's call that day stayed with me because he had asked me, for the very first time, if I was recording our conversation (I was not). And I had to wonder, given Boustany's deep familial roots in both local and national politics (his father was the coroner of Lafayette Parish, he's related to former Louisiana governor Edwin Edwards, and to Vicki Kennedy, the widow of the late senator Edward Kennedy) and his prominence on Capitol Hill (he is the chair of the Tax Policy Subcommittee of the Ways and Means Committee in the House), just what Frankie's tip was all about.[2] Frankie himself was of little help. On that day in June, just as soon as he'd asked me if I was taping our telephone conversation, he hung up on me.

Because I lacked any specific information about Boustany's involvement with the Jeff Davis 8, I shelved any search into his possible connections with the slain women. But then, more than two years later, right around the time that I received the tip about Big G and the Boudreaux Inn, I interviewed a former Jennings sex worker and discovered what Boustany's connection to the Jeff Davis 8 may have been. The sex worker, who had been interrogated by the Taskforce, told me that Boustany was a well-regarded client of at least three of the Jeff Davis 8 victims as well as Tracee Chaisson. "Tracee, Loretta, Kristen, Muggy, all said that he [Boustany] was a good trick," she told me. "He was at the Boudreaux Inn. He had money and he had the dope."

Then in the spring of 2015, a Jennings woman with close ties to some of the victims contacted me to share memories of her deceased friends. She recounted the numerous conversations she had had with Kristen about her clientele, whom she described as "lawyers, judges, and cops." The Jennings woman—whose identity I'm concealing out of concern for her safety—said that both Kristen and Loretta admitted that Boustany was a client. Kristen, she told me, specifically characterized Boustany as an important client whom she frequently rendezvoused with at the Boudreaux Inn. Kristen described Boustany to her friend as a man who "works in government, in high places," and that she was concerned about her relationship with him because if he had any problems, "all he gotta do is say one thing to one person and it'll be taken care of."

I later learned that in the fall of 2012, a witness contacted the Taskforce to pass along information that Boustany engaged in sexual activity with at least one of the Jeff Davis 8 victims. I will call this witness Boustany Witness A. Taskforce investigators took Boustany Witness A seriously enough to interview her over several days in October of 2012. Boustany Witness A kept meticulous logs of her visits with the Taskforce, and according to these logs, she was interrogated by the upper echelon of the Taskforce, including Jefferson Davis Parish Sheriff's Office commander Christopher Ivey, and Edward W. Reed, a senior resident agent at the FBI's Lake Charles office. In an August 2015 meeting at the FBI's Lake Charles office, I asked Agent Reed about his meeting with Boustany Witness A, and he refused to confirm or deny that such a meeting occurred. Agent Reed also refused to confirm or deny that the feds have received information that Boustany patronized any of the Jeff Davis 8.

On May 9, 2016, I asked Boustany if he was aware of Martin Guillory's role at the Boudreaux Inn and/or criminal activity occurring there, if he had ever visited the Boudreaux Inn in any capacity, or if he'd engaged in sexual relationships—or relationships of any nature—with any of the women of the Jeff Davis 8. On May 16, 2016, I received the following reply from Boustany's Communications Director, Jack Pandol, via e-mail: "Dr. Boustany had no knowledge of Martin Guillory's prior involvement at the establishment you mentioned. After double checking our office's records, Dr. Boustany has never had any contact with any of the eight victims you mentioned. Obviously this case is a tragedy and Dr. Boustany is saddened something like this could happen in southwest Louisiana." When I told Pandol that I believed there was one question unanswered—has Congressman Boustany ever visited the Boudreaux Inn in any capacity, and if so, when?—he replied "To my knowledge the congressman hasn't ever visited that establishment [the Boudreaux Inn]."[3]

Before taking these allegations to Boustany, I obtained documentary evidence that could place him in the Jeff Davis 8 milieu. On a gray day in March of 2015, I made the three-hour drive from New Orleans to Jennings to research the property records of the Boudreaux Inn, the motel where the Taskforce witness told me that Boustany patronized Tracee Chaisson, Kristen, Muggy, and Loretta. Property records from the Assessor's Office are housed in a sprawling space on the first floor of the parish courthouse at 300 North State Street. Because I'm accustomed to searching property records by name, I was surprised to find that one could not do the same in Jefferson Davis Parish. Instead, I had to search by address on a computer terminal, which then directed me to a conveyance book. According to the conveyance records, the Boudreaux Inn was owned by Justin Boudreaux, who died in 2006 at the age of seventy-seven. Boudreaux leased the space from November of 1999 to November of 2004 to a trio of business partners working under an LLC named Tri-Tech.[4] The lease terms set the monthly rent at $4,000. According to Tri-Tech's business filing with the Louisiana Secretary of State, Tri-Tech LLC's principals included Martin P. Guillory—Big G—and Toby Leger.[5]

Guillory and Leger leased the Boudreaux Inn at the height of its role in the Jennings sex-and-drug trade—1999 to 2004—according to their lease terms but actually several years beyond that because, according to a lawsuit filed by the Administratrix of the Boudreaux estate after Tri-Tech's lease expired in 2004, they "continued to occupy the premises on a month-to-month basis."[6]

Big G has a phone number in Boustany's office on Capitol Hill and makes public appearances on behalf of Boustany.[7] In October 2013, Big G attended a groundbreaking ceremony for an oil-field manufacturing facility in Boustany's stead.[8] Big G is currently working for Boustany on his run for the United States Senate, according to Schedule B—"Itemized Disbursements"—forms that Boustany filed with the Federal Election Commission.[9] Boustany is now running for a Senate seat vacated by David Vitter, who in 2007 admitted to involvement with a Washington, DC, escort service. Vitter's run for Louisiana governor in 2015—he was beaten by a largely unknown Democrat from a rural part of the state named John Bel Edwards—failed in large part because of the specter of his involvement with sex workers, even though he was never charged with a crime. Boustany representative Big G is also connected to former Louisiana governor Bobby Jindal. In 2008, Jindal appointed him to the Louisiana's State Parks and Recreation Commission.[10]

Big G's partner at the Boudreaux Inn, Toby Leger, is a similarly notable public figure in southwest Louisiana. In 2006, he ran for alderman of Ward 5 in Church Point, a tiny town of approximately 4,036, miles northeast of Jennings, which is also where Tri-Tech is registered with the Louisiana Secretary of State. He's served as a member of the Jeff Davis Business Alliance and the Calcasieu Parish Police Jury.[11] A position on a governing body such as a police jury carries with it both enormous prestige and significant power.

After I returned home from my visit to the courthouse, I decided to review the hundreds of pages of records I'd received from Sheriff Edwards documenting the arrests of all of the women of the Jeff Davis 8. What I discovered stunned me, even after investigating the case for years. From the late 1990s to the end of 2004, the period when Big G's Tri-Tech was leasing the motel, Frankie Richard and several of the slain workers were constantly involved in incidents resulting in police presence at the Boudreaux Inn. Incident reports I've obtained from the Sheriff's Office read like a diary of the Jeff Davis 8. I've summarized key points below.

- On October 12, 1998, Loretta and a Jennings woman, Norma Dubroc, rented a room at the Boudreaux Inn. Loretta's husband arrived and knocked on the motel room doors looking for her. When he found Loretta, he allegedly beat her and then fled the scene.[12]
- On December 22, 1999, a man complained to the Sheriff's Office that he brought Loretta to the Boudreaux Inn for a threesome, but when he woke up the next morning, his money and wallet were missing.[13]
- On December 19, 2000, Boudreaux Inn management found Loretta in Room 206 despite her being previously told that she was no longer allowed on the property. Detective Terrie Guillory arrested Loretta, but because the jail was full, she was released.[14]
- On January 10, 2000, a fight broke out between Loretta and another woman at the Boudreaux Inn. After the women refused orders to stop fighting, the Sheriff's Office was called. Loretta was told—again—not to return. Warden Guillory noted in his report that Loretta was "very intoxicated."[15]

- On May 11, 2000, Toby Leger called the Sheriff's Office after spotting Loretta getting into a truck that was parked by one of the rooms. "In speaking with Mr. Leger," wrote a sheriff's deputy, "I was informed that Mrs. Chaisson has caused trouble there in the past and was told by a Deputy not to return to the Boudreaux Inn and he wants charges pressed on her."[16]

- On February 7, 2002, a fight broke out at the Boudreaux Inn between Frankie Richard and Andrew Newman, the father of Jeff Davis 8 victim Kristen Gary Lopez. Frankie allegedly put ex-wife Jill Richard in a headlock, and when Newman attempted to stop the assault, Frankie broke his nose. The incident report notes that the "Boudreaux Inn did not want to file report and allowed them [the Richards] to remain in the restaurant and stay in room 206."[17]

- On March 11, 2002, Jill Richard reported that her former husband had threatened to burn down her house and "whoever was in it." Jill said that Frankie had "come to the trailer park hunting for her and told her neighbors that he was going to kill her." Jill confronted Frankie at the Boudreaux Inn, where he allegedly warned her that he was going to "burn her down in the trailer while she was sleeping." After this incident, Jill obtained a restraining order.[18]

- On April 2, 2002, Jill called the Sheriff's Office because Frankie allegedly violated the restraining order by pulling into the parking lot of the Boudreaux Inn while she was staying in a room there.[19]

- On August 15, 2004, Loretta called the Sheriff's Office

from the Boudreaux Inn. When a sheriff's deputy arrived, he found her in the lobby. Loretta said that her husband, Murphy Lewis, "got mad at her and put her in a head lock beating her on top of the head." The deputy on the scene noted bumps on her head and a cut lip. Murphy Lewis was later located in Jennings, where he allegedly admitted that he'd struck Loretta.[20]

- Just before midnight on December 31, 2004, Muggy Brown rented Room 105 at the Boudreaux Inn. Moments later, she pulled the fire alarm on the outside of the room and fled to her grandmother Bessie Brown's home in South Jennings. According to a report written by Mike Janise—the same officer from the Sheriff's Office who discovered Muggy's body in 2008—she admitted that she pulled the alarm.[21]

- On April 8, 2006, detectives responded to a call from the Boudreaux Inn about a stabbing in Room 204. When they questioned the occupants of the room, Whitnei and Bootsy Lewis, Lewis said that he had gotten into a fight with a man and that another woman stabbed Whitnei in the head. Whitnei was transported by ambulance to the Jennings American Legion Hospital, where she was treated. Whitnei's head wound was approximately two inches long and one-quarter of an inch deep. Investigators photographed the wound. It's unclear if anyone was ever arrested or charged in the incident.[22]

These many incidents demonstrate that the Boudreaux Inn played a central role in the lives of the Jeff Davis 8. Furthermore, the persistent string of incidents involving the Jeff Davis 8 would have all but guaranteed that management was aware of their presence. Indeed, Tri-Tech's Toby Leger chased Loretta off the Boudreaux Inn property on May 11, 2000, though she continued to patronize the business—and engage in sex work there—until just before she was murdered in 2005. "It was a whorehouse," a former deputy with the Sheriff's Office told me. "That's exactly what it was."

I contacted one of the Boudreaux Inn's former managers, Suzette Bouley Istre of Jennings, to understand the day-to-day operations at the Boudreaux Inn better. Istre managed the Boudreaux Inn from 2000 until the motel closed in 2008. She told me that Kristen, Muggy, Loretta, and Frankie Richard were all frequent habitués of the business.[23] "Loretta, she was a regular," Istre told me. "She was thrown off the property for a couple of years. But she came back. She wasn't allowed on the property [even] before I got there. I don't remember Kristen in the rooms, but Kristen would come and eat. . . . Muggy gave me trouble a few times; she pulled a fire alarm and scared everybody in the middle of the night. People were running everywhere. Frankie would come to the bar and rent a room." Istre insisted, however, that because she worked at the Boudreaux Inn mostly during the daytime hours, she "didn't always see" what was occurring at the motel, especially at night between the likes of the Jeff Davis 8 and Frankie.

When I asked Istre whom she reported to at the Boudreaux Inn, she named Tri-Tech LLC's Toby Leger and Martin Guillory as her bosses. "They were both in politics," Istre said. "Toby had ran in Church Point, for mayor. Martin is a representative for Charles Boustany. . . . I met Boustany over there [at the Boudreaux Inn]. It was [with] other people working for him and they were campaigning. He came and met a lot of people; he talked and he answered a lot of their questions. He didn't stay long because he was campaigning from town to town that day. I think it was just one time he was over there if I'm not mistaken. He didn't stay very long, like I said. He came and then he had to go to another little town."

Indeed, Boustany's first campaign for Congress occurred in 2003–4 when Guillory was at the helm of the Boudreaux Inn. On December 4, 2004, Boustany was elected to represent Louisiana's Seventh Congressional District after he defeated Democratic state senator Willie Mount in a much-contested runoff—an endorsement from Vice President Dick Cheney gave Boustany a late campaign boost.[24] Boustany became the first Republican elected from southwest Louisiana since 1884, and in the fall of 2009, he delivered the Republican Party's rebuttal to President Obama's address to a joint session of Congress on health care.[25]

Istre told me that both Leger and Boustany staffer Big G were at the Boudreaux Inn on a weekly basis. "Every week Toby would come," Istre told me. "On Thursday, he'd come and do the payroll. There were poker machines in there, and when someone would win a certain amount of money, they [Leger and Big G] would have to come in. They was there pretty often."[26] The Boudreaux Inn era ended in 2008 after a lengthy legal battle between owner Justin Boudreaux's heirs and Tri-Tech LLC. Boudreaux's heir Jacqueline Granger served Big G and Leger with an eviction notice, but the pair claimed that they had exercised an option to extend the five-year term of the initial lease and that the extended term had not yet expired. The Louisiana Supreme Court ruled in Granger's favor in April of 2008, and the Boudreaux Inn subsequently closed.

Istre was not the only person to encounter Boustany field representative Big G at the Boudreaux Inn. Kristen Gary Lopez's father, Andrew Newman, told me that he saw Big G there constantly and even knew him by his nickname. Newman told me that Big G was at the Boudreaux Inn "on a weekly basis maybe two to three times a week, if not more," and that Big G told him that he was particularly concerned about the slaying of the eighth victim, Necole Guillory, because her body had been dumped in Acadia Parish, where he is based.[26] Frankie Richard, similarly, told me that he had had drinks with Big G at the Boudreaux Inn. "I talked to Big G at the bar," Frankie told me. "He used to be over there all the time."

Documentary evidence establishes that not only was Big G at the Boudreaux Inn but also, on at least one occasion, he was armed. In the summer of 2015, I received a long-awaited response to a request I'd made under Louisiana's Public Records Act to the Sheriff's Office for any and all incident reports related to the Boudreaux Inn from the late 1990s to 2010. Among the documents—they spanned eleven hundred pages—was a July 22, 2003, incident report of the Sheriff's Office being called to the motel because "Martin Guillory pointing gun."[27] When detectives arrived on the scene, the complainant—whose name was redacted in the report—said that Big G "pulled a black pistal [sic] on him" during an argument. Big G's handgun was taken and placed into evidence and he was issued a citation for aggravated assault (the disposition of the case is unclear from the Sheriff's Office's records). The Sheriff's Office's response to my public records request also documents multiple incidents involving drugs at the Boudreaux Inn when Big G and Leger helmed the business. In one incident report, dated December 27, 2001, a caller to the Sheriff's Office complained of a "crack party going on at the Boudreaux Inn."[28]

On May 10, 2016, I spoke with Big G about illegal activity at the Boudreaux Inn, his relationships with Frankie Richard and the Jeff Davis 8, and Boustany. In an earlier, introductory phone call, Big G had requested that I e-mail him with background information about me and my work. During that call, Big G confirmed that he is Martin Guillory, former proprietor of the Boudreaux Inn who currently serves as a field representative for Congressman Charles Boustany.

When I asked Big G if he was aware of criminal activity occurring at the Boudreaux Inn or if he was aware of any of the Jeff Davis 8 engaging in prostitution, he said, "No, sir"; he added, however, "I've met one or two [of the Jeff Davis 8]" though he could not recall which specific women he had met.[29] "I didn't know the rest of 'em," he insisted. Guillory then said that he met Frankie Richard "on one occasion," but "Frankie mostly stayed in Lafayette: he told me he had a business in Lafayette."

I asked Big G if he could recall Congressman Boustany visiting the Boudreaux Inn in any capacity, and he said, "Not that I can remember," but that he "may have." Of the 2003 incident where he allegedly pointed a gun at someone while inside the Boudreaux Inn, Big G insisted, "I was never arrested," and that he was simply "took in [to the Jefferson Davis Parish Sheriff's Office] to write a statement." Big G then downplayed his role at the Boudreaux Inn—"I half owned a business in the Jennings area"—but then admitted that he was on the premises "maybe once a week." When I asked Big G if Congressman Boustany had engaged in relationships of any nature with the women of the Jeff Davis 8, he replied, "Well, of course not, that I know of. Why would that man deal with any of the women at the Boudreaux Inn?" Big G then angrily concluded the call, told me to never call him back, and warned, "I assure you when you come out with all of these allegations we're gonna file suit against you."

And while FBI agent Reed would not comment on his meeting with Boustany Witness A nor any Taskforce interviews regarding Boustany's involvement with the Jeff Davis 8, he did, however, appear interested in the connections between Boustany and Big G, and Big G and the Boudreaux Inn. So, per his request, on August 3, 2015, I furnished Agent Reed a précis of Jeff Davis 8 arrests at the Boudreaux Inn; the Boudreaux Inn property records/its lease; Martin Guillory's business registrations with the Louisiana Secretary of State as "Big G"; Big G's staff listing with Charles Boustany on Capitol Hill; LLC documents filed with the LA Secretary of State for Tri-Tech LLC, leased by Big G and Toby Leger; and a copy of the July 22, 2003, incident report involving Big G at the Boudreaux Inn. Because the Jeff Davis 8 case is an open investigation, it's unclear if the feds have acted upon any of the information provided by me, Boustany Witness A, or other Taskforce witnesses connecting Boustany to the Boudreaux Inn and the Jeff Davis 8.

To be clear, there is no evidence that either Congressman Boustany or Big G and his partners had any involvement with the murders of the Jeff Davis 8. And while a number of witnesses maintain that Boustany enjoyed the services of at least two of the victims, he has denied, through his office, any involvement, and no doubt, while I have found the reports credible, his accusers can be challenged. Nevertheless, the clear evidence of Big G's involvement with the Boudreaux Inn and the allegations concerning Congressman Boustany do provide yet another indication of how intertwined the powerless Jeff Davis 8 victims were, or were believed to be, with those who hold power in Louisiana.

CHAPTER 14

Whistle-Blower in White Robes

On August 25, 2015, Lake Arthur police detective Raymond Mott, who had only been on the force for a few months but had made more arrests than any other officer in the twelve-man department, was called into a surprise meeting with Police Chief Ray Marcantel, newly hired Assistant Chief Terrie Guillory, and Chris Myers, an investigator for the Jefferson Davis Parish DA. The lawmen confronted Mott about a photograph taken of him at an August 2014 anti-immigration rally held by the Loyal White Knights of the Ku Klux Klan in North Carolina. In the photograph, Mott, a balding man with a thick build and an engaging, dimpled smile, is dressed in all-black KKK garb, his arm extended in a Nazi-style salute; a burning cross is in the background, and he is flanked by an unidentified man in an all-white robe with a pointed hat. "They brought up the Klan rally picture," Mott told me. "And they said that I was going to be fired."[1]

Indeed, just days later, after the photo of Mott at the KKK rally went viral on social media—a tweet about Mott from activist Shaun King was retweeted nearly four thousand times, inspiring coverage ranging from the *Huffington Post* to the *New York Daily News*—a motion to terminate Mott's employment passed unanimously.[2] On the surface, it appeared that a devilishly bad cop had met an appropriate fate. But like every story about Jefferson Davis law enforcement, the truth is more complicated.

Mott told me that in the weeks before the meeting with Chief Marcantel, he was called out to the home of Crystal Benoit Zeno's former neighbor, who was having a monetary dispute with Crystal's sister. "Me and Chief Marcantel went out on the call," Mott remembers, "and when we arrived, Crystal's sister was screaming and panicking at the sight of us. She was irate and screaming and crying. She said, 'Terrie Guillory killed my sister.'"

Mott says he wrote up an incident report regarding the call—a minor dispute between the neighbor and Benoit's sister, whom the neighbor said owed her $5. Then Mott viewed a cell phone video, taken by one of Crystal's family members, in which a witness claimed that "seven [of the Jeff Davis 8] were selling narcotics for Terrie Guillory." Beyond this, Mott has no understanding of why Crystal's sister blamed Terrie for her death.

A short while later, Mott was called into a meeting, this time with Terrie and Marcantel. There Guillory told him, "Stop doing drug busts. People are tired of reading about you and your drug busts in your newspaper."

Mott couldn't believe what Terrie was saying to him: "This was a direct order to stop making drug busts."[3] Mott told me that he refused Terrie's order, and worse, in the days after the meeting, he saw Terrie embracing a big-time meth dealer and murder suspect, Vaughn Robinson. In May of 2015, Robinson had been arrested and charged with accessory after the fact to first-degree murder and accessory after the fact to armed robbery.[4] In August, Robinson bonded out, but quickly caught new drug charges thanks to an arrest by Mott. Those charges were mysteriously dropped after cops at the Lake Arthur Police Department failed to write up an incident report regarding Robinson's arrest. After the drug case against Robinson fell apart, Mott says he saw Terrie embracing Robinson.

Having refused Terrie's order, Mott was hauled into another meeting with the town's top cop. Here he was presented with the KKK photo, though Mott believes the department had been in possession of it much sooner, waiting to use it as leverage. "This photo has been in the hands of my supervisor for nearly six months, yet no one is willing to step up and tell the truth about that," Mott told a reporter from *Vice* in September of 2015.[5] Mott, then, insists that he was disciplined and fired not for his involvement with the Klan, but for challenging the police power structure, which he says protects drug dealers, not the public. "When Terrie told me that people were tired of reading about my drug busts, I told him I don't care who it pisses off," Mott told me. "This is the job I'm supposed to do." Mott's account is confirmed by an associate, Trey Gordon, who insists that Guillory told Mott, "I'm onto you — and then the next day the Klan photo was released to the *Jennings Daily News*."[6]

But Mott is not, in fact, a white supremacist. He is an FBI informant, working to take down the KKK. After the August 2014 KKK rally he gave the FBI "everything I knew about the Klan — names, codes, everything. I basically ended the KKK in Louisiana." It's a bold claim, but it's backed by Gordon, who says, "If it had not been for Ray, there would be a very active Klan in Louisiana." The Klan itself (sources in the

Loyal White Knights) confirmed to *Vice* that Mott's informing led to the withering away of the Louisiana branch of the
organization and a halt to its recruitment efforts there. More
important, the FBI confirmed Mott's account to *Vice*.

Both Mott and Gordon also told me that they fed information about the corrupt practices of Jefferson Davis Parish
lawmen such as Terrie Guillory to the FBI. "I immediately
contacted the agent with whom I was working on the KKK
stuff about Terrie Guillory," Mott told me. A law enforcement source confirms that the FBI, from its Lafayette office,
has opened wide-ranging investigations into Jefferson Davis
Parish's law enforcement.

Mott's claims about Terrie—specifically the allegation of
his chumminess with a murder suspect—strongly echo allegations about him in the Jeff Davis 8 case. At the peak of the
murders in 2009, Terrie and his ex-wife, Paula, were observed
at Frankie Richard's house. And the firing of whistle-blower
Mott has much in common with the fall of detective Jesse
Ewing and nurse Nina Ravey, who also crossed Terrie. "Do
not trust them," Gordon remembers warning Mott of Jefferson Davis Parish law enforcement. "They destroyed a man
named Jesse Ewing."

Gordon maintains that he and his family had their own
history with Terrie Guillory. Gordon told me that a family
member used to ferry drugs into Jefferson Davis Parish with
Guillory serving as an escort; that a friend was booked into
the jail when Terrie was warden and was sodomized with a
flashlight by one of its guards; and that Terrie was a "frequent
visitor" to the Boudreaux Inn and "would go in and offer free
rides in exchange for sex."

A woman who carried on a long-term relationship with
Terrie told me that he is extremely close with both Frankie

Richard and Tracee Chaisson. That a high-ranking member of law enforcement such as Terrie would have a relationship with Tracee is telling because she, like Frankie, has a history of beating significant charges (recall that in 2007 charges were dropped against her in the murder of Kristen). Tracee is also, notably, one of the sole surviving sex workers from the 2005–9 era. I reached out to her on multiple occasions during the writing of this book, but she refused to comment.

Terrie's partner told me that she overheard multiple late-night personal conversations between Terrie, Frankie, and Tracee, including one where Frankie threatened to kill a relative. During the call, Terrie advised Frankie to harm—and not kill—the family member so "he [Terrie] could take care of it legally." The partner says she was fearful of Terrie because he strangled her during sex (the suspected cause of death in many of the Jeff Davis 8 cases is asphyxia).

Terrie is a perennial power player in Jefferson Davis Parish, a status that appears to be confirmed by a bizarre August 31, 2015, suspension letter to Mott that is ostensibly from Chief Marcantel—it bears his name and signature—but is written in the third person.[7] "The initial letter provided to you by Chief of Police Ray Marcantel on August 28, 2015," it reads, "is supplemented by this letter." Mott says that the third-person style of the letter is no accident and that it was actually authored by Terrie Guillory, who, Mott says, while officially second-in-command, is actually the de facto police chief of Lake Arthur, Louisiana. That a lawman who has connections to unsolved murders in a parish serves as police chief in that very parish is a bone-chilling reality in an area already haunted by decades of police corruption.

Acknowledgments

Thank you: my family, particularly my wife and my son, a beautiful, loving little soul who has made my life immeasurably richer; Mark Lotto, Kate Lee, David Patterson, Brett Martin, Brett Michael Dykes, Campbell Robertson, Ryan Holiday, the late Michelle McNamara at *True Crime Diary* (and Patton Oswalt), William Sothern, Nikki Page, Karen Gadbois, Scott Lewis, Josmar Trujillo, Robert Levine, Robert Kolker, Tom Lowenstein, Angel Polachek, Bill Loehfelm, Jarret Lofstead and the NOLA Fugees folks, Susan Larson, Rachel Conner, Mariame Kaba, Lil Boosie, Hashim Nzinga, Michael Arria, Michael Friedman, Greg Augarten, Michael Perlstein, Kade Crockford, Joseph Corcoran (RIP), Susan Kaplow, Mark Healy, Raven Rakia, Jim Boren, Kirk Menard, Seth Ferranti, Cormac Boyle, Annie Preziosi, Richard Bourke, Christine Lehmmann, David Simon, John McWhorter, Glenn Loury, Evan Wright, George Pelecanos, Richard Price. Thanks to the phenomenal team at Scribner for their hard work, patience, and support with this project, particularly my editor, John Glynn.

Ferguson, we see you. Dellwood, we see you. Jennings, we see you. Kinloch, we see you.

—2015 Ferguson protesters' chant

ACKNOWLEDGMENTS

The August 9, 2014, shooting of unarmed teen Michael Brown by police officer Darren Wilson in Ferguson, Missouri, provoked a nationwide and ongoing revolt against police killings. Though the Department of Justice declined to indict Officer Wilson on civil rights charges in 2015, the Ferguson Police Department was lambasted in an extensive report by the DOJ for its pattern and practice of unconstitutional policing. Officer Wilson came to the Ferguson PD from a police department in Jennings, Missouri, that was so troubled—it was rocked by a number of incidents of excessive force by its officers—that the city council there disbanded it. And in July of 2016, Jennings, Missouri, paid out a $4.7 million settlement to two thousand people over a lawsuit alleging that the city's practice of jailing citizens for unpaid fines and fees was unconstitutional.[1] Jennings, Louisiana, and Jennings, Missouri, have many parallels: both are small towns where police have historically treated the citizenry as revenue generators and where excessive force is commonplace. As protests against unconstitutional policing have emerged everywhere from North Charleston, South Carolina, to New York City, and, most recently, Baton Rouge and Falcon Heights, Minnesota, where Alton Sterling and Philando Castile were killed by police, sparking the most intense protests since the summer of 2014, which saw the murders of Eric Garner and Mike Brown, it's apparent that problems with policing aren't confined to the Jenningses of the United States.

So I have to express my incredible thanks and boundless gratitude to the protesters in the Ferguson/St. Louis area for bringing the issue of law enforcement misconduct into the public discourse. In a few months, you made possible what criminal justice system reformers have been unable to achieve for decades. Thank you. The future belongs to folks like y'all.

ACKNOWLEDGMENTS

Thanks also to Louisiana's Public Records Act, La. R.S. 44:1–41, and Article XII, Section 3, of the Louisiana Constitution, which grants any person the right to examine and copy public documents in the possession of the state and its political subdivisions. I couldn't have deeply investigated the Jeff Davis 8 case without it.

Special thanks to Nic Pizzolatto for his words of encouragement about my *Medium.com* piece about this case, "Who Killed the Jeff Davis 8?"

Victim Data

VICTIM DATA

Victim	Date Found	Date of Death (Estimated)	Location of Body	
Loretta Chaisson	Friday, May 20, 2005	May 17, 2005	Highway 1126, the Grand Marais Canal	
Ernestine Patterson	Friday, June 18, 2005	June 16, 2005	Highway 102, the Aguillard Canal	
Kristen Gary Lopez	Sunday, March 18, 2007	March 6, 2007	Highway 99, the Petitjean Canal	
Whitnei Dubois	Saturday, May 12, 2007	May 11, 2007	Near the intersection of Earl Duhon and Bobby Roads, on road, near crawfish ponds	

VICTIM DATA

Clothing	Toxicology	Findings
Blue jeans, blue panties, short-sleeve white pullover blouse	ETOH 0.16; cocaine; Zoloft; Celexa	Undetermined manner of death; mixed-drug intoxication; presence of blood under scalp; no evidence of significant injuries or natural disease
Blue-jean shorts	ETOH 0.08; cocaine	Homicide; three incised wounds to the neck; three cuts across front of neck; bruises on left hand; postmortem injuries from marine predators; no evidence of other significant injuries or natural disease
White sock on right foot bearing red hearts; yellow metal ring on finger	ETOH 0.06; cocaine; meprobamate (Soma)	Manner of death undetermined; extensive postmortem injuries caused by marine predators; no evidence of significant injuries or natural disease
Brown elastic band and white elastic band on right wrist; earring found on ground at crime scene	ETOH 0.42; cocaine; alprazolam (Xanax)	Undetermined manner of death; mixed-drug intoxication; nonspecific bruises on left and right lower extremities; no evidence of significant injuries or natural disease

Victim	Date Found	Date of Death (Estimated)	Location of Body	
Muggy Brown	Thursday, May 29, 2008	May 27, 2008	Racca Road, east of Highway 102	
Crystal Shay Benoit Zeno	Thursday, September 11, 2008	Unknown	Lacour Road, one mile south of Highway 1126	
Brittney Gary	Saturday, November 15, 2008	November 4, 2008	Keystone Road, south of Highway 1126	
Necole Guillory	Wednesday, August 19, 2009	August 17, 2009	Off I-10, between mile markers 73 and 74; Acadia Parish	

Clothing	Toxicology	Findings
Peach tank top with white discoloration around left hip; blue denim shorts with white discoloration around left hip; purple brassiere; purple panties; ankle bracelet with colored beads	ETOH 0.04; cocaine	Multiple incised wounds to the head and neck; three cuts behind right ear; approximately seven cuts across the front neck; no evidence of significant other injuries or natural disease
No clothing or jewelry	Unknown	Homicide
No clothing; gray beaded bracelet on right ankle	ETOH 0.03; cocaine	Manner of death: asphyxia; mixed-drug intoxication; no evidence of other significant injuries or natural disease
Partially clothed	Tramadol; cocaine; alcohol	Manner of death: asphyxia; postmortem cuts on left face, left eyebrow, and left clavicle; mixed-drug intoxication; possible sperm in vagina

The Timeline

Date	Event
3/29/1993	Former Jefferson Davis Parish sheriff Dallas Cormier pleads to one count of obstruction of justice in federal court in the Western District of Louisiana. Cormier had been hit with thirty-five charges related to corruption at his office.
11/28/1995	Hispanic couple Albert and Mary Gonzales pulled over by Jefferson Davis Parish Sheriff's Office on I-10. The Gonzaleses sue the Sheriff's Office in federal court, claiming that there was no probable cause for the stop and that the Gonzaleses were detained longer than similarly situated Caucasians.
1/3/1997	*Dateline NBC* runs exposé on the Jefferson Davis Parish Sheriff's Office. The department is caught on camera making traffic stops without probable cause and illegally seizing cash from motorists.
2/14/1998	Jennings Police Department informant Sheila Comeaux is beaten to death near a funeral home in Jennings. Her murder remains unsolved.
October 1999	Incumbent Jefferson Davis Parish sheriff Ricky Edwards faces challenger Arnold Benoit in the race for sheriff. Edwards is reelected; Benoit claims he was subjected to threats of violence near the campaign's conclusion.

2/5/2000	Jennings police officer Phil Karam kills Jennings police officer Kenneth Guidry and his wife, Christine. A standoff ensues. During the standoff, Karam kills Officer Burt LeBlanc and wounds Officer Johnny Lassiter. Karam is later tried and convicted on first-degree murder charges.
8/19/2003	Jennings police chief Donald "Lucky" DeLouche resigns due to allegations of rampant sexual misconduct at the department.
10/29/2003	Female officers with the Jennings Police Department file civil rights complaints against the department in federal court in the Western District of Louisiana. Female cops claim that they suffered a hostile work environment, including violence and rape at the hands of male cops.
4/20/2005	A South Jennings home suspected of being a hub for prescription-pill trafficking is raided by the Louisiana State Police, Jefferson Davis Parish DA's office, Jefferson Davis Parish Sheriff's Office, and the Jennings Police Department. During the raid, an addict named Leonard Crochet—who was unarmed and had no weapon anywhere near him—was shot to death by John Briggs Becton of the Louisiana State Police. Witnesses to the killing of Crochet at the hands of law enforcement include Harvey Burleigh and Kristen Gary Lopez, both of whom were later murdered.
5/20/2005	Body of Loretta found floating in Grand Marais Canal near Jennings. Her murder remains unsolved.
6/17/2005	Body of sex worker Ernestine Daniels Patterson is found in drainage canal near Jennings. Her murder remains unsolved.
3/18/2007	Kristen Gary Lopez, witness to the 2005 Crochet killing by law enforcement, found floating in canal outside Jennings. Kristen was questioned by cops in the 2005 murder of Loretta and was a witness in that case. Her murder remains unsolved.

3/30/2007	Warren Gary, the Jefferson Davis Parish Sheriff's Office chief investigator, purchases from a female inmate a truck suspected of being used to transport the body of murder victim Kristen Gary Lopez by suspects Frankie Richard and Tracee Chaisson for $8,748.90.
4/20/2007	Warren Gary sells the truck for nearly $15,500.
5/12/2007	Body of Jennings sex worker Whitnei Dubois found near crawfish ponds on the outskirts of Jennings. Boyfriend Alvin Lewis witnessed 2005 Leonard Crochet killing by law enforcement, and Whitnei was in the same small circle of drug users as Crochet. Whitnei's murder remains unsolved.
6/9/2007	Steven Gunter, from Lake Arthur, Louisiana, shot to death by Jefferson Davis Parish warden Terrie Guillory during an alleged domestic dispute. Guillory claimed Gunter was armed and pointing a weapon at him—this claim is called into question by the autopsy report by the Calcasieu Parish coroner.
7/25/2007	Harvey Burleigh, witness to 2005 Leonard Crochet killing, stabbed to death in Jennings. Prior to his death, Burleigh told friends that he was pursuing promising leads on the murdered women. His murder remains unsolved.
10/9/2007	Female prisoner Lisa Allen files a civil rights lawsuit in federal court claiming that jailer Mark Ivory sexually abused her at Jefferson Davis Parish jail. Ivory commits suicide on the same day that Allen passes a polygraph test administered by the Louisiana State Police.

December 2007	Jennings PD sergeant Jesse Ewing takes recorded statements from female inmates who say that Jefferson Davis Parish Sheriff's Office chief investigator Warren Gary, who purchased the truck suspected of being used to transport the body of 2007 murder victim Kristen Gary Lopez, worked hand in hand with the prime suspect in the case, Frankie Richard, to destroy physical evidence from the truck.
5/29/2008	Body of sex worker Laconia "Muggy" Brown found on a dirt road on the outskirts of Jennings. Brown witnessed the 2005 murder of Ernestine; her cousin Lawrence Nixon was suspected of aiding Byron Chad Jones in Patterson's killing. Brown's murder remains unsolved.
6/26/2008	Louisiana Board of Ethics rules on Warren Gary's purchase of truck suspected of being used in the commission of 2007 Kristen Gary Lopez killing: Gary abused his office and improperly received gifts when he bought and sold the truck in 2007.
9/11/2008	Body of sex worker Crystal Benoit Zeno found in wooded area outside Jennings. Her murder remains unsolved.
11/11/2008	A Jennings sex worker tells the Taskforce that Jefferson Davis Parish Sheriff's Office deputy Danny Barry and his wife trolled South Jennings for sex workers. Other Taskforce witnesses say that Barry had a dungeonlike room as well as rolls of plastic sheeting in his home.
11/15/2008	Body of sex worker Brittney Gary, first cousin to 2007 murder victim Kristen Gary Lopez, found in field outside Jennings. Gary's murder remains unsolved.
5/28/2009	Multiagency raid on the home of Frankie Richard at 811 McKinley Street in South Jennings. Raid is related to ongoing theft-of-drugs investigation; participants in the raid include Taskforce members Ramby Cormier and Paula Guillory.

July 2009	Paula Guillory and husband Terrie Guillory (warden of parish jail) surveilled by local private investigator Kirk Menard at the home of drug kingpin and murder suspect Frankie Richard *and* at a South Jennings home frequented by the murdered women.
7/7/2009	Internal investigation into Paula Guillory initiated at Jefferson Davis Parish Sheriff's Office after thousands in cash goes missing from May 28, 2009, drug raid on Frankie Richard's home.
8/11/2009	Paula Guillory terminated from Jefferson Davis Parish Sheriff's Office because of missing evidence from raid on Richard's home; drugs and theft case against Richard collapses as a result of Guillory's misconduct.
8/19/2009	Body of Jennings sex worker Necole Guillory found by I-10 in Acadia Parish. Guillory witnessed the 2005 murder of Loretta Chaisson. Just prior to Guillory's murder, she told her mother, Barbara, that "it was the police who were killing the girls."
12/28/2009	Then Jefferson Davis Parish sheriff Ricky Edwards orders that all investigators working the Jeff Davis 8 homicides be swabbed for DNA.
January 2010–early spring of 2010	Shootings plague the South Jennings drug scene. Alan West and Kenneth Pelican among victims.
10/10/2010	Lafayette, Louisiana, resident Russell Carrier struck and killed by Burlington Santa Fe train in Jennings. Carrier had called in a tip to the Jefferson Davis Parish DA's office regarding the 2008 murder of Crystal Benoit Zeno. Carrier saw three men, all drug dealers connected to homicide suspect Frankie Richard, emerging from the woods where Zeno's body was discovered.

7/8/2011	Drug dealer David "Bowlegs" Deshotel shot to death in his South Jennings home. Deshotel was an associate of Jeff Davis 8 victims Necole and Brittney. Deshotel's murder remains unsolved.
1/11/2013	Jennings police chief Johnny Lassiter arrested by Louisiana State Police. Lassiter is charged with obstruction of justice, malfeasance in office, and injuring public records because of items missing from the evidence room.
1/31/2014	Body of Lake Arthur, Louisiana, twenty-seven-year-old Lacie Fontenot found in a shallow ditch in that town. Cause of death is drowning as a result of hypothermia.

Notes

1 Ida B. Wells, "Lynch Law in All Its Phases," 1893. http://www
   .blackpast.org/1893-ida-b-wells-lynch-law-all-its-phases.

Chapter 1: Loretta

1 http://www.statesymbolsusa.org/Louisiana/fish_white_perch
   .html.
2 Interview with Jerry Jackson, December 21, 2011.
3 http://quickfacts.census.gov/qfd/states/22/22053.html.
4 Jefferson Davis Parish Sheriff's Office, Incident Report
   #2005050144, May 20, 2005.
5 Calcasieu Parish Coroner's Office and Forensic Facility, Terry
   Welke, MD, Autopsy Report, Case #CPCO-095-2005; May 23,
   2005.
6 Interview with Barb Ann Deshotel, August 23, 2014.
7 Data on Lake Arthur from US Census Bureau: https://www
   .google.com/publicdata/explore?ds=kf7tgg1uo9ude_&met_y=
   population&idim=place:2241050&hl=en&dl=en.
8 Interview with Murphy Lewis, July 21, 2011.
9 *State of Louisiana v. Loretta Lynn Chaisson Lewis*; Jefferson
   Davis Parish Sheriff's Office, Case Number 2005-03-0110.
10 Ibid.
11 Doris Maricle, "New Jeff Davis Parish Jail One Step Closer to
    Reality," *American Press*, June 17, 2013, http://www.american
    press.com/New-Jeff-Davis-Parish-Jail-one-step-closer-to-reality.
12 Welke, Autopsy Report, Case #CPCO-095-2005.
13 Ibid.
14 http://www.boudincapitaloftheworld.com/.

15 http://www.2theadvocate.net/louisiana_facts.php; and Bryan P. Piazza, *The Atchafalaya River Basin: History and Ecology of an American Wetland* (Texas A&M University Press, 2014).

16 Al Jazeera, "Future of Louisiana Community Uncertain as Chemical Plant Expands, March 28, 2014," http://america.aljazeera.com /watch/shows/the-stream/the-stream-officialblog/2014/3/28 /future-of-louisianacommunityuncertainaschemicalplantexpands .html.

17 Louisiana Bucket Brigade, "Citgo Petroleum Accidents," http:// rav.labucketbrigade.org/map.php.

18 Letter/flyer from Robert S. Mueller III, FBI Director: "Seeking Information: Murder Victims, Jennings, Louisiana, Area. A Multi-Agency Investigative Team led by the Jefferson Davis Parish Sheriff's Office in Jennings, Louisiana, is seeking information regarding the murders of eight women: Loretta Lynn Chaisson Lewis, Ernestine Daniels Patterson, Kristen E. Gary Lopez, Whitnei Charlene Dubois, Laconia Shontell Brown, Crystal Shay Benoit Zeno, Brittney Gary and Necole Guillory. The victims, who range from 17 to 30 years old, were found deceased in and around the Jennings area from May 2005 through August 2009."

19 Sheila Smith, "Cassidy, Miller Face Public Forum," *Jennings Daily News*, October 10, 2014. Cassidy's full remarks: "We certainly don't have any inpatient treatment here. . . . Drugs account for eighty to eighty-five percent of our cases."

20 Kadi Hanes, "116 Pounds of Marijuana Found after Traffic Stop," KPLC-TV, December 22, 2011.

21 Lee Peck, "Authorities Make Arrests in Largest Anti-Drug Operation in History of Southwest Louisiana," KPLC-TV, May 5, 2014.

22 Theresa Schmidt, "Jennings Women Turn Out for Self-Defense Seminar," KPLC-TV, November 26, 2008.

23 "Jennings Press Conference on Mystery Murders," KPLC-TV, December 18, 2008, http://www.kplctv.com/story/9550151/ jennings-press-conference.

Text of December 18, 2008, Taskforce press conference:

I would like to take this opportunity to introduce the formation of a Multi-Agency Investigative Team. This team is composed of law enforcement agents from many different agencies. They will work full-time on the investigations of the seven women who have been found dead in our community over the last three and a half years. Since May of 2005, when Loretta Lewis was found off of LA 1126, the members of this task force worked to trace Loretta's whereabouts and find out what happened to her. Since that time and when we have found the other six victims, these dedicated men and women have worked tirelessly to determine who is responsible for their deaths and why.

Many man-hours over the years have been logged and every law enforcement agency in this area from local to national has assisted. To the many people who have already assisted, I say, "Thanks." The formation of this group today will allow eight to ten people to work full-time and exclusively to these cases. We will continue to search for leads, follow those leads and tips that we receive, and act upon those leads aggressively utilizing every resource that is available to us. The citizens of Jennings, Jefferson Davis Parish, State of Louisiana, and the United States of America have our word on that.

We have opened a new work center where tips can be called in. Our collective hope is that our community will take note of their surroundings, report suspicious behavior, and if they know for fact the reasons why these young ladies of our community have died, to come forward and give that information to this Investigative Team, so that we can bring the individual or individuals to justice. The number to call is 337-824-6662. We will soon be opening a website that will give information about these young ladies and will allow you to report information via the Web.

I would like to thank the media for their coverage of these deaths. Sometimes opinions differ as to what and why things are happening. Please understand that I will never speculate or give you my opinion on what is going on in these cases. I will always give you the facts that I have, and only if those facts will not compromise the investigation or the future prosecution of these cases. We are not here to speculate; we are and have taken an oath to investigate fully and uphold the Constitution and laws of the United States, State of Louisiana, Parish of Jefferson Davis, and the City of Jennings. This isn't to say that speculation is not used in law enforcement, but the primary basis for decision making will be based on *fact*.

Our united concern and mission has been and will always be to catch the killer or killers responsible for taking the lives of seven of our citizens, who were daughters, sisters, friends, and some of them mothers in our community. I ask you the media to continue to help us put out the facts of the cases, not to speculate or sensationalize, and to quickly put out the information when we ask you.

You have all asked whether or not this is a serial killer. The facts that we currently have do not allow me at this time to say with certainty that these cases are all linked. We are working on them individually and collectively. I caution you that the term *serial killer* is complicated and conjures images based on "Hollywood shows" of a frightening-looking maniac. However, most of the time, the offender or offenders in a serial case end up looking as normal as you and me, the typical guy next door. So, when we ask you to call in with information or tips, keep in mind that whoever is responsible for some—if not all—of these cases is likely someone who lives in this community or at least visits here and is familiar with the area. Sadly, we need to look to the right and left of us. It could be someone's uncle or father, and that is what is painful for our community. I will always give you the facts and pray that you assist us and not speculate.

We will continually try to educate our community on what behavioral characteristics to look for. We know with cases like this which have occurred in the United States, this type of offender will have attempted to approach, even hurt, other women, but those women got away or maybe didn't even realize they were in jeopardy or at risk. We know that the offender or offenders has made mistakes. We are holding that information close to the investigation. Although this person looked "normal," there was likely something about him that caused concern. Maybe you described it as the "creep factor." This is someone we believe comes across as somewhat arrogant as well. If you have had an experience like this, we want you to please come forward and talk to us. Please don't shrug off an event and just say, "Oh, that was nothing." Maybe it was, maybe it wasn't. Let law enforcement make that call.

Do you know someone who is:

Superficially glib and charming

Self-confident

Appears nonthreatening initially

Physically strong—not to be confused with someone who works out every day at the gym

Frequents the area where the girls go missing from

Quick to anger especially if rejected

Lures girls with alcohol and drugs—crack cocaine

May have a formal criminal record involving assaultive behavior with a knife and may include burglary

May not necessarily have a violent criminal history

Our community is hurting and grieving the deaths of seven women. We ask your media audience to pray for our community and for the souls of our seven citizens. Our investigative team only wants the truth. Once we get the truth, then we can bring the individual or individuals to justice.

Our team is comprised of very experienced investigators from eight separate agencies, local, state, and federal. These men and women have years of experience in working very complicated cases, some of which are serial investigators. Most of these law enforcement officers live in our community or have family that live in our community. We are *all* anxious to solve these cases and bring those responsible to justice.

I also currently have the commitment of every sheriff in the State of Louisiana and the LA Sheriff's Association task force to provide manpower as needed during this investigation.

Again, to report information on the deaths of Loretta, Ernestine, Kristen, Whitnei, Muggy, Shay, and Brittney, please call 337-824-6662. If you are being stalked, harassed, or followed, please call 911 immediately and report it. Jennings and Jefferson Davis Parish will survive these tragic events. My hope and prayer is that we will also grow together as a community, continue to work together, and bring those responsible to justice.

24 October 28, 2009, Taskforce press conference text:

Members of the team investigating the eight deaths in Jeff Davis Parish held a press conference Wednesday morning in Jennings.

The press conference was held to update the details of the investigation, and to announce an increase of the reward that is being offered.

The reward for information that leads to the arrest and successful prosecution of the person responsible for the murders has been increased from $35,000 to $85,000. The reward money is being offered by the Jeff Davis Parish District Attorney's Office, the Jeff Davis Parish Sheriff's Office and the FBI.

Below is the text of the press conference from the Jeff Davis parish task force:

"The agencies comprising the Multi-Agency Investigative Team have called you here today to provide you with an update regarding where we are in the investigation, to give you facts as we have them, and to announce an increase in the reward that is being offered. We will take no questions today and we thank you for your continued efforts to release factual information, not opinions or gossip.

"Representatives of each agency of the Investigative Team are here and will provide you with information regarding their involvement in this investigation. Although all agencies are independent, each has made all of its resources available in support of other Investigative Team agencies as needed.

"I would like to introduce you to Special Agent in Charge David Welker, FBI, New Orleans Office; Captain Barry Branton, LA State Police; Calcasieu Parish sheriff Tony Mancuso; Jennings police chief Johnny Lassiter; Acadia Parish sheriff Wayne Melancon; Director of Investigations Mike Thompson, Louisiana Department of Justice.

"As you know, there are other agencies involved in this investigation that could not be here with us today. There are also many people behind the scenes who work on this case twenty-four/seven along with us here in Jennings.

"This investigation pertains to the murders of Loretta Lewis, Ernestine Daniels Patterson, Kristen Gary Lopez, Whitnei Dubois, Laconia 'Muggy' Brown, Crystal Benoit Zeno, Brittney Gary, and Necole Guillory. I use the term *murder* because we are treating them all as murders unless we can prove otherwise. As we have stated in previous releases, it is the collective opinion of all agencies involved in this investigation that these murders may have been committed by a common offender. For that reason, the label *serial murder* is applicable; however, we have not used that label when referring to this investigation because it does not benefit us in our goals to identify and apprehend the offender, nor does it prevent further loss of life. Labels are sometimes confusing and are subject to misinterpretation.

"A number of individuals have been considered possible suspects or persons of interest in the course of this investigation. None of these people have been ruled out completely, and they continue to be on the Investigative Team's 'radar.' At this time, we do not have a particular suspect who we are focusing on exclusively; therefore we will continue to consider other suspects.

"This investigation is ongoing. Investigators have followed nearly one thousand leads, interviewed approximately five hundred people, and fielded countless telephone calls providing information on these cases. Some of the information received in the course of this investigation has lead to progress in other unrelated cases such as narcotic and burglary cases.

"All available resources from our federal, state, and local agencies have been continuously applied in the investigation of these murders.

"The reward for information that leads to the arrest and successful prosecution of the person responsible for these murders has been increased from thirty-five thousand dollars to eighty-five thousand dollars. The reward money is being offered by the Jefferson Davis Parish District Attorney's Office, the Jefferson Davis Parish Sheriff's Office, and the FBI. Lamar Advertising has partnered with us to use electronic and paper billboards in SW Louisiana.

"There have been more than forty-eight thousand investigative hours logged in this case. We are working collectively as a team with the shared and mutual goals of bringing closure for the families of Loretta, Ernestine, Kristen, Whitnei, Muggy, Shay, Brittney, and Necole and bringing the responsible party to justice. Additionally, since November 2008, the Investigative Team has been tasked to find approximately thirty females who were reported missing.

"Collectively, law enforcement has been working on these cases for over four years. Investigators have covered and then rechecked leads upon entering them into the FBI's lead-management system. Investigations of this type make up less than one percent of all crimes. They are complex, arduous, and time-consuming. The Investigative Team members have worked around the clock, sometimes spending many days and nights away from their families to do so. I want to personally thank all of the men and women who have worked extremely hard and will continue to work hard until this case is successfully resolved. I would also like to thank the families of these men and women who support their law enforcement members.

"As I previously mentioned, all of these independent agencies are joined in support of the investigation centered at the Jefferson Davis Parish Sheriff's Office. We speak with one voice and will bring the offender to justice as one *team*. The complete facts and evidence gathered thus far are only known to law enforcement. The integrity of this investigation must not be compromised by disclosing evidence and/or other investigative results.

"We ask that the public contact the Investigative Team with any facts, suspicions, or other information about these crimes. We want the public to understand that the Investigative Team is the *only* appropriate recipient of such information. We are aware of others who have represented themselves as cooperating with the Investigative Team in the investigation; such is *not* the case. We are unable to confirm whether all information is being relayed. Reporting case information to individuals who are not members of the Investigative Team could delay or even prevent that information from being acted upon. This could result in irreparable harm to the investigation, and possibly in further loss of life.

"Our other partners in this investigation are you, the citizens of Jennings, Jefferson Davis Parish, and all of the surrounding towns and parishes. We have had a tremendous response from the public and we ask for your continued support. If you have any information on any of these cases, or that you think may be helpful to the investigation, please call. Even if you think your information is unimportant, or that someone else has reported what you know, please contact us. Your call may be the one that helps us to solve these cases. Our tip line is 337-824-6662, our website is www.jeffdaviscrimes.net. Thank you."

25 Letter/flyer from Mueller, "Seeking Information."

26 October 28, 2009, Taskforce press conference text.

27 Marty Briggs, "Does Jeff Davis Parish Have a Serial Killer?" KPLC-TV, http://www.kplctv.com/story/9307177/does-jeff-davis-parish-have-a-serial-killer.

28 *CNN Newsroom*, rush transcript, September 27, 2009, http://edition.cnn.com/TRANSCRIPTS/0909/27/cnr.03.html.

29 Campbell Robertson, "8 Deaths in a Small Town, and Much Unease," *New York Times*, January 1, 2010, http://www.nytimes.com/2010/01/02/us/02serial.html?_r=0.

30 Mike Pearlstein, "Jennings 8: Unsolved Murders Haunt Town, Police," WWL-TV, January 30, 2014.

31 Jill Leovy, "The Underpolicing of Black America," *Wall Street Journal*, January 23, 2015, http://www.wsj.com/articles/the-underpolicing-of-black-america-1422049080.

32 Jim Polk, "DNA Test Strengthens Atlanta Child Killings Case," September 6, 2010. http://www.cnn.com/2010/CRIME/06/09/williams.dna.test/.

33 Brad Hamilton, "After Up to 17 Victims, Cops Still Can't Find the Gilgo Beach Killer," the *New York Post*, January 3, 2015.

34 Jeremy Tanner, "New Shannan Gilbert Autopsy Reveals 'Disturbing' Findings in Gilgo Beach Case, Medical Examiner Says," PIX 11, February 12, 2016, http://pix11.com/2016/02/12/new-shannan-gilbert-autopsy-reveals-disturbing-findings-in-gilgo-beach-case-medical-examiner-says/; and Joseph Goldstein, "Ex–Suffolk County Police Chief's Arrest Comes amid a Broader Federal Inquiry," the *New York Times*, January 3, 2016.

35 Interview with Louis Schlesinger, January 28, 2012.

36 Jefferson Davis Parish Sheriff's Office incident report, #200590170, September 24, 2005.

37 Interview of Muggy by Detective Danny Semmes, July 7, 2005.

38 Interview of Melissa Daigle, July 12, 2011.

39 Interview of Ricky Edwards, December 19, 2011.

NOTES

Chapter 2: Boom and Bust

1 Calcasieu Parish Police Jury, "History of Calcasieu Parish," http://www.cppj.net/index.aspx?page=218.

2 http://www.nola.com/crime/index.ssf/2000/05/edwin _edwards_guilty_ex-govern.html; *New Orleans Times-Picayune* staff, "Edwin Edwards Guilty; Ex-Governor Faces Forfeiture of Millions, Long Jail Term," the *Times-Picayune*, May 10, 2000.

3 Scott Lewis, eleven-part series, "The Zigler Legacy," *Jennings Daily News*, April 6, 2011, http://www.jenningsdailynews.net /2011/04/archive-6734/.

4 Bureau of Labor Statistics, "Databases, Tables & Calculators by Subject; Louisiana."

5 Economic Innovation Group, "Distressed Communities Index," http://eig.org/dci/report.

6 *New Orleans Times-Picayune* staff, "Ex-Sheriff Seeks Pardon to Hunt," *New Orleans Times-Picayune*, August 13, 1994.

7 Interview with Ginger Deshotel Reiley, April 9, 2014.

8 Ibid.

9 Interview with Ty Anthony Cornelius, March 30, 2014.

10 *Richard Alan Breaux v. Jefferson Davis Parish Sheriff*, Court of Appeal of Louisiana, 3rd Circuit, February 5, 1997.

11 Interview with Mike Dubois, July 1, 2011.

12 *Dirks et al. v. Ricky Edwards*, US Western District Court of Louisiana, Civil Docket 2:93-CV-00810-JTT-APW.

13 "Mayor Advises South Cutting Residents to Change Address," the *Jennings Daily News*, April 12, 2008, http://www.jennings dailynews.net/2008/04/archive-1106/.

14 *Karen Bryant v. Dennis Fontenot*, US Western District Court of Louisiana, Civil Docket 2:93-CV-1800-JTT-APW.

15 "Probable Cause? Police in Louisiana Harass Motorists and Seize Their Property for No Apparent Reason, Claiming It Is All Done in the War against Drug Trafficking," *Dateline NBC*, August 22, 1997.

16 *Gonzales et al. v. Darrell Pierce*, US Western District Court of Louisiana, Civil Docket 2:96-CV-01335-JTT-APW.

17 "Probable Cause?," *Dateline NBC*.

18 National Drug Strategy Network, "Louisiana Law Enforcement Stops Innocent Motorists and Seizes Their Property, Reports NBC's 'Dateline,'" February 1997, http://www.ndsn.org/FEB97/LOUSIANA.html.

19 Ibid.

20 Ibid.

Chapter 3: Lucky and LeDoux

1 "Ellender Murders Investigation," Calcasieu Parish Sheriff's Office, Complaint #91-005805.

2 Ibid.

3 Interview with Huey Littleton, January 7, 2015.

4 Christopher Prudhomme suicide note, Calcasieu Parish Sheriff's Office files, March 10, 1993.

5 "Statement of Littleton Witness" (name redacted), August 24, 1993.

6 Steve Sandlin, *Unsolved Mysteries*, http://unsolved.com/archives/steve-sandlin.

7 Michael Perlstein, "Search for Justice," *New Orleans Times-Picayune*, June 4, 1998.

8 *State v. Cisco*, Supreme Court of Louisiana, decided December 3, 2003.

9 Lake Charles Police Department, Offense Report 97-55698, July 23, 1997.

10 "Wanted for Questioning: Triple Homicide at KK's Grocery on July 6, 1997," Violent Crimes Task Force, Calcasieu Parish Sheriff's Office.

11 Theresa Schmidt, "Cisco Sentenced to 90 Years in Prison," KPLC-TV, March 26, 2010.

12 Sulphur Police Department, Offense Report, October 22, 1997.

13 Ibid.

14 Taskforce witness, April 21, 2015, statement.

15 Interview with Arnold Benoit, February 1, 2014.

16 "Jennings Mayor Appoints New Police Chief," KPLC-TV, undated news segment, http://www.kplctv.com/story/148093/jennings-mayor-appoints-new-police-chief.

17 *Martha Amie et al. v. City of Jennings, Louisiana, Chief of Police*

Donald "Lucky" DeLouche, US Western District Court of Louisiana, CV-03-2011.

18 *State v. Karam*, Court of Appeal of Louisiana, 3rd Circuit, Case #02-0163, July 31, 2002.

19 Graham Winch, "Jennings Police Chief Resigns," KPLC-TV, August 19, 2003.

20 "Delouche Appointed asst. Chief in Welsh," *Jennings Daily News*, January 8, 2011. http://www.jenningsdailynews.net/2011/01/archive-6308/.

Chapter 4: Frankie

1 Interview with Frankie Richard, March 31, 2012.

2 Interview with Mike Dubois, July 1, 2011.

3 Eric Onstott, "Local Pain Clinic Doctor Has License Suspended," *Orange Leader*, May 20, 2007.

4 Tom Aswell, "State Police Launch Internal Affairs Investigation of Troop D Commander after Public Records Requests by the *Louisiana Voice*," *Louisiana Voice*, September 5, 2015, http://louisianavoice.com/2015/09/05/state-police-launch-internal-affairs-investigation-of-troop-d-commander-after-public-records-requests-by-louisianavoice/.

5 Ibid.

6 Louisiana State Police, Bureau of Investigations, Western District Detectives, Case #WDD004505, "Police Involved Shooting, Jefferson Davis Parish."

7 State of Louisiana, Parish of Jefferson Davis, 31st Judicial Court, Negligent Homicide Case against John Briggs Becton, July 9, 2005.

8 Andrew Siff, "Grand Jury Declines to Indict NYPD Officer in Eric Garner Choke Hold Death," NBC 4 New York, December 4, 2014, http://www.nbcnewyork.com/news/local/Grand-Jury-Decision-Eric-Garner-Staten-Island-Chokehold-Death-NYPD-284595921.html; and Monica Davey and Julie Bosman, "Protests Flare after Ferguson Police Officer Is Not Indicted," the *New York Times*, November 24, 2014, http://www.nytimes.com/2014/11/25/us/ferguson-darren-wilson-shooting-michael-brown-grand-jury.html.

Chapter 5: Ernestine

1 Jefferson Davis Parish Sheriff's Office, Case Summary Report, Case Number 2005-06-00111, June 18, 2005.
2 Calcasieu Parish Coroner's Office and Forensic Facility, Case CPCO-116-2005; Name: Ernestine Patterson; Date of Examination: June 18, 2005; Time of examination: 10:15 a.m.
3 Jefferson Davis Parish Sheriff's Office, Case Summary Report, Case Number 2005-06-00111, June 18, 2005.
4 Interview with Jessica Daniels, July 11, 2011.
5 State of Louisiana, Parish of Jefferson Davis, Conspiracy to Commit Forcible Rape Case against Laconia Shontell Brown, Lawrence Nixon and Jarriel L. Palfrey. CR-114-06.
6 Affidavit of Rosalyn Breaux, March 27, 2006.
7 State of Louisiana, Parish of Jefferson Davis, Second Degree Murder Case against Byron Chad Jones and Lawrence Nixon, June 23, 2006.
8 Case Summary Report, Case Number 2005-06-00111, June 18, 2005.
9 Ibid.
10 Interview with Kirk Menard, July 1, 2011.

Chapter 6: Kristen

1 Interview with Roxanne Alexander, August 25, 2014.
2 Jefferson Davis Parish Sheriff's Office, Case Number 2007030140, March 18, 2007.
3 Autopsy of Kristen Gary Lopez by Richard Dupont, March 20, 2007.
4 Jefferson Davis Parish Sheriff's Office, Case Number 1999090114, September 14, 1999.
5 Interview with Nancy Gary, July 7, 2011.
6 Jefferson Davis Parish Sheriff's Office, Criminal Investigations Division, Case Number 2007030140.
7 Interview with Frankie Richard, March 31, 2012.
8 Interview with Melissa Daigle, July 12, 2011.

NOTES

Chapter 7: Whitnei

1 Interview with Mike Dubois, July 1, 2011; and Rebecca Loretta, "She Deserved Better," *Jennings Daily News*, September 25, 2009.
2 Loretta, "She Deserved Better."
3 *State v. Whitnei Chalene Dubois*, Case #5271-01-01.
4 Jefferson Davis Parish Sheriff's Office, Case Number 2006040077, April 8, 2006.
5 Interview with Brittany Jones, March 21, 2012.
6 Interview with Frankie Richard, July 13, 2011.
7 Interview with Scott Lewis, May 16, 2016.
8 Lee Peck, "Woman's Body Discovered in Jeff Davis Parish," KPLC-TV, May 12, 2007.
9 Interview with Frankie Richard and Brandon Wise, March 21, 2012.
10 Jennings Police Department files, Case #E-02456-07, May 14, 2007.
11 May 16, 2007, warrant for Frankie Richard, on second-degree murder charges, State of Louisiana, Parish of Jefferson Davis.
12 Interview with Frankie Richard, March 21, 2012.
13 Affidavit of Elizabeth Clemens, July 30, 2007, State of Louisiana, Parish of Jefferson Davis.
14 "Jennings Man Fatally Stabbed," *Jennings Daily News*, July 26, 2007.
15 Interview with Scott Lewis, August 30, 2014.

Chapter 8: Gunter and Guillory

1 Louisiana State Police, Bureau of Investigation, Western District Detectives, Case #WDD00507-1, August 31, 2007.
2 Deposition of Lorritta Lacoste in *Johnnie Thomas Gunter v. Jefferson Davis Parish*, C-488-08, February 3, 2009.
3 Interview with Beth Trahan, February 17, 2016.
4 *Lisa Allen v. Ricky Edwards, Mark Ivory, Terry [sic] Guillory*, US Western District Court of Louisiana, 2:07-CV-01675-CMH.
5 Interview with Nina Ravey, March 4, 2015.
6 "Ewing, Ravey Respond to Arrests," *Jennings Daily News*, December 22, 2007.

7 Audiotaped statements taken by Jesse Ewing, December 2007; and interviews with Jesse Ewing, July 8 and 9, 2011.

8 Louisiana Board of Ethics, "In the Matter of Warren Gary," June 26, 2008, Opinion No. 2007-489.

9 Interview with Ricky Edwards, December 19, 2011.

10 "Jennings Man Booked on Seven Counts of Aggravated Rape," KATC, November 3, 2015.

11 Deputy Terrie J. Guillory, "Whereabouts of Hanna, Month of March 2007," July 11, 2007.

Chapter 9: "Death on Me":
Muggy, Crystal, and Brittney

1 Interview with Roxanne Alexander, August 25, 2014.

2 Alexandra Natapoff, written testimony for the US House of Representatives, Committee on the Judiciary, Subcommittee on Crime, Terrorism, and Homeland Security, and the Subcommittee on the Constitution, Civil Rights and Civil Liberties, July 19, 2007.

3 Radley Balko, "A Drug Informant Lied, SWAT Pounced, a Man Died," the *Washington Post*, December 31, 2014.

4 Jennings Police Department, Complaint Card, Case #02-457-98C, February 14, 1998.

5 Interview with Marie Comeaux, August 21, 2014.

6 Interview with Gail Brown, July 7, 2011.

7 Interview with Bessie Brown, December 21, 2011.

8 Jennings Police Department, "Calls for Service Report," Item #E-03034-8, May 29, 2008, signal: 30, homicide.

9 Interview with Scott Lewis, May 16, 2016.

10 Interview of South Andrew Street resident, December 19, 2011.

11 Jefferson Davis Parish Sheriff's Office, Case #2008070145, July 17, 2008.

12 Semien-Lewis Mortuary, Jennings, LA, "Death Notice, Kenneth Patrick Drake, Sr., August 9, 1963–August 25, 2012."

13 "Unsolved: Mystery in Jeff Davis Parish," KPLC-TV, October 28, 2009.

14 Interview with Barb Ann Deshotel, August 23, 2014.

15 Jefferson Davis Parish Sheriff's Office, Case Number 2006010183, January 24, 2006.

NOTES

Interview with Velvet Gary, August 24, 2011.

17 Louisiana State Police, Case #09-576.

18 Interview with Butch Gary, August 21, 2014.

19 Interview with Melissa Daigle, July 12, 2011.

20 Jefferson Davis Parish Sheriff's Office, Case #2008110110, November 15, 2008.

21 Ibid.

22 Lee Peck, "Jennings Teen Identified as 7th Victim," KPLC-TV, November 17, 2008, http://www.kplctv.com/story/9367809/jennings-teen-identified-as-7th-victim.

23 Tina Marie Macias, "Taskforce," *Daily Advertiser*, December 25, 2008.

24 Interview with Frankie Richard, July 13, 2011.

25 Ricky Edwards, December 18, 2008, Taskforce press conference.

26 Letter/flyer from Mueller, "Seeking Information."

27 Interview with Ramby Cormier/Taskforce witness interview with Cormier, April 23, 2015.

Chapter 10: The Undoing

1 *Richard Alan Breaux v. Jefferson Davis Parish Sheriff*, Court of Appeals of Louisiana, 3rd Circuit, February 5, 1997.

2 Dina Temple-Raston, "Bulger's Case Changed FBI's Role with Informants," NPR, September 1, 2008, http://www.npr.org/templates/story/story.php?storyId=94117338.

3 Michelle McPhee, "'Whitey' Bulger Defense Cites 'Unholy Alliance' of FBI Killers and Liars," ABC News, August 5, 2013, http://abcnews.go.com/US/whitey-bulger-defense-cites-unholy-alliance-fbi-killers/story?id=19872366.

4 Brad Heath, "Exclusive: FBI Allowed Informants to Commit 5,600 Crimes," *USA Today*, August 4, 2013.

5 Alexandra Natapoff, "Snitching: The Institutional and Communal Consequences," Loyola Law School, Los Angeles, Paper 2004-24, November 2004, https://www.aclu.org/sites/default/files/images/asset_upload_file744_30623.pdf.

6 Jefferson Davis Parish Sheriff's Office, Case #2009050064, May 22, 2009.

7 State of Louisiana, Parish of Jefferson Davis, Arrest Warrant for Frankie Richard, May 26, 2009.

8   Vermilion Parish Sheriff's Office investigation of Paula Guillory, July 8, 2009.

9   Letter from Ricky Edwards, August 11, 2009.

10 Interview with Paula Guillory, January 24, 2014.

11 Interview with Frankie Richard, March 21, 2012.

12 Interview with Brittany Jones, March 21, 2012.

13 Michael Hill, Jennings Police Department, Incident Supplemental Report, #01-006281, September 30, 2001.

14 Jennings Police Department, Case #4241-02, June 12, 2002.

15 Interview with Barbara Guillory, July 9, 2011.

16 Jefferson Davis Parish Sheriff's Office, Case #2009080173, August 19, 2009.

17 Acadia Parish Sheriff, Initial Police Report, Case 09-562, August 19, 2009.

18 Calcasieu Parish Coroner's Office and Forensic Facility, Case #189-2009, August 20, 2009.

19 Brandon Richards, "Police, Investigator Swabbed for DNA in Jeff Davis Case," KPLC-TV, December 28, 2009.

20 Sheriff Ricky Edwards, October 28, 2009, Taskforce press conference (page 227).

21 "Unsolved: Mystery in Jeff Davis Parish," KPLC-TV, October 28, 2009.

22 Interview with Mike Dubois, July 1, 2011; and Lee Peck, "Dubois Transferred to Jeff Davis Parish Jail," KPLC-TV, November 10, 2009.

23 Lee Peck, "Outspoken Jeff Davis Task Force Critic Speaks Out from Jail," KPLC-TV, March 16, 2010.

24 Brandon Richards, "Violence in Jennings: Are Things Getting Worse?" KPLC-TV, January 9, 2010.

25 Crystal Price, "Jennings Police Investigating Shooting Death," KPLC-TV, February 25, 2010.

26 Ibid.

27 Adam Hooper, "Lake Arthur Woman Stabbed in the Mouth," KPLC-TV, June 14, 2010, http://www.kplctv.com/story/12647449/lake-arthur-woman-stabbed-in-the-mouth.

28 Campbell Robertson, "8 Deaths in a Small Town, and Much Unease," the New York Times, January 1, 2010, http://www.nytimes.com/2010/01/02/us/02serial.html?_r=0.

29 Interview with Barb Ann Deshotel, August 23, 2014.

NOTES

Chapter 11: "Frankie Richard's Coming and Hell Is Coming with Him"

1 Interview with Frankie Richard, July 13, 2011.

2 "Jennings Man Arrested after Shooting, 1 Person Wounded," KPLC-TV, April 1, 2011, http://www.kplctv.com/story/14364295 /jennings-man-arrested-after-shooting-1-person-injured.

3 Interview with Scott Lewis, August 30, 2014.

4 Jefferson Davis Parish Sheriff's Office, "Administration," http:// www.jdpso.org/page.php?id=1&PHPSESSID=e10827b9044c 1767d8165e4788e19bd5.

5 Doris Maricle, "Unsolved Deaths Priority for Candidates," *American Press*, September 28, 2011.

6 Lee Peck, "Ivy Woods Voted New Jeff Davis Parish Sheriff," KPLC-TV, October 22, 2011.

7 Interview with Joy Huvall, December 19, 2011.

8 Interview with Frankie Richard, March 21, 2012.

9 Interview with Joy Huvall, July 31, 2012.

10 E-mail from Kirk Menard to Ramby Cormier, May 10, 2012.

11 Interview with Ramby Cormier, April 23, 2015.

12 Semien-Lewis Mortuary, "Kenneth Patrick Drake, Sr., August 9, 1963–August 25, 2012."

13 Ben Wallace, "An Inmate's Final Struggle Caught on Video; Some Raising Questions about Death at Baton Rouge Jail," *Acadiana Advocate*, April 19, 2015.

14 https://twitter.com/MiaFarrow/status/592368604395532288.

15 "Sentencing for Former Jennings Chief on Hold," Associated Press, December 31, 2013.

16 Denver Brown, "Lassiter Sentenced to Five Years Hard Labor," *Jennings Daily News*, June 24, 2014.

17 Jefferson Davis Parish Sheriff's Office, Number 2008010131, January 22, 2008.

Chapter 12: "The Past Is the Past"

1 Ethan Brown, "Who Killed the Jeff Davis 8?" https://medium .com/matter/who-killed-the-jeff-davis-8-d1b813e13581.

2 Drew Grant, "Did the Jeff Davis 8 Inspire *True Detective*?" the *New York Observer*, February 25, 2014.

3 Campbell Robertson, https://twitter.com/campbellnyt/status /429419170812293120?lang=en.

4 Doris Maricle, "Authorities Identify Body Found in Lake Arthur," *American Press*, February 2, 2014.

5 Ibid.

6 Interview with Crochet family member, March 22, 2012.

7 Sheila Smith, "Officials, Investigators Respond to New Coverage, Rumors about JD Eight," *Jennings Daily News*, February 9, 2014.

8 Kevin Millican, September 28, 2011, e-mail to Ethan Brown.

9 Ivy Woods, Jefferson Davis Parish Sheriff, "From the Desk of Sheriff Woods," http://www.jdpso.org/message.php?id=4.

10 Ric Oustalet, March 28, 2014, Facebook post.

11 Theresa Schmidt, "Jeff Davis 8: Why A.G. Buddy Caldwell Doesn't Intervene," KPLC-TV, February 6, 2014, http://www .kplctv.com/story/24658592/jeff-davis-8-why-ag-buddy-cald wells-doesnt-intervene.

12 Sheila Smith e-mails to Ethan Brown, January 31, 2014.

13 "Rayne Police Investigate Shooting Death of 32-Year-Old Man and Other Acadiana Crime Blotter News," the *Acadiana Advocate*, March 30, 2015.

14 KFLY, "Rayne Police Arrest Two Lafayette Men in Christopher Tent Homicide," April 29, 2015, http://klfy.com/2015/04/29/rayne -police-arrest-two-lafayette-men-in-christopher-tent-homicide/.

Chapter 13: Coda: Boustany and the Boudreaux Inn

1 Phone call from Frankie Richard to Ethan Brown, June 25, 2012.

2 Lauren French, "Charles Boustany Slams IRS for 'The Apprentice' Parody," *Politico*, September 6, 2013, http://www.politico.com /story/2013/09/charles-boustany-irs-apprentice-parody-96397 .html.

3 Jack Pandol, Communications Director, Congressman Charles W. Boustany Jr., MD, e-mail to Ethan Brown, May 16, 2016.

4 United States of America, State of Louisiana, Parish of Jefferson Davis, Commercial Lease and Option to Purchase between Tri-Tech Inc. and Justin Boudreaux.

NOTES

5 Tri-Tech LLC, Charter Number 34807754K, registration date, June 25, 1999, Louisiana Secretary of State.

6 *Jacqueline Granger as Independent Administratrix of the Estate of Justin Boudreaux v. Tri-Tech, LLC*, Case #07-1392, State of Louisiana, Court of Appeal, 3rd Circuit.

7 Sunlight Foundation, House Staff Directory, http://staffers.sun lightfoundation.com/staffer/martin-p-guillory-1.

8 Paul Kedlinger, "Oilfield Manufacturer Begins New Facility in Duson," *Rayne-Acadian Tribune*, October 3, 2013.

9 "Charles Boustany Jr. MD for Congress Inc.," Schedule B (FEC Form 3), "Itemized Disbursements," page 279 of 312, date of disbursement: June 1, 2015.

10 States News Service, "Governor Bobby Jindal Appoints Members to State Parks and Recreation Commission," April 25, 2008.

11 Louisiana Secretary of State, Official Election Results, November 7, 2006.

12 Jefferson Davis Parish Sheriff's Office, Case #1998100060, October 12, 1998.

13 Jefferson Davis Parish Sheriff's Office, Case #1999120176, December 22, 1999.

14 Jefferson Davis Parish Sheriff's Office, Case #2000120139, December 19, 2000.

15 Jefferson Davis Parish Sheriff's Office, Case #20000010089, January 10, 2000.

16 Jefferson Davis Parish Sheriff's Office, Case #2000005082, May 11, 2000.

17 Jefferson Davis Parish Sheriff's Office, Case #2002020063, February 7, 2002.

18 Jefferson Davis Parish Sheriff's Office, Case #2002030078, March 11, 2002.

19 Jefferson Davis Parish Sheriff's Office, Case #2002040016, April 2, 2002.

20 Jefferson Davis Parish Sheriff's Office, Case #2004080114, August 15, 2004.

21 Jefferson Davis Parish Sheriff's Office, Case #2004120191, December 31, 2004.

22 Jefferson Davis Parish Sheriff's Office, Case #2006040077, April 8, 2006.

23 Interview with Suzette Istre, March 31, 2015.

24 http://www.nationaljournal.com/almanac/member/53?print =true.

25 https://www.youtube.com/watch?v=VAuPB54ObU8.

26 Interviews with Andrew Newman, spring of 2015.

27 Jefferson Davis Parish Sheriff's Office, Case #20003070156, July 22, 2003.

28 Jefferson Davis Parish Sheriff's Office, Case #2001120206, December 27, 2001.

29 Interview with Martin P. Guillory, May 10, 2016.

Chapter 14: Whistle-Blower in White Robes

1 Interview with Raymond Mott, September 2, 2015.

2 Valerie Ponseti, "Motion to Terminate Raymond Mott Unanimously Carried by Lake Arthur Council," KATC-TV, September 2, 2015.

3 Interview with Raymond Mott.

4 Laura Heller, "Four More Arrested in Lake Arthur Homicide," KPLC-TV, March 2, 2015 (with May 1, 2015, update).

5 Nate Thayer, "Was Louisiana Cop Accused of Being KKK Fired for Objecting to Corrupt Police," *Vice*, September 4, 2015, http://www.nate-thayer.com/was-louisiana-cop-accused-of-being-kkk-fired-for-objecting-to-corrupt-police/.

6 Interview with Trey Gordon, September 2, 2015.

7 Ray Marcantel, Chief of Police, Town of Lake Arthur, "Re: Termination Letter Dated August 28, 2015."

Acknowledgments

1. Campbell Robertson, "Missouri City to Pay $4.7 Million to Settle Suit Over Jailing Practices," The New York Times, July 15, 2016. http://www.nytimes.com/2016/07/16/us/missouri-city-to-pay-4-7-million-to-settle-suit-over-jailing-practices.html?_r=0.